GARDENING WEEKENDS

Better Homes and Gardens®

GARDENING WEEKENDS

Strategies for the Busy Gardener

Olwen Woodier

Better
Homes
and Gardens
BOOKS

®

BETTER HOMES AND GARDENS® BOOKS
An Imprint of Meredith® Books

Vice President and Editorial Director:
Elizabeth P. Rice
Executive Editor: Kay Sanders
Managing Editor: Christopher Cavanaugh
Art Director: Ernest Shelton

President, Book Group: Joseph J. Ward
Vice President, Retail Marketing:
Jamie L. Martin
Vice President, Direct Marketing:
Timothy Jarrell

MEREDITH CORPORATION
Chairman of the Executive Committee:
E. T. Meredith III
Chairman of the Board and Chief Executive
Officer: Jack D. Rehm
President and Chief Operating Officer:
William T. Kerr

All of us at Meredith® Books are dedicated to
providing you with the information and ideas
you need to garden successfully. We guarantee
your satisfaction with this book for as long as
you own it. If you have any questions, comments,
or suggestions, please write to us at:

MEREDITH® BOOKS, Garden Books
Editorial Department, RW 240
1716 Locust St.
Des Moines, IA 50309-3023

GARDENING WEEKENDS
Strategies for the Busy Gardener
was prepared and produced for Meredith
    Corporation by
Michael Friedman Publishing Group, Inc.
15 West 26th Street
New York, New York 10010

Editor: Karla Olson
Production Editor: Loretta Mowat
Art Director: Jeff Batzli
Designer: Edward Noriega
Photography Editor: Emilya Naymark
Illustrator: Jennifer Markson
Garden Designer: Dorothy Schmitt

Copyright © 1995 by Michael Friedman
    Publishing Group, Inc.

All Rights Reserved.
First Edition. Printing Number and Year:
    5 4 3   98 97 96

Library of Congress Catalog Card Number
94-79048

ISBN: 0-696-04649-0

Color separations by Fine Arts Repro House
    Co., Ltd.
Manufactured in the United States

Dedication

To my mother, Joyse, for nurturing my love for the earth, and to my brother, Francis,
for sharing his gardening wisdom.

Acknowledgments

First, I thank my husband, Richard Busch, for moving mounds of mulch and constructing bird-houses, ponds, raised beds, fences, and the many other elements that made my garden a reality.

I thank Mary Bean and Dr. Rajandra Waghray for being such dedicated and inspirational leaders in the Master Gardener's Program of Fairfax County, Virginia. Indeed, I am grateful to many who have shared their horticultural knowledge with me, particularly my master gardening colleague and British compatriot, Dorothy Schmitt, who also created the garden designs for this book; the people at Wayside Gardens in Hodges, South Carolina; and at Gardener's Supply Company in Burlington, Vermont.

I also appreciate the efforts of all those who worked on this book. I especially recognize the editorial support received from Karla Olson, and the creative aspects produced by Jeff Batzli, Ed Noriega, Emilya Naymark, and Jennifer Markson. Final thanks go to Loretta Mowat, whose painstaking efforts kept the project moving along.

To all of these people, and those I have not mentioned by name, my sincere thanks.

CONTENTS

CHAPTER ONE

WORKABLE WEEKEND GARDENS

A special kind of pleasure is gained when you nurture the earth around your own back door. You are creating a place where you can escape from the pressures of the everyday world. But if you can garden only on the weekends, you have another goal—to create an environment that, once established, can be maintained in just a few hours a week. That way you can spend your time enjoying it. The key is to choose the right plantings, to design your gardens so they require a minimum of maintenance, to use gardening techniques and materials that drastically reduce the chores of cultivation, and to set and maintain realistic goals and expectations for your garden.

LEFT: A mix of perennials and annuals capture the colorful combinations typical of a carefree cottage garden. Here, delphiniums, poppies, lupines, and pansies add charm to the shutters found on this cottage in Crested Butte, Colorado.

Realistic Expectations

Before you start to plan and prepare your garden, make a realistic assessment of the amount of time you have—or want—to spend looking after your garden each weekend. Your answer, whether two hours or 10, will affect the size, number, and types of your beds, borders, and plantings. Keep in mind, however, that a garden that almost looks after itself will take extra time and money in the beginning.

Start Small and Go Slow

When establishing your low-care garden, start small and go slow. Plant one bed, then spend some time—at least several weeks—making sure that the plants you've chosen are suited to the site and that you are comfortable with the maintenance level the plot requires. When the bed is well established and you feel capable of taking on more, move on to the next garden area.

Working on only one small area at a time has an economic advantage. You can fill a small bed with low-cost annuals, bulbs, and ornamental grasses, then slowly expand it to include the more expensive perennials, shrubs, and specimen trees. And, you can spread your cost out over years, if you prefer.

Low-Care Garden Styles

Contrary to what you might think, a weekend garden can be almost any garden style. You can even choose a formal style, as long as it abandons the rigid lines and symmetry that show every flaw.

Generally, the characteristics of a true low-maintenance garden include curves and contours planted with low-care varieties that don't need frequent shearing, pruning, or other special treatment. Keep the design natural and soft around the edges and no one will notice a few weeds or errant runners.

ABOVE: Low-maintenance plantings spill over and soften the edges of this perennial bed. The stone walkway keeps the weeds at bay.

OPPOSITE PAGE: The heat-tolerant flowers of purple lantana, society garlic (Tulbaghia violacea), yellow Euryops daisy, and pinkish red paper flower (Bougainvillea glabra) create an exciting contrast with the lime green shrubs of Pittosporum. When plantings are suited to the climate, even a formally designed garden such as this one in Laguna Beach, California, can be maintained with a minimum of care.

A BACKYARD WATER GARDEN

Home to gliding goldfish and starred with beautiful water lilies, a water garden attracts birds, dragonflies, frogs, toads, and small turtles. Whether you choose to install a molded fiberglass pond or a free-form pond lined with polyvinylchloride (PVC) or butyl rubber, it's a job you can accomplish in a weekend. If you'd like a pond over 20 feet long, rent a small earth-scooping backhoe to help with the excavation. If your design is more modest, you should be able to dig out the shape with a shovel.

Choose a site near your house so the pond is easy to watch. For a thriving plant and animal environment, position it where it will get at least six hours of sun. Hardy water lilies require a minimum of five to six hours of sun; tropical water lilies respond far better to all-day sun and warm water temperatures. Take into consideration your pond's proximity to deciduous trees. Once the trees leaf out, they'll cast shade and in the autumn will drop their leaves into the pond, which could clog the pump.

The shape and design of your pond should reflect the rest of your garden. For a naturalistic look, choose a kidney, an oval, or any shape with a curvy perimeter, and plant thickly around the edges. A rectangular or square pond adds a formal, ornamental air. Filled with floating leaves and taller clumps of iris, and edged with stones and some creeping plants, formal ponds will still appeal to several forms of wildlife.

Fiberglass forms range from 2 X 3 feet and 12 inches deep to 15 X 25 feet and 2 feet deep. A depth of 2 feet is considered adequate for fish and amphibians in zones where the water doesn't freeze more than a few inches. Be sure to check local zoning regulations, however. To safeguard children in the neighborhood, many states and counties require a fence around a pond deeper than 2 feet.

Some fiberglass pond shells come with molded shelves 9 inches wide and about 9 inches below the water, where marginal plants can be grown. Despite these options, you may prefer to customize your pond and line it with 32- to 45-mil-thick PVC or butyl rubber.

The gentle murmur of moving water is soothing and hypnotic. You can have moving water quite easily by installing a pump and a small fountain that simply spurts a steady stream. If you prefer a more forceful tumble, erect a waterfall. Where the pump-to-fountain hookup requires assembly only, the waterfall will need minor, but simple, construction. Whichever method you choose, be sure to plant water lilies at the opposite end of the pond, away from the flow or cascade of water.

STEP-BY-STEP INSTRUCTIONS FOR CONSTRUCTING A FREE-FORM POND

1. Using garden hose or rope, make an outline of your pond. Remove a 12-inch width of sod on the outside of the hose. Start digging straight down inside the hose formation to a depth of 9 inches and make a shelf 9 inches wide to hold pots of marginal water plants. Excavate the rest of the pond, throwing the earth at the end where you want to construct a rock garden or a waterfall. Slope the sides down to a center depth of 24 inches.

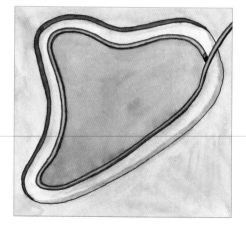

2. Place a plank of wood across the length of the pond and use a level to make sure that the pond is not sloping in one direction. Do the same across the width.

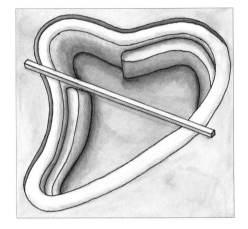

3. Remove any stones from the pond's interior and layer the hole with special fabric pond liner, 1 inch of damp sand, unfolded newspapers, or large pieces of carpeting—anything to create a smooth surface free of sharp objects.

4. Calculate the amount of PVC or butyl liner you need by adding twice the depth of the pond to both the length and the width. If your pond is 10 x 16 feet by 2 feet deep, you need a liner that is 14 x 20 feet.

5. Fit the liner into the pond hole and over the shelf. Bring it up over the edges and across the 12-inch width where the sod was removed. Secure temporarily with a few rocks along the edges while the pond fills with water.

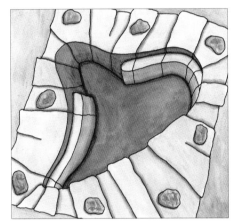

6. As the pond fills, trim the plastic so it overlaps and fits neatly across the 12-inch ledge.

7. Remove the temporary rocks. Replace the cutaway sod and cover with large, heavy flat rocks (such as fieldstones or flagstones) that jut a little over the rim to hide the plastic liner.

8. If the pond is to have a waterfall, position the tubing so it comes over the edge of the pond (disguise it with a few extra edging rocks and plantings). Then bury it under earth or rocks until it comes out at the top of a waterfall, which may have one, two, or three 6- to 12-inch steps. Use a piece of PVC liner under the rocks where the water will run down over the waterfall and into the pond.

9. When a simple fountain is the main source of cascading water, situate the fountain at the edge of the pond or on a few raised blocks in the pond. There is no need to bury the tubing—it will remain submerged and hidden in the water.

To plant your water garden, see Weekend Project #2.

PLANTING THE WATER GARDEN

You spent last weekend constructing the pond. Now all you have to do is fill your water garden with water and plants. Most large nurseries sell water lilies and several other varieties of water plants. For a really good selection of water plants, visit an aquatic plant specialist or request a catalog and order by mail. The plants arrive with precise planting information.

When you grow a variety of aquatic plants, your pond will develop a natural ecological balance. Oxygenating plants such as CABOMBA • ANACHARIS • SAGITTARIA • and DUCKWEED absorb fish and plant wastes and release oxygen into the water. By consuming carbon dioxide, they also restrict the growth of free-floating algae, which turns pond water into "pea soup." If floating plants cover about 60 percent of the surface, they reduce the amount of sunlight reaching the bottom and prevent the loss of oxygen. When not enough water surface is covered, sheet or "hair" algae start to grow. When there's too much shade, free-floating brown algae takes over.

Oxygenator plants also provide protection for fish eggs and newly hatched fry. Fish and Japanese black snails are essential to pond life, too—they eat algae and decaying leaves. You don't need to feed them commercial fish food because they thrive on other micronutrients naturally available in a balanced pond. But don't add them to the pond until the plantings have been in place for four to five weeks so they have a source of natural food. Add one 2-inch fish per square foot of water surface.

The best method of planting in a small pond is to use plastic pots and perforated baskets. This controls plants with rampant roots (cattails, rushes, dwarf bamboos) and makes it easy to move and repot floaters and tropical plants. Oxygenators can be planted in small pots or simply anchored with stones to submerge them.

Plant water lilies and other aquatics in heavy garden soil enriched with slow-release fertilizer tablets. Don't add compost or manure; they encourage the growth of algae. Top with a 1-inch layer of small pebbles to keep the soil in the pot and out of the water. Marginal bog plants grow in 4 to 12 inches of water and can be placed on a shelf or on concrete blocks (place an extra piece of PVC or butyl rubber underneath the blocks to prevent tearing of the pond liner). Though many marginal bog plants will grow with only three to five hours of sun, most need five to six hours to bloom.

Water lilies and deep-water floating plants grow best when their crowns are about 18 inches under water. When adding new plantings with little or no foliage, however, start them off at 4 to 6 inches below the water. As growth reaches the surface, keep on submerging them until they are at the desired depth. This way, you'll get good blooms early in the season.

If you want to grow tropical water lilies, they need 70°F water to start growth and bloom only when the temperature reaches into the 80s. If winter

temperatures drop below 30°F, transfer tropicals to a tub in a greenhouse or sunroom, or store the pots in damp sand at temperatures 55° to 60°F. This will induce dormancy.

Hardy water lilies will survive the winter in the pond if the soil in their pots doesn't freeze. If you know it will, overwinter them in a cool area in the cellar. Wrap the pots in damp newspaper and place in a plastic garbage bag. Open the bag once a month to air the plant and check that the newspaper is still damp. When you see new growth in the spring, repot if necessary, add slow-release fertilizer tablets, and return to the pond. Lily tubers put out new growth when the water temperature is around 55°F and produce blooms when the water reaches 70°F.

If you want frogs and other amphibians to overwinter in your pond, add a little earth to the bottom where they can bury themselves.

The water in your newly filled pond may appear cloudy and greenish for about two months while natural nutrients and microorganisms develop. When they are established the water will slowly clear. If, after three months, the water is still very green and cloudy, you may safely use Acurel-E or AquaRem to clear

the water of floating algae without harming plantings, pond animal life, or beneficial microorganisms.

Once your pond is established, periodically remove decaying plants, including leaves fallen from nearby trees. A balanced water garden doesn't need draining and cleaning. If necessary, during summer months replace the water that evaporates.

ABOVE: Designed to attract wildlife, this naturalistic-looking pond requires minimal upkeep.

Some garden designs initially require more work, but once incorporated, their requirements dwindle. You'll put in two weekends of hard work installing a water garden, for instance, but once established, it requires little upkeep. The most you will have to do is remove debris from the pump and pond periodically and divide the water lilies or other water plants every few years. (See Weekend Projects #1 and #2.)

When considering garden design possibilities, begin by examining the existing elements of your landscape. Pinpoint high-care areas, as well as those that present special problems or challenges. Your first step will be to convert these spots to low-maintenance areas. Here are some typical problems and some low-care solutions you should consider.

- Replace part of a close-clipped lawn—traditional but time-consuming—with care-free ground covers, ponds, groupings of shrubs and trees, wildflowers, stones, and rocks. Scatter a section of your yard with wildflower seeds. It may take a weekend to prepare and seed the soil (see Weekend Project #3), but unlike the lawn, a meadow of wildflowers needs mowing only once or twice a year. If it is essential that you have an area of lawn,

plant it with a low-care grass and mow it with the blades set high.

- A water garden is a creative way to replace lawn space. In fact, you could use this strategy to reduce the lawn to only a ribbon encircling the pond and its plantings.

- Plant a slope that is difficult to mow with fast-spreading ground covers or shrubs.

- Avoid large, formal beds full of floppy or fragile annuals and perennials. They demand constant attention with deadheading, staking, and cutting back. Choose, instead, more naturalistic designs with soft lines and overlapping plants that disguise the inevitable imperfections

that are inherent in a living, growing landscape.

- Forgo angular hedges that require constant clipping or shrubs that must be trimmed to form perfect globes. Choose instead ARBORVITAE • YEW • LEYLAND CYPRESS • HOLLY • and FORSYTHIA, all popular for their natural shape and beauty.

- A windswept area is vulnerable to chilling breezes and to frost. It also will dry out quickly. To overcome these problems—and add privacy at the same time—install a basket-weave fence or a hedge of fast-growing evergreens.

- If you have a boggy spot, don't fight it. Enhance it by planting it with varieties that thrive in wet soil.

- A rock outcropping can be integrated into a rock garden. Or, you can make it the focal point in an Oriental-style garden. In the traditional Asian garden, fine gravel or sand is constantly raked into a design, but the weekend version should use small pebbles poured over a weed barrier.

Most gardens can be converted to low-care designs simply by curving the straight beds or by obscuring sharp lines with fast-spreading round-shaped plantings. The idea is to mimic nature by blurring boundaries and creating forgiving lines.

PLANTING A LOW-CARE MEADOW

Brighten your landscape with the glorious hues of YELLOW GOLDENROD • PURPLE ASTERS • ORANGE BUTTERFLY WEED • RED POPPIES • WHITE-AND-YELLOW OXEYE DAISIES • BLACK-EYED SUSANS • BLUE CORNFLOWERS • PINK CONEFLOWERS • and other wildflowers native to your area. These annual and perennial wildflowers grow in poor soil, don't need fertilizing or watering, and need mowing only once a year in late autumn or early spring.

Depending on the size of the area you want to turn into a meadow, this project could take one day or two. The best time to seed a meadow of perennials and annuals is spring. The annuals will flower and reseed themselves for the following year. If you seed a meadow in late summer or early fall, seed with perennials only. Some will germinate quickly and overwinter; others will not germinate until early the following spring.

Before planting, scoop off the sod (if you have not killed it by covering it with black plastic) and turn over the soil. You don't need to enrich or fertilize, but the soil should be fine enough to allow seeds to germinate and take hold.

Sprinkle the area with twice as many seeds as is recommended, walk over the bed to tread them in, then cover with a light layer of straw. This will help with germination, prevent birds from stealing the seeds, and deter animals from digging in the freshly turned earth. Water the seeds with a sprinkler. If there is a dry spell, water periodically to speed germination.

Most wildflowers reseed profusely. However, it may be necessary to spot-seed some of the annuals periodically. You may want to fill in a few bare patches with mature plants.

Mow the meadow once a year in spring or autumn. A tractor-mower will cut down young tree growth, and shred all the woody vegetatation and dried plant stems. Do not rake, but leave the shredded material to act as a natural fertilizer and mulch.

Discovering Low-Care Plants

It is important to the success of your weekend garden that you learn all you can about the growth habits of different plants and how they respond to your climate. This will help you determine which plants are best for your weekend garden, and which to avoid. Many weekend gardens are doomed from their beginning because of poor plant choice. Take time now to educate yourself so you don't make costly mistakes.

Reading about plantings is one way to learn. Study plant catalogs, not just for possible purchases, but to learn everything you can about what to expect from a particular plant and what specific conditions it requires.

Visit local nurseries, especially those that have display beds of shrubs, flowers, and ornamental grasses. Stop by during each of the seasons and note whether plants you are interested in grow bushy and low or thick and tall, whether they usually are positioned in the front, middle, or back of the bed, and what color changes they bring with the seasons. Also pay attention to which shrubs and flowers bloom for weeks on end. Speak to the horticulturalist to get more specific information about plants you are

considering. Explain that you are cultivating a low-care garden and want to know whether a plant would be appropriate. Ask whatever questions you need to feel certain that you won't waste time and money on the wrong plant or put it in the wrong spot in your garden. If you hear anything that makes you uncertain, forget that plant and choose another.

Though plant species indigenous to your region are most likely to thrive in your garden, you also can consider many Asian and European varieties. Just find out all you can to make sure they are low maintenance. Plant breeders throughout the world are constantly developing new strains of old favorites that are more

disease free, resistant to pests, and tolerant to drought and other environmental stresses, all essential qualifications for low-care plants. Investigate these as possibilities for your garden.

Choosing Low-Care Plants

You should follow a number of rules when selecting plants for the weekend garden. Choose only varieties that follow these guidelines, and if they don't, move on to another plant. If you have established plantings that don't meet these guidelines, be ruthless and get rid of them.

HERE ARE THE RULES:

- Find and adopt the plants—flowers, vegetables, shrubs, and trees—that demand little attention, including a mininal amount of fertilizing and watering.

- Choose only varieties that are disease and pest free.

- Avoid varieties that need frequent cutting back, deadheading, or watering. However, all vegetables need deep watering at least weekly, so plan to use an irrigation system.

- Avoid plants that must be staked and tied repeatedly. Staking is acceptable if done only once, at the beginning of plant growth. For special plants that need their branches secured as they put out new growth (tomatoes, for example), caging, rather than staking, is the best alternative.

- Select good low-care plants that have strong stems to withstand wind and heavy rain.

- Choose fast-growing varieties, but avoid plants that are so invasive they crowd out other plants, thus requiring constant cutting back.

- Pick varieties with the longest bloom time. If you are away or busy during the week, you are likely to completely miss the show of a short-bloom variety. If you must have a short-blooming plant in your garden, make sure it has pretty foliage.

- Avoid plants that require heavy pruning, fertilizing, and spraying, such as peach, apricot, apple, or pear trees. Avoid large beds of strawberries as well. Strawberry runners need constant pruning, and you will have to replace mature plants periodically,

OPPOSITE PAGE: Plantings of penstemon thrive in full sun and gravelly, well-drained soil. To create a low-maintenance garden, choose those varieties native to your region. Although naturally hardy, indigenous species can be tempermental when conditions differ from their native environment.

ABOVE, LEFT: Annual sunflowers are available in numerous varieties. One of the easiest flowers to grow, they bloom for weeks and provide seeds for birds, nectar for butterflies, and pollen for honeybees.

ABOVE, RIGHT: A colorful mixed border is planted with petunia, gloriosa daisy (Rudbeckia hirta), *and small ornamental grasses.*

both of which take time. The ideal fruit for the weekend garden is the blueberry. The berries ripen slowly, and, even if you share them with the birds, you will enjoy their reddish purple foliage into autumn. If you must have strawberries, plant a few in large containers or cylinders (see Weekend Project #19). The upkeep will be minimal. Also, be sure you choose everbearing day-neutral plants so you'll enjoy the fruits of your labor through the summer.

Low-Maintenance Materials and Strategies

Besides choosing low-care plants, take advantage of the low-maintenance materials and techniques available today. Some of these strategies mean investing extra time and money initially, but you'll probably make up for it in just a few weekends.

- Install drip irrigation or soaker hoses equipped with a water timer, especially in the vegetable garden, where regular and deep watering is essential to the growth of healthy edibles. Program the timers to water as often as needed—hourly, daily, or weekly. Timers allow the weekend gardener

to direct-seed and have beds of lettuces, green beans, root vegetables, onions, and other vegetables requiring a constant supply of moisture.

- Raised beds make gardening much easier (see page 34 for advantages), so use them for vegetables, flowers, and herbs. See page 40 for advice on how to build and install a raised bed, or, if you are not handy, buy ready-made frames.

- Mulch is the weekend gardener's best friend and should be piled around every plant to retain moisture and keep weeds out. Organic mulches such as wood chips and shredded bark also enrich the soil as they

decompose. The cost of a truckload of mulch can be high, but the advantages are priceless. (See Weekend Project #41 for ideas about where to get free wood chips and shredded organic matter.)

- You might also want to lay down fabric weed barriers. Fabric barriers provide frost, weed, and insect protection while allowing sunlight to reach the plants and water and air to reach their roots. Some special plastics also block weed growth while allowing water and air to penetrate and nourish roots.

- If you are a serious container gardener, look into self-watering planters with built-in reservoirs and water level indicators. They keep the soil moist for a week or longer.

- If you are interested in year-round growing, look into self-ventilating cold frames and greenhouses. When temperatures climb, an automatically operated thermostat opens vents to admit cooling air and closes the vents when temperatures drop.

- For the true weekend gardener, who is away from the garden all week, insulated growing trays mean that starting plants from seed is possible. Equipped with domed plastic covers and capillary matting that wicks up water, these trays create a warm, moist environment for fast germination. The water reservoir holds a seven-day supply, ensuring that the seeds or seedlings receive a constant source of water. When the seedlings are sturdy and have outgrown the miniature greenhouse but conditions do not permit you to plant them directly into the garden, transplant them into larger pots also containing water reservoirs with a one-week water supply.

- Another way to keep transplants watered while you are away is to mix the soil with water-absorbing polymar crystals and binding materials. Able to absorb up to 400 times their weight in water, they release moisture into the soil as needed. Add these materials to window boxes, hanging baskets, and raised beds so the soil won't dry out during your absence.

- Another method for storing water in the soil is to spray the surface with a special biodegradable liquid that reduces the plants' water needs up to 50 percent. This can be used for the soil in pots or in beds or plots.

With all the specialized landscaping materials and equipment available today, a low-maintenance weekend garden is easy to attain. As always, the best way to find out what is going to work for you is to start small and go slow, then build on when you are comfortable. For example, after installing a successful watering system in one area, expand the system to another. This way you won't feel overwhelmed by the cost of time and money spent, especially if a technique does not work for you.

OPPOSITE PAGE: Thanks to a thick layer of straw mulch, the hollyhocks in this bed are strong and healthy. Mulch keeps the soil moist and the weeds at bay, and also enriches the soil when it breaks down.

LEFT: A small greenhouse can add months to the growing season. Choose one that is thermostatically controlled so that the vents will open and close automatically when there's a rise or fall in temperature.

ROCK GARDENING MADE EASY

Planted with dwarf evergreen shrubs and trees, seasonal bulbs, annuals, and perennials, a rock garden can become the year-round focus of your garden. A rock garden adds color and interest to any area, whether located in semishade, full sun, or filtered sunlight. Once you've made your plans and found a source for rocks, it's easy to construct and plant a rock garden in one weekend.

A steep slope, which presents erosion problems and is difficult to mow, is a wonderful site for a rock garden.

To prepare a steep slope: Rip out weeds and sod and embed large flat stones into the soil to form terraces. Slant the stones toward the hill to prevent soil loss during water runoff. Embed the bottom third of some boulders or large rocks into the soil between the terraces. Fill the terraced levels with a layer of free-draining soil mixture (see below), spreading it around the upright rocks and boulders. Plant around the bases and in rock crevices.

To make a free-draining soil mixture: Combine equal parts of loam (rich soil that can break down easily into smaller particles), peat moss or leaf mold, and ¼-inch stone chips or coarse builders' sand. If you need to accommodate plants that require a more acidic soil,

add a little extra peat moss to their immediate area.

Use to fill an uninteresting corner site or an undeveloped area below a deck or picture window, or construct a rock garden along a boring stretch of lawn parallel to the driveway or street.

To construct a rock garden on flat land: Take a hose or length of string and make an outline of the desired shape and size of your site. Dig a channel through the center for a narrow pathway and throw the excavated soil on either side to give height to your rock garden. Add a free-draining soil mixture to the site. Working from the bottom to the top of the mounded soil, add several large rocks, embedding their bases several inches into the soil. Tilt the rocks backward to direct rainwater to the roots.

A small pond and a rock garden are perfect companions.

To construct a pond and a rock garden: Dig the pond (see Weekend Project #1), piling the earth on one side. Arrange rocks and plants in the pile leading down to the water.

Other ways to construct rock gardens with even less work include:

Plant a rock garden in a raised bed: Alpines (plants that grow above the timber line) and saxatiles (plants that grow

among rocks) will thrive in the humus-rich, slightly acidic soil of a raised bed.

Plant a rock garden in a drystone wall: You have a ready-made rock garden if you have a drystone wall (one not held together with cement). Plant alpines, saxatiles, low-growing herbs, and maidenhair ferns between the crevices. To plant between the stones, place a small plant on a trowel with roots facing the tip and slide it into place between the stones. Gently remove the trowel, then use it to cover the plant's roots with soil. Pack the soil in place with a wooden stick or dowel.

PLANTS FOR ROCK GARDENS

SHRUBS: *CEDRUS DEODARA* 'AUREA PENDULA' (CEDAR) • *CRYPTOMERIA JAPONICA* 'COMPRESSA' (DWARF JAPANESE CEDAR) • *ABIES BALSAMEA* 'HUDSONIA' (COMPACT BALSAM FIR) • *PICEA ABIES* 'NIDIFORMIS' (SPRUCE) • *ILEX CRENATA* (HOLLY) • *PINUS MUGO* 'COMPACTA' (DWARF MOUNTAIN PINE) • *RHODODENDRON* (AZALEA) • *CHAMAECYPARIS LAWSONIANA* 'MINIMA AUREA' (CYPRESS) • *TSUGA CANANDESIS* 'PENDULA' (WEEPING CANADA HEMLOCK) • and *JUNIPERUS CHINENSIS* 'COMPRESSA' (JUNIPER).
PERENNIALS: *AJUGA* (BUGLEWEED) • *AURINIA SAXATILIS* (BASKET-OF-GOLD) • *ASTER*

ALPINUS (ASTER) • *ASTILBE SIMPLICIFOLIA* (STAR ASTILBE) • *A. CHINENSIS* (CHINESE ASTILBE) • *CAMPANULA CARPATICA* (TUSSOCK BELLFLOWER) • *C. ELATINES* (ADRIATIC BELLFLOWER) • *C. PORTENSCHLAGIANA* (DALMATION BELLFLOWER) • *DICENTRA EXIMIA* 'LUXURIENT' (BLEEDINGHEART) • *IBERIS SEMPERVIRENS* (CANDYTUFT) • *AQUILEGIA DISCOLOR* (COLUMBINE) • *A. FLABELLATA* • *COREOPSIS VERTICILLATA* (COREOPSIS) • *GERANIUM SANGUINEUM* (CRANESBILL) • *G. CINEREUM* • *G. DALMATICUM* • *TIARELLA CORDIFOLIA* (FOAMFLOWER) • *CHRYSOGONUM VIRGINIANUM* (GOLDEN STAR) • *GENTIANA SCABRA* (GENTIAN) • *SEMPERVIVUM* (HENS-AND-CHICKENS) • *HOSTA TARDIFLORA* (HOSTA or PLANTAIN LILY) • *H. VENUSTA* • *IRIS CRISTATA* (CRESTED IRIS) • *I. GRAMINEA* (IRIS) • *ALCHEMILLA ALPINA* (DWARF LADY'S-MANTLE) • *THALICTRUM KIUSIANUM* (DWARF MEADOW RUE) • *PHLOX SUBULATA* (MOSS PINK) • *DIANTHUS* (PINKS) • *PRIMULA SIEBOLDII* (PRIMROSE) • *P. VULGARIS* (ENGLISH PRIMROSE) • *ARABIS ALPINA* (MOUNTAIN ROCK CRESS) • *A. STURII* (ROCK CRESS) • *ANDROSACE SARMENTOSA* (ROCK JASMINE) • *SAXIFRAGA PANICULATA* (SAXIFRAGE) • *S. AIZOON* • *SAPONARIA OCYMOIDES* (SOAPWORT) • *VERONICA PECTINATA* (SPEEDWELL) • *V. PROSTRATA* • *V. REPENS* • *V. SPICATA* •

SEDUM DASYPHYLLUM (STONECROP) • *S. SIEBOLDII* (OCTOBER DAPHNE) • *S. KAMTSCHATICUM* • *ARMERIA JUNIPERIFOLIA* (ARMERIA) • *A. MARITIMA* • and *ACHILLEA TOMENTOSA* (WOOLLY YARROW).

BULBS: CROCUS • MINIATURE DAFFODILS • SCILLAS • GRAPE HYACINTHS • DWARF TULIPS • GLORY-OF-THE-SNOW • and AUTUMN CROCUS.

House

Pathway

Steps

ROCK GARDEN

KEY	QTY	NAME
1	1	*Ilex crenata* 'Latifolia' (big-leaf holly)
2	2	*Rhododendron* 'Roseum elegans' (rhododendron)
3	1	*Chamaecyparis pisifera* 'Boulevard' (false cypress)
4	1	*Chamaecyparis obtusa* 'Nana variegata' (false cypress)
5	1	*Picea abies* 'Little Gem' (dwarf spruce)
6	1	*Berberis thunbergii* 'Rose Glow' (dwarf barberry)
7	1	*Yucca* 'Color Guard' (yucca)
8	6	*Rhododendron* species (*Azalea* 'Gumpo')
9	3	*Buxus sempervirens* (English boxwood)
10	1	*Pinus mugo* 'Compacta' (mugo pine)
11	3	*Calluna* (heather)
12	24	*Muscari liriope* (lilyturf)
13	100	*Narsissus* 'Thalia' (daffodil)
14	12	*Iberis sempervirens* (candytuft)
15	24	*Primula sieboldii* (primrose)
16	3	*Dianthus chinensis* (rainbow)
17	35	*Iris cristata* (crested iris)
18	100	*Tulipa* species *(tarda, kaufmanniana, greigii)*
19	9	*Astilbe simplicifolia* (astilbe)
20	5	*Arabis alpina* (rockcress)

ABOVE: A border that includes care-free perennials such as coneflowers, golden-rod, asters, and penstemon will be in bloom for weeks on end. These self-maintaining varieties don't need dead-heading or watering and can be cut back in late autumn or early spring.

OPPOSITE PAGE: Mature plantings of ground covers, mosses, bulbs, and other care-free flowering perennials have multiplied and spread to form drifts and dense carpets in this informal, low-maintenance rock garden.

Weekend Garden Styles

A gardener's choice of garden style and design usually is one of personal preference. As a weekend gardener, your decisions will be influenced by the amount of time you can—or want to—spend caring for your garden. Existing site conditions also will play a major role in your choice, for it is much easier to establish a low-maintenance garden when you work with—instead of against—the natural range of light, soil, and microclimates in your yard. You will be even more successful if you choose plants best suited to each microcondition, and group together plants with similar maintenance requirements.

Here are observations about several garden styles, all from the weekend gardener's view; all are described in greater detail, with garden blueprints, later. These are not the only styles you can adopt for a care-free garden, however. Almost any style can be adapted if the golden rules of plant choice are followed and the edges of the garden are kept soft and easy.

A care-free flower garden should include bulb varieties that keep coming up year after year. They should be complemented by trouble-free perennials that bloom for weeks on end, such as PURPLE CONEFLOWER • BLACK-EYED SUSAN • ASTER • and TICKSEED. Annuals that spread quickly and bloom from spring to hard frost are a good choice for a low-maintenance flower garden.

Self-heading or self-cleaning annuals such as IMPATIENS are great for the weekend garden because they relieve the gardener of yet another chore. In the flower garden, as in any design, crowd out weeds with mulches, and fill larger spaces with a few compact shrubs that rarely, if ever, need trimming. Good shrub choices for sunny borders include small flowering cultivars of DAPHNE • POTENTILLA • AZALEA • SPIRAEA • and MINIATURE DOGWOOD.

A design filled exclusively with perennials will cost more the first year and will not be as colorful as a mixed border. During the following years, however, you won't have to spend money buying plants, and you won't have the work of planting. In three to five years, when it comes time to divide the perennials, you'll have plenty of plants to fill spaces elsewhere in the garden. Choose the trouble-free perennials already mentioned (or if you have shade, see Chapter 5) and include other care-free varieties such as SIBERIAN IRIS • PHLOX • BEE BALM • LIATRIS • and BLUE SALVIA.

You may decide that you'd rather plant small, compact perennials suitable to a rock garden. If this is the case, turn to Weekend Project #4 for a rock garden design and plantings.

A cottage garden may be the perfect weekend garden, for its unstructured, care-free form requires little maintenance and allows for visual flaws. Start out with a diverse and colorful mixture of annuals, perennials, and herbs. Your cottage garden design will evolve as these plants reseed and spread to fill spaces. Slowly add vines such as CLIMBING ROSES and CLEMATIS, flowering shrubs such as BUTTERFLY BUSH, and small trees, such as LILAC. Usually the tallest plantings are positioned behind the shorter ones, but in the cottage garden that rule can be broken. (See page 156 for a detailed cottage garden plan.)

A rose garden might seem to require too much care for a low-maintenance garden. However, several cultivars are low care and long blooming. SHRUB ROSES (RUGOSAS and FLORIBUNDAS), which are used more and more as hedge roses, and CLIMBING ROSES, which will ramble up walls and over fences and arbors, are more resistant to diseases and pests and don't need a lot of fertilizer. They also do not need constant watering, as long as their roots are covered with thick layers of an enriching, moisture-retaining organic mulch.

A beautiful water garden will feature an ornamental or natural-looking pond surrounded by low-care shrubbery, ground covers, drifts of spreading perennials and wildflowers, punctuated by a few large rocks. To make a pond, fill an excavated hole with a fiberglass form or line it with heavy-duty plastic lining. Both are care-free and simple to install. Planted with hardy water lilies and other plant varieties that go dormant in the colder months, this garden requires virtually no help from you. Just add a few Japanese snails and some goldfish to eat decaying plant matter. Your pond also will attract water-loving creatures that thrive on mosquito eggs and larvae.

An ornamental grass garden is a low-maintenance dream. Ornamental grasses add beauty and texture through-

out the year and require no upkeep other than cutting back in the early spring. They will grow in poor soils and in full sun, and they don't need a drop of water, even during the hottest summer. These grasses grow into large clumps, spread to fill a large area, and will reseed. (For an ornamental grass garden design, see page 80.)

The small woodland lot, once thought to be too shady to support much growth other than trees, can be turned into the perfect low-care weekend garden. Plant it with shade-loving shrubs such as RHODODENDRONS and AZALEAS. Many ground covers, including LIRIOPE • VINCA MINOR • and EUONYMUS

love shady spots, and the flowers of ASTILBE • FOXGLOVE • BLUEBELLS • and BLEEDING-HEART will provide vertical interest. When the trees give up their leaves in autumn, you don't need to rake them. Leave them to form a beautiful carpet of natural mulch for the shade-loving shrubs and woodland flowers.

Shade also is ideal for a garden full of FERNS or HOSTAS, which thrive without any care other than trimming back. Plant them in the woodland garden or under a grouping of trees such as DOGWOODS • JAPANESE MAPLES • or WILLOW OAKS. Or install this low-care garden along the foundation on the northeast side of the house. Choose a variety of

LEFT: These fast-spreading Miscanthus *grasses create an easy-care planting to relieve the hard, rigid lines of this concrete wall.*

OPPOSITE PAGE: Blue-green Drumhead cabbages and red Lollo Rosso lettuces are laid out in squares of artful color in this formal vegetable garden. The surrounding stone blocks keep the pathways weed free and clean.

ferns with tall and short fronds and include variegated hostas and shade-loving ground covers.

The easiest way to achieve success in the weekend vegetable garden, besides installing soaker hoses or other forms of drip-irrigation systems and keeping a 4- to 8-inch layer of mulch around the plantings at all times, is to make small raised beds and plant them in rows or blocks. This is an ideal method, because in raised beds, you can seed, plant, and harvest without stepping on the garden soil. It will remain soft and crumbly, so you won't need to till it every year.

Although most vegetable beds follow the more traditional rectangular lines, take advantage of space and sun in your garden by constructing the beds as a series of squares. Or make raised beds in the shape of triangles that form a circle or square, surrounded by a low picket fence.

Be sure to choose high-yield plants with low-maintenance needs, such as PEPPERS • LETTUCES • BEANS • RADISHES • SNAP PEAS • SUMMER SQUASH • and TOMATOES, and plant just enough for your family. (Two squash plants will produce a bountiful harvest for four.) As a weekend gardener, you need to resist overplanting or you'll spend too much time cultivating and harvesting vegetables you can't eat. (See Chapter 4 for more.)

A weekend gardener can have any style of garden, as long as the words of American philosopher and naturalist Henry David Thoreau are followed:

"Simplify, simplify, simplify." Start with simple garden styles and gradually increase the number of plantings to expand the designs that you find to be most care-free. And keep your garden in balance in terms of time and desires. If you want a large vegetable bed (which means more vegetables but also more work), fill the rest of the garden with no-care ornamental grasses and install a self-sufficient pool. In a meadow that doesn't need mulching or weeding, plant wildflowers. For every plant or bed you install that requires the least bit of effort, include one that requires no effort at all.

Planning Your Weekend Garden

Once you have learned all you can about your garden space, the style you prefer, the plants you want to include, and the techniques and strategies available to you, it is time to plan your garden. Consider the needs of each plant. Does it need full sun or part shade? How will it influence the position of other plants and the overall scheme of the bed? How can you take advantage of the low-care elements that already exist in your garden? Consider the following, too, when developing your garden plan:

- The more sun most vegetables get, the better, so locate your vegetable garden where it will receive at least eight hours of full sun a day. It also should be close to the house and accessible to a water supply. When you plan your vegetable garden, make a detailed diagram of the plot. Place the tallest plants where they won't cast shade on the smaller varieties. Allow for growth habits of bushy plants like tomatoes, peppers, and squash. Zucchinis, for example, need to be planted 3 feet apart. Also make note of plants that will replace other crops as they are harvested. This way you will be able to plant more varieties in a small plot. Because vegetable crops need rotating annually to avoid diseases and pest infestations, save your vegetable garden plans so you can refer to them year after year.

- An area with mature deciduous trees is perfect for a low-care woodland garden. If the tree canopy creates dense shade (no sun at all), consider removing a few branches or thinning out a few saplings.

- The perfect spot for an herb garden is right outside the kitchen door, where you can dash for a handful of basil while the spaghetti sauce simmers. Make sure your herb garden receives full sun and is sheltered from wind.

- A pool surrounded by colorful annuals, perennials, and flowering shrubs will attract butterflies and hummingbirds, so you will want it within view of a window or the patio. Position it away from large deciduous trees, if possible, to keep leaves from covering the pond's surface. Also, hardy water lilies need at least six hours of sun a day.

- Remember to plan for walkways and paths that will lead viewers to the different parts of your garden. Low-care

OPPOSITE PAGE: Densely planted with vegetables and flowers, these rectangular beds are surrounded by low-maintenance stone walkways. Narrow pathways separate mounded blocks of soil, allowing the gardener to harvest vegetables without stepping on the growing area.

ABOVE: This herb garden incorporates the traditional design of small square beds intersected by brick pathways. When located in full sun and protected from wind by a wall or hedge, herbs grow into large, lush plants providing a steady harvest from spring through autumn.

walkways can be made from a thick layer of gravel or crushed stone, flagstones, irregular slabs of stone, wood decking, or bricks embedded in sand (see Weekend Project #37). Paths planted with slow-growing grasses are easy to maintain because they don't need to be mowed often.

- The easiest path of all to install is one made of a thick layer of wood chips. Just renew the layer once a year to keep weed growth at a minimum. Use wood chips as a pathway through a woodland area or a shaded spot where little else will grow. In sunny areas, make the pathways of thickly layered shredded bark, which does a better job of smothering weeds.

When you have your ideas down on paper, sit back and think about the changes you have planned. If it is winter and too early to start work outside, study garden catalogs and make a list of the plants you would like to grow. Do some research to make sure they are low care. Visit your local nursery for a talk with the resident horticulturalist, visit a public garden, or get your neighbor's recommendations on what grows well locally. Researching thoroughly and learning from others' successes and failures will save you time and money when you break ground.

GET YOUR PLAN ON PAPER

Now that you've considered your garden from every necessary angle, get your plan down on paper. Begin by measuring your property, then transfer this information onto graph paper using the scale of one square to represent 1 square foot. Next, mark the house, other buildings on the property, and other permanent components such as the driveway, paths, walls, shade and specimen trees, hedges, and established beds. Indicate which direction is north and identify the areas that receive full sun, those that get a few hours of sun, and those that are mostly in the shade. You'll also want to make note of areas that are sheltered or windy, as well as any areas that dry out quickly or often are subject to early frost. All of these factors will influence where you put your beds and what plants you fill them with.

After recording the existing elements, take a sheet of tracing paper and tape it over the top. Sketch out your ideas for raised beds, an ornamental pond, specimen plantings, an herb garden, or any other specific garden designs. Repeat with several sheets until you're satisfied

with the results. Transfer the final scheme to the graph paper and make several copies to mark up in the future as you expand your garden or your plans change.

Next, test the soil for available nutrients and acidity and alkalinity levels (the soil pH). Take samples from different parts of the garden and mix them together to get a general reading. The most accurate way to test your soil is to take the sample to a professional laboratory or to your county extension service. State colleges also usually have soil-

LEFT: While the grass pathway that has been chosen to set off this formal garden will need occasional mowing, the perennial border is planted for low maintenance. The many varieties massed throughout the bed crowd out weeds and the plantings of orange montbretias and lamb's-ears soften the straight lines of the border, eliminating the need for frequently trimming the edges.

testing facilities. For a small fee, they will interpret the results and make recommendations on how you can amend and improve your soil. You also can buy a commercial soil kit for home testing. Make sure you get one that will give levels of nitrogen, phosphorus, and potassium, as well as pH readings. (To learn how to change the pH and enrich your soil organically, turn to "Earthworks" on page 167.)

Site Preparation

If any part of your garden is covered with weeds, your first step is to get rid of them. Do this by mowing or using a weed eater over the entire area, then cover it with black plastic for several weeks to kill the roots. The roots of some plants, such as pokeweed, thistle, poison ivy, and bindweed, are long and go deep. Even if your basic approach to gardening is organic, you may find it necessary to use a noninvasive weed killer to get rid of these and other noxious roots. Once the roots have died, dig the area or use a rototiller to turn the soil.

Now you know that with good planning, realistic expectations, and the right strategies and plants, you can have a weekend garden. It might not look after itself entirely, but with the proper start and a few hours of help each weekend, it will be low maintenance. And it will always be a welcome haven from the pressures and responsibilities of the rest of the week.

CHAPTER TWO

EASY-CARE BEDS

Using raised and mounded beds is one of the most important strategies for the weekend gardener. Unlike traditional large beds, raised and mounded beds are small and manageable. They provide better drainage, have rich soil that remains loose and crumbly, have fewer weeds, and are easier on your back—and your time. These and many other advantages add up to low-maintenance gardening.

Contained by raised frames or left free-form, mounded beds ignore the traditional rules of removing turf and digging the earth. Instead, fertile soil is mounded aboveground and covered with a thick layer of mulch. You can create a raised or mounded bed in just one day, offering all kinds of possibilities for instant gardens. It is a quick fix when you move into a new

LEFT: *Raised beds constructed out of stone are attractive and long lasting. This one, approximately 18 inches high, also acts as a low retaining wall to a terraced slope. Raised beds are ideal for growing plants that require good drainage such as the lavender, hens-and-chickens, stock, and Shirley poppies shown here.*

house surrounded by compacted sub-soil. Filled with IMPATIENS • PETUNIAS • MARIGOLDS • GERANIUMS • and PANSIES, it is a charming spring setting. Massed with colorful CHRYSANTHEMUMS, it can fill an empty space in the fall garden. Create a raised bed on Saturday, then enjoy it on Sunday and every weekend thereafter.

Advantages of Raised and Mounded Beds

Once you start using raised and mounded beds, you'll find they have many advantages:

- After the initial work of filling the raised bed or mounding the free-form bed with soil and composted organic matter, you'll rarely have to dig again. Because you don't walk on the soil, it remains loose. Planting is as easy as scooping a hole with a trowel or your hand.

- Seeding is easier because the soil doesn't need breaking up; you only need to rake it smooth.

- The loose, crumbly soil allows better aeration for plant roots.

- Because they are higher than the surrounding ground, they provide better drainage. This is an advantage for gardeners with heavy soils where water percolates slowly and may drown plant roots.

- They can be planted intensively in squares and rectangles instead of long, narrow rows. Besides affording a better yield in a smaller space (as much as four times that of a traditional garden), plants grown close together shade the soil so it retains moisture and discourages weed growth, both essential in the weekend garden.

- The frames stop the spread of weeds from pathways and lawns, so you spend less of your weekend weeding.

- They can be planted earlier in the spring because the soil thaws, dries out, and warms up faster than it does in ground-level beds. This extends the season by giving the gardener a head start of two or three weekends.

- The entire raised or mounded bed can be tented over with clear polyethylene in the spring to hasten seed germination and in autumn to prolong the growing season.

- They can provide extra gardening space. When filled with soil enriched with organic matter from the compost pile, they can be located on rock bound earth, in a parking area, or on blacktop—even on a flat garage roof.

- They take the pain out of gardening. If you build them 2 feet high or higher, you won't have far to bend—great relief for anyone, but even better if you suffer from chronic backaches or arthritis, or are confined to a wheelchair.

Raised-Bed Garden Styles

Raised beds can be contained with wood or stone frames or made by mounding earth. They can be positioned to take advantage of a sunny spot and used for growing vegetables, small bush fruits, and flowers. Placed in the shade, they make a wonderful showcase for a thick bed of IMPATIENS • a variety of HOSTAS or FERNS • or DWARF RHODODENDRONS.

Asian farmers and many British and European gardeners have used unconstrained raised beds for centuries to grow vegetables and small fruits in confined spaces. The mounded beds usually are about a foot wide and separated by narrow pathways. They can be planted intensively, allowing more plants in the bed. The weekend gardener can take advantage of this simple method to create a no-frame raised bed.

Raising or mounding the soil also is an excellent way to prepare island beds in a sea of lawn. An added advantage is that it reduces high-maintenance lawn care. When located in a prominent position, islands frequently are planted with specimen trees and shrubs such as *ACER PALMATUM* 'DISSECTUM FLAVESCENS' (JAPANESE THREADLEAF MAPLE) • *CHAMEACYPARIS OBTUSA* 'CRIPPSII' (GOLDEN HINOKI CYPRESS) • *COTONEASTER APICULATUS* (STANDARD FORM COTONEASTER) • *JUNIPERUS HORIZONTALIS* 'MOTHER LODE' (GOLDEN PROSTRATE JUNIPER) • and *CORYLUS AVELLANA* 'CONTORTA' (HARRY LAUDER'S WALKING STICK). They also are filled with drifts of perennials that bloom from spring to autumn such as *LIATRIS* 'KOBOLD' (GAY-FEATHER) • *PLATYCODON GRANDIFLORUS* 'DOUBLE BLUE' (BALLOON FLOWER) • *PYRETHRUM* (PAINTED DAISY) • *SALVIA X SUPERBA* 'EAST FRIESLAND' (MEADOW SAGE) • and *STOKESIA LAEVIS* 'BLUE DANUBE' (CORNFLOWER ASTER). When a mounded bed is anchored with large rocks or a boulder or two, it makes an eye-catching rock garden. Plant it with compact perennials that love the sun such as *VERBENA RIGIDA* 'FLAME' (HARDY VERBENA) • *VERONICA* 'SUNNY BORDER BLUE' (SPEEDWELL) • *SEDUM SPECTABILE* 'METEOR' (STONECROP) •

OPPOSITE PAGE: A variety of herbs thrive in the well-drained soil contained by wood-framed raised beds.

ABOVE: By mounding a light layer of soil around and under trees, it's easy to create an island garden in a sea of lawn. The trees in the middle of this lawn have been underplanted with shallow-rooted ground covers and flowers.

MAKING A WINDOW BOX

A perfect project for a rainy weekend is to make a couple of window boxes. Purchased metal and plastic ones are inexpensive and sturdy, but not very pretty. Use them as liners for a simple wooden exterior that you make yourself.

Unless you are planning to paint the box, choose redwood, cedar, locust, or another wood that can tolerate some moisture.

Measure your liner to determine the sizes of the pieces you will need, then have the lumberyard cut the wood to your specifications. If desired, stain or treat the wood with a preservative before you assemble the box.

Using ¾-inch-thick wood, you will need five pieces:

Two sides 2 inches longer than the liner and 1 inch higher

Two end pieces 2 inches wider than the liner and 1 inch higher

A base the same width as the liner and 1½ inches longer than the two wood sides

Twelve 2-inch screws

Woodworking glue

Drill or awl

STEP-BY-STEP INSTRUCTIONS FOR CONSTRUCTING A WINDOW BOX

1. Predrill holes for the screws to prevent the wood from splitting. Drill a hole at the top and bottom of each end piece to correspond with holes drilled into the top and bottom of each end section of the side pieces. See illustration. Drill two more holes in the bottom of each end piece 3 inches inward toward the center. Drill two holes in each end section of the bottom piece to line up with the two center holes of the end pieces. See illustration.

2. Position the two end pieces on the outside of the two side lengths so that the corners and drilled holes on the top and bottom line up. Attach with glue and secure with four screws in each end section (one in each corner).

3. Position the bottom piece so that it sits inside the two end pieces, leaving an equal space on both sides to allow excess water to drain out of the box and preserve the life of the wood. (You can also drill drainage holes in the wooden base to line up with those in the plastic container.) Attach with glue and secure with two screws on either side.

4. Attach the window box to a deck railing, ledge, or windowsill with the aid of two L-shaped brackets screwed into the window frame. Or, use a strong wire in front of the box and anchor to the window frame with eye screws.

PLANTING THE WINDOW BOX

1. Place a layer of stones or broken pottery in the bottom of the box for drainage.
2. Fill to within 1 inch of the rim with potting soil enriched with compost, peat moss, and fertilizer.

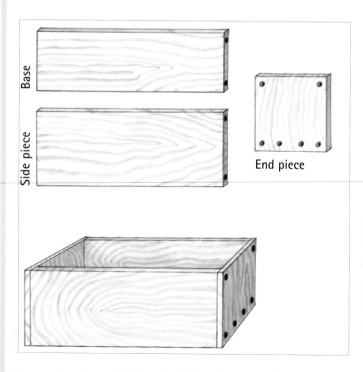

Base

Side piece

End piece

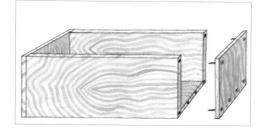

WEEKEND PROJECT #5

3. Plant the box with flowers in a variety of colors, shapes, and foliages. Place taller plants at the back or in the center, and add shorter or bushy plants around the sides and at the front. Tuck some trailing plants along the front. For year-round interest, plant evergreens such as *HEDERA* (IVY) • *VINCA* (PERIWINKLE) • *PACHYSANDRA* (JAPANESE SPURGE) • and *EUONYMUS* (WINTERCREEPER). If your window box is 8 inches wide and at least 10 inches deep, plant a very small evergreen shrub and add a few spring-blooming bulbs such as CROCUS • *MUSCARI* (GRAPE HYACINTHS) • and DWARF *TULIPA* (TULIP). In May, plant with colorful annuals.

4. Mulch heavily with shredded bark or leaves during the winter months and whenever the container is not fully planted.

5. Water whenever the soil is dry to a depth of 1 inch. Window boxes located in full or even partial sun require daily watering, so if you can only water on the weekends, position your box in the shade and fill it with shade lovers (see Weekend Project #14).

6. Frequent waterings leach out nutrients, so feed the box twice a month with a diluted 10-10-10 fertilizer. Remove dead and faded heads to keep the blooms coming.

ABOVE: Herbs and vegetables grow in lush profusion in a series of mounded raised beds. This method of using stones and rocks to contain the soil places the design within easy reach of the gardener who lacks wood construction skills.

and *LIMONIUM LATIFOLIUM* (SEA LAVENDER).

A raised bed is perfect for a culinary herb garden—herbs don't need a lot of space, but they do require well-drained soil. Fill it with perennial varieties such as CHIVES • SAGE • OREGANO • TARRAGON • and THYME, then complement these with annuals such as BASIL • PARSLEY • DILL • and CILANTRO. You can position small raised beds right outside the kitchen door or on the deck so the herbs are at your fingertips when you're cooking.

Use one of your raised beds to start flowering annuals and perennials from seed. Watering is easier when seedlings are grown in one area and not dotted all over the garden. Also, seedlings that aren't transplanted from cell packs or growing trays into an interim space grow sturdier faster. Move them to their permanent location when they are 6 to 8 inches tall.

A small framed garden is perfect for a beginning garden for children. Position it near their play area and let them seed it with fast-growing flowers, such as ZINNIAS • SUNFLOWERS • DAISIES • MARIGOLDS • or flowers that will attract butterflies. Let them grow easy vegetables such as RADISHES • LETTUCES • and BEANS. They will have fun planting an onion bulb, cloves of garlic, a chunk of gingerroot, and a sweet potato, and seeing these familiar foods send up green tops and multiply underground.

Raised beds make attractive aboveground water gardens when lined with a fiberglass mold. Or, if the frame is fitted with a wooden bottom, you can line it with less expensive 20-mil thick plastic. These small aboveground pools are perfect for a deck or patio. (See Weekend Project #35.)

How to Build Raised Beds

Build your raised beds as long and high as your space and needs dictate. The height can range from 8 inches to 2 feet or more. Keep the width to 4 feet or less so you can reach the center without walking on the bed. If you want beds that are wider, use planks, flagstone, or some other permanent material to create a path so you don't compact the bed's soil.

If someone in a wheelchair will be working in the beds, take chair dimensions into consideration and space the raised beds accordingly. In any case, space them wide enough to accommodate a wheelbarrow, lawnmower, and other garden equipment.

Construct the beds from materials that complement the rest of your landscape. Choose from redwood, cedar, cypress, locust, pressure-treated pine, bricks, stone, cinder blocks, logs, or metal and plastic edging lengths. Redwood is the most expensive, but durable—it lasts for 20 years. Cedar, locust, and cypress are other rot-resistant woods that, like pressure-treated pine, can last up to15 years.

RIGHT: This raised bed is being constructed from cedar posts. The 4-inch-diameter posts are braced with wooden stakes and are joined together with 6-inch-long spikes.

OPPOSITE PAGE: Raised beds can be constructed to any shape desired. This irregularly shaped bed, formed from 10 X 2 inch wood, is being constructed directly on top of uncultivated earth. The finished beds will be filled with topsoil and composted materials.

Using pressure-treated wood for edible plant beds is controversial. To prolong the life of a soft wood, it is treated with a chemical preservative such as pentachlorophenol, copper naphthenate, or chromated copper arsenate (CCA). During the last decade, research has shown that low levels of arsenic migrate from treated woods into soil. For this reason, organic-gardening authorities do not recommend using pressure-treated wood in vegetable beds. The Environmental Protection Agency, however, considers the levels of arsenic low enough and approves pressure-treated wood for use in vegetable gardens. Also, studies conducted by the Master Gardeners from Bexar County in San Antonio, Texas, and the Texas A & M Soil and Plant Analysis Laboratories show that the arsenic content of soil near CCA-treated timbers was well below the danger level. However, never use railroad ties or telephone poles treated with creosote, a chemical highly toxic to plants, animals, and humans.

See page 40 for specific instructions on how to build a raised bed.

Preparing the Ground for Raised Beds

You will want to rototill or dig the area where you plan to locate the raised-bed frames. Do this before you move the frames into place. If you use a rototiller, go over the ground once or twice until the earth is broken up but not powdery. When digging, turn the earth to the depth of a shovel—about 9 inches. Break up any clods with a fork; the soil doesn't have to be perfectly smooth. Remove weedy roots and large rocks.

Next, half-fill the frames with soil from another area of your garden or from a garden center, then add composted organic matter, aged shredded leaves, or another soil enrichment such as aged horse manure. If you are creating a vegetable garden, add a layer of peat moss to increase the nutrient value of the soil. Completely fill the frames. Combine the mixture with a fork, then water it so it settles. Add more soil or composted organic materials as needed to top off the bed. Your raised beds are now ready to plant. Because of all the organic materials incorporated in the beds, you shouldn't have to add chemical fertilizers. However, have the pH level checked and adjust it if necessary.

You can save a lot of time and energy by constructing raised beds directly over lawn or hard, uncultivated earth. Follow the Instant No-Dig Garden method on page 49 and you eliminate the need to rototill or dig.

BUILDING A RAISED BED

If you are handy with a hammer, make wooden raised beds yourself. They're simple to construct and go in easily in a weekend. Measure your space and buy your wood on Saturday morning; by late afternoon, you can have two raised beds constructed and filled with soil. Spend Sunday morning planting or seeding—or leave that job until the following weekend.

If you're not handy with a hammer, you can order raised-bed kits from a garden catalog. All you have to do is position them where you want them.

Here's what you need to make two raised beds 8 feet long, 4 feet wide, and 1 foot deep:

- Four 8-foot lengths and four 4-foot lengths of 2 X 12-inch wood

- Thirty-two 16d nails

Construct the beds where they are to be installed so you do not have to lug them around the yard after putting them together. Balance two of the 8-foot lengths upright, parallel to each other and 4 feet apart. Fit a 4-foot length between the 8-foot lengths at each end and secure by hammering nails 1 inch from the edge of the 8-foot lengths at 3-inch intervals.

To make a 2-foot-deep raised bed, construct two 8-foot frames, then set one on top of the other. Have someone hold them together while you nail eight 23 X 2 X 2-inch strips of wood vertically, approximately 2 feet apart, to the interior of the two frames. You'll need thirty 4d nails for this job.

If your raised bed is going on a rocky, concrete, or asphalt surface, make sure it is at least 2 feet deep. Provide drainage by layering the bottom with 6 inches of crushed rock or gravel. Top this with the soil/organic matter mixture.

If you want a garden on your deck, place a raised bed against the railings. Make it no more than 2 to 3 feet wide so you can reach the back easily. You also will need to add a bottom section to prevent the soil and moisture from rotting the deck. To do so, nail long-lasting wooden boards across the bottom, then use several bricks to support the frame. Or use bricks to support a sheet of metal, slab of slate, or flagstones and lay a bottomless raised frame on top. Fill with the gravel and soil/organic mixture.

LEFT: Soil has been mounded into small island beds to create easy-to-manage mini gardens.

MOUNDED ISLAND BED OF DWARF EVERGREENS

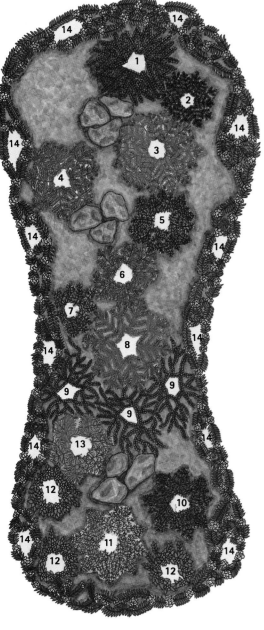

KEY	QTY	NAME
1	1	*Buxus sempervirens* (English boxwood)
2	1	*Picea abies* 'Little Gem' (spruce)
3	1	*Picea pungens* 'RH Montgomery' (blue spruce)
4	1	*Chamaecyparis pisifera* 'Boulevard' (false cypress)
5	1	*Chamaecyparis obtusa* 'Nana varigata' (false cypress)
6	1	*Picea glauca* 'Conica' (Alberta spruce)
7	1	*Chamaecyparis pisifera* 'Mops' (false cypress)
8	1	*Picea pungens* 'Glauca' (blue spruce)
9	3	*Berberis thunbergii* 'Rose Glow' (dwarf barberry)
10	1	*Chamaecyparis obtusa* 'Mariesii' (false cypress)
11	1	*Chamaecyparis* 'Hinoki Golden' (false cypress)
12	3	*Potentilla fruticosa* 'Mandshurica' (shrubby cinquefoil)
13	1	*Chamaecyparis thyoides* 'Andelyensis' (false cypress)
14	100	plants (two flats of 2-inch cellpacks) *Iberis sempervirens* (candytuft)
15	9	Large rocks

How to Make Mounded Beds

Mounded beds are raised beds with no frames. They are made by mounding soil about a foot higher than the rest of the garden, with the sides sloping down. If you don't slope the sides when you make the bed, it will occur naturally as the soil settles.

To create mounded beds, bring in topsoil and aged shredded leaves (see Weekend Project #41), dump them in the chosen location, and fork and rake them into the desired shape. Spread a thick layer of composted organic material over the top. You can heighten the beds even more by digging pathways between or around them and throwing the soil into the beds.

Planting Raised or Mounded Beds

Planting in a raised or mounded bed is a breeze. Because you don't walk on the soil, it remains soft and loose, and is easy to work—an important feature for low-maintenance gardening. The enriched soil nurtures strong specimens that require much less care and suffer from fewer soil-related diseases.

When planting for the first time in beds enriched with composted materials, simply scoop a hole with a shovel or trowel, put in the plant, and tamp down. Water plants and cover the bed with several inches of organic mulch. Six to 8 inches of straw is a good choice for veg-

Right: Raised beds can be planted intensively, which is a distinct advantage. These narrow beds are each planted with one variety. They could, however, be planted in smaller blocks to accommodate at least two varieties of greens.

Below: When there's not enough horizontal space, build up in tiers and utilize vertical space by growing crops up grids and trellises of wire, twine, nylon, or wood.

etables—it's inexpensive, airy but thick, and only needs topping up when you plant the fall garden. Use 2 or 3 inches of shredded leaves or shredded bark around flowers, and wood chips around shrubs and trees. Pull the mulch aside when adding plants later on. Water the plants and surround with additional mulch, as necessary.

To make the most of the space in your raised beds, plant compact varieties and use intensive-gardening and double-cropping techniques (see pages 44–46).

Using these techniques means no part of the garden will be barren at any time. With intensive gardening, vegetables and flowers are planted close together, then young vegetables and early flowers are harvested to thin the patch and allow the rest of the plants to grow to maturity. In double cropping, after a particular plant is harvested, the same area is planted or seeded again with the same or a different plant. Your vegetable bed, in particular, will benefit if you use these methods.

STARTING YOUR OWN SEEDS INDOORS

Sowing seeds indoors hastens the season and is a particularly good way to grow new and hard-to-find varieties. It also saves you money, especially if you sow annuals and perennials.

Start seeds two months before you want to transplant outdoors. Depending on your planting zone, this means you'll start your seeds in mid-February to late March.

Many different types of seed-starting kits are available from mail-order garden companies as well as from garden centers. You also can use plant pots, or recycle the styrofoam and clear plastic containers that you get from the supermarket or deli; the lids act as mini greenhouses. Your containers should be about 3 inches deep.

If they do not have them, punch several drainage holes in the bottoms of the containers. Fill with a soilless growing mixture (make your own of equal parts perlite, vermiculite, and shredded sphagnum moss). Moisten the mix and sow seeds evenly over the top. Cover with a sprinkling of the mix and pat down.

Fit the container with a clear top, or place in a clear plastic bag. Set in a bright area, where the temperature is 65° to 75°F; do not place them in direct sunlight.

Speed germination with bottom heat: Place the containers on special heating cables, an electric heating pad set on "low," or the top of the refrigerator (don't put them on top of radiators or other heating units; they'll dry out too

quickly). When the seeds germinate, remove the bag or top.

You can place the seedlings in a south-facing window, but unless they get at least eight hours of direct sun, they will grow into weak, leggy plants. To get sturdy and healthy plants, keep them in a greenhouse that gets full sun, or place them 6 inches below fluorescent lights. Use two warm-white 40-watt tubes and two cool-white 40-watt tubes. Most vegetables grow best when they receive 12 to 14 hours of direct light. For best results, keep the temperature 65° to 70°F and the soilless mix moist. Fertilize weekly with a water-soluble plant food diluted to one-fourth of its recommended strength.

When the seedlings have developed their first set of leaves or are about 2 inches high, transplant them to individual pots or space them at least 2 inches apart in larger pots. Continue to water and fertilize. When the plants have four sets of leaves, harden them off by setting them outside (in a protected area) on warm, sunny days and bringing them in at night.

TO GARDEN INTENSIVELY IN A RAISED BED

- If the raised bed is 4 feet wide by 8 feet long, divide it into eight 2-foot-square sections. Rake each section smooth, broadcast the seeds on top of the soil over a section, then sprinkle ½-inch of soil over the top. Or seed at the depth recommended on the seed packet. For an early-spring garden, seed the blocks with greens such as LETTUCE • SPINACH • MUSTARD • COLLARDS • ARUGULA (ROCKET) • and SCALLIONS, and use two squares to sow two rows of DWARF PEAS.

- Start to thin the lettuce when it is 3 to 4 inches high. Use the thinnings in the salad bowl or plant them in another raised bed. If directions for traditional row planting suggest spacing the lettuce 8 inches apart, set them 4 inches apart; the leaves of one plant should touch another plant's leaves when they are mature. Transplant lettuce to fill any spare spaces in the beds—between rows of ONIONS or near TOMATOES • PEPPERS • and EGGPLANTS.

- RADISHES • CARROTS • and BEETS also can be seeded in blocks; POTATOES and ONIONS can be planted in blocks. If you prefer to plant in rows, plant across the width of the raised bed and reduce the recommended row spacing by 50 percent. If you plant CARROTS and BEETS in rows, seed RADISHES between them. Radishes grow quickly and won't interfere with the beets and carrots.

- For more efficient use of space, plant warm-weather vining crops—CUCUMBERS • MELONS • POLE BEANS • or heat-resistant MALABAR SPINACH—on the north side of the bed on a string trellis supported by a wooden, metal, or plastic pipe frame. You can grow tomatoes this way, too, but use 4- to 6-inch wire mesh instead of string to give them more support.

ABOVE: *Raised beds can dry out unless the soil is mulched. Drip irrigation can be installed on top of the soil before the mulch is laid down. For more efficient use of space, plant vining varieties on trellises and confine others in cages.*

OPPOSITE PAGE: *Bathed in full sun, this flagstone patio is a wonderful example of a no-care herb garden. The islands of herbs are so densely planted that there are no spaces for weeds to take hold.*

ERECTING A SPLIT-RAIL FENCE

Charming, attractive, and natural are the words that come to mind when you think of split-rail fences. Split-rail fences are also fast, easy, and inexpensive to construct. They are assembled from simple prenotched posts and precut rails so you don't have to use a saw, hammer, or nails. Set aside one Saturday morning to pick up the lumber, and by late afternoon your fence will be in place.

Depending on whether you want a two- or three-rail fence, you'll need to sink 5½- to 6½-foot-high posts 24 inches into the ground. The rails are available only in 10-foot lengths.

Buy pressure-treated posts and rails, so you won't need a wood preservative. However, you can treat the wood with a stain to give it a weathered gray appearance. If you'd rather keep your fence looking new, use a sealer.

Before installing the posts, mark the fence line with stakes and string. Using a shovel or a special posthole digger, excavate a hole that is not much wider than the post and is 24 to 30 inches deep (depending on how far off the ground you want the lowest rail). Set the post into the hole, then fill it halfway with soil. Tamp the soil down firmly with the end of a stake or shovel handle. Use a level to ensure that the post is perpendicular. Continue filling and tamping until the hole is completely closed, and the post is level and firm.

Set the posts 10 feet apart. After the second post has been inserted and backfilled with soil, set the rails into the slots. Use a level to check that the rails are parallel with the ground. Work on one section at a time so that you get a good fit.

TO DOUBLE CROP

- Harvest one square or row, then reseed with the same or a different vegetable. You can reseed lettuce varieties every two weeks and beets and carrots every three weeks to provide a summer-long supply. Make the final seeding at the end of August. This also is the time to seed cool-weather crops, such as COLLARDS • SPINACH • MUSTARD • PEAS • and RADISHES.

- Other crops to reseed at two- to four-week intervals include BUSH BEANS • DILL • and CILANTRO. Seed these varieties May through August.

- By June, when you have harvested radishes and early cool-weather greens and removed the spent pea plants, replace them with any of the warm-weather varieties, such as compact CHERRY TOMATO plants (seed lettuces in spaces around them) • HOT and SWEET PEPPER PLANTS • JAPANESE EGGPLANTS • SUMMER SQUASH • heat-resistant NEW ZEALAND and MALABAR SPINACH varieties • BUSH BEANS • POLE BEANS • and CUCUMBERS.

- Use either or both of these methods to make your raised beds as productive as possible and your weekend gardening as pleasurable as possible.

Watering Raised Beds

Higher than the rest of the garden, the soil in raised beds tends to dry out more quickly. This is a plus in early spring because these higher beds are ready to be planted when the lower ground is still saturated from winter snow and rain. In the hotter months, however, raised beds will dry out too quickly if the surface is not shaded with plants' leaves and protected with thick mulch.

The absentee gardener should install a timed drip or soaker system. This kind of watering system is more practical than an overhead sprinkler because it gets the water where the plants need it most—at their roots. Like any other watering system, it can be hooked up to a timer to water your garden while you are away. Although it normally is best to water in the morning, with a drip or soaker system covered with mulch, watering can be done any time of the day.

An overhead sprinkler system is an efficient watering method for seeds and tiny seedlings. Set the timer to water every day for 15 minutes in the morning before the sun is directly over the bed. In hot sun, water evaporates quickly, and watering in the cool of the evening encourages the growth of fungus and mildew (especially on larger, leafy plants).

ABOVE: Gardeners who live in arid regions rely on drip irrigation snaked among plants in raised beds. Frames can be draped with floating row covers to shield tender plants from the hot summer sun.

INSTALLING DRIP AND SOAKER WATERING SYSTEMS

Drip-irrigation systems made specifically for raised beds are available. The kits contain the rigid drip hoses and a connector that attaches to a feeder hose, which is connected to the faucet. However, a length of flexible soaker hose without the special connector is just as effective. Lay either system directly on top of the soil in a U- or W-shape and cover with mulch. During the hottest and wettest days of summer, when mulch is not effective enough to stop weed growth, cover the drip/soaker hoses with black plastic (which prevents weed growth and locks in moisture) or a weed barrier fabric. The weed fabric is the better choice because it allows air, rain, and water-soluble fertilizers to reach the plants' roots. Finally, cover the plastic or fabric with straw, shredded bark, or wood chips. Although the plastic prevents moisture from evaporating from the soil, it must be covered with mulch to prevent it from absorbing too much sun and overheating the plants' roots.

LEFT: A densely planted bed of flowering perennials is a welcome change from the usual formal foundation plantings of evergreen shrubs. To create such a garden, plant the shallow-rooted perennials in a thick layer of composted materials, and mulch heavily with shredded bark.

A No-Dig Garden

A no-dig garden may sound impossible, but actually is easy to create. By laying newspapers in the bottom of the bed and topping them with 8 to 12 inches of enriched soil, the weekend gardener gets crumbly, healthy soil without hours of digging. This no-dig method can turn any uncultivated area into an oasis, such as an "island" in the middle of a lawn, a border along a driveway, or a kitchen garden outside the back door.

• Decide on the size and location of your no-dig garden, then outline the bed with a garden hose. Mow the grass and weeds as close to the soil level as possible.

• Cover the site with a thick layer—about 40 pages—of newspaper. Wet it, then cover with 6 inches of shredded bark, shredded leaves, or wood chips. Saturate the mulch with water. Deprived of light and air, the grass and weeds under the newspapers and mulch will die. The decayed roots will add nutrients to the soil and attract earthworms, which will help break down the earth. During the warmer months, decay and soil breakdown is accelerated, and in about four to six weeks you'll be ready to plant. When you prepare a no-dig bed in early spring or in autumn, the colder earth conditions slow down microorganism and earthworm activity, causing the weed and soil breakdown to be much slower. Once warmer weather arrives, however, the breakdown process takes place rapidly.

• To plant, pull back the mulch and use a trowel or shovel (depending on the size of the plant) to push through the rotting newspapers into the soil. Form a hole, loosen the soil, and set in the plant. Tamp down the soil and water thoroughly. Draw the mulch around the plantings or add additional mulch.

This no-dig method works well for herbs, annuals, perennials, shrubs, trees, and vegetables. When planting a tree, however, still dig a hole and loosen the soil in a wide area to allow for lateral root growth. Or plant trees and shrubs before you lay down the newspapers and mulch, then wait four to six weeks to add the more delicate annual and perennial flowers, whose root systems require soft, loose earth.

An Instant No-Dig Garden

There is a way to shortcut even the no-dig method just described. Use the *instant* no-dig method to create a garden in no time for flowers, vegetables, and herbs. Make it in the morning and plant it in the afternoon—it's that fast.

- Mow the lawn or weeds, then lay down a thick layer—about 40 pages—of newspapers.

- Wet the newspapers, then cover them with 8 to 12 inches of compost-enriched soil. By adding the loose soil, you don't have to wait for the earth under the newspapers to break down; plant it immediately with shallow-growing plants. Turn it into an herb garden or a border of annuals and perennials, small shrubs, ground covers, and a mixture of spring and summer bulbs.

- To plant, use a trowel to make a hole in the soil, gently pull apart the plant's roots, and place the plant in the enriched soil. Tamp down and water thoroughly.

- When all the plants are in place, add several inches of mulch to the bed.

By keeping your garden contained and controlled in raised and mounded beds, you will eliminate many of the time-consuming chores that plague every gardener, but especially the weekend gardener. Instead, by using these simple methods, you can concentrate on the real purpose of developing your garden—relaxing and enjoying its beauty and bounty.

WEEKEND PROJECT   #8

PLANTING A MAILBOX GARDEN

Welcome your friends and the mail carrier by planting a seasonal garden around the mailbox. The following design will work for sun or partial shade, and it will provide interest all year round.

MAILBOX GARDEN

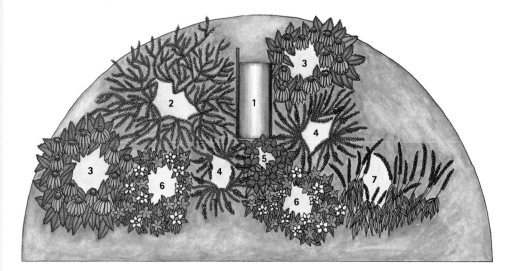

KEY	QTY	NAME
1	1	Mailbox
2	1	*Juniperus procumbens* 'Nana' (creeping juniper)
3	2	*Echinacea purpurea* (purple cone-flower)

KEY	QTY	NAME
4	2	*Erica* 'Winter Beauty' (heath)
5	1	*Clematis* 'Jackmanii' (leather flower)
6	6	*Vinca rosea* (Madagascar periwinkle)
7	1	*Salvia purpurea* (annual purple salvia)

CHAPTER THREE

EASY-CARE PLANTS

When you garden only on the weekends, it makes sense to use plants that require minimal care and offer maximum return for your time and effort. When you visit a nursery or browse through a catalog, look for plant and seed varieties that are resistant to diseases and garden pests and that require little or no fertilizing and watering. Beware of plants with invasive root systems or those that need deadheading or staking. Choose plants with the longest bloom time. Finally, be sure you select the right plant for the right place. Buy fast-spreading varieties for large spaces, and compact or slow-growing cultivars for small areas. Follow these rules and you'll get a lot of pleasure and satisfaction with little effort.

LEFT: Pincushion flowers, ornamental onions, flax, and bellflowers are long-blooming perennials. Here they tumble together in a symphony of blues to create an informal, low-maintenance border.

This chapter highlights numerous low-care plants. Among these plants you'll find fast-growing ground covers that will spread over bare spots, and annual flowers that will fill in spaces and bloom from spring until frost. You also will learn which flowers reseed prolifically to provide additional new plants the following year. If you live in a hot or dry climate, read about the varieties that are particularly water thrifty.

The section on bulbs shows that they are some of the ultimate low-care flowers. You plant them once—under trees, in mixed beds and borders, by entryways—and they'll spread and bloom for years and years with little or no upkeep.

For plantings that deliver year-round interest, look to low-care ornamental grasses. Check out the many varieties available. You'll find a good selection suited to wet or dry soil conditions, as well as short and straight varieties that spread to form ground covers, small and mounding plants that cascade over a pond edge or soften a stark pathway, and tall and feathery selections that add interest as accent plantings, create a dramatic backdrop, or form an inexpensive and fast-growing hedge.

From annuals to ornamentals, the possibilities for the weekend gardener

are endless. Choose carefully and yours will be a low-maintenance garden full of variety, beauty, and interest.

Great Ground Covers

Although often planted for decorative effect, most ground covers are a practical addition to the weekend garden. They need no watering or fertilizing, and once established rarely need weeding because many form dense mats that act as weed barriers. Their various

ABOVE: Ajuga spreads quickly in sun or partial shade to form dense mats of rosy-purple foliage bearing short spikes of blue flowers. Use it to fill in bare spots and crowd out weeds.

OPPOSITE PAGE: Pansies thrive in cooler weather. Pick up several packs in early spring and again in autumn; they will provide color for many months of the year. These compact plants are good choices to plant in window boxes and hanging baskets.

heights, shapes, colors, and textures will add new dimension to forgotten corners of your garden. Perennials, evergreen ground covers in particular, offer a speedy solution to problem sites. Use them to fill in bare spots, to replace a section of lawn, or to control erosion. Plant them in shady areas and on sunny slopes and banks too steep to mow. Planted next to rocks or concrete steps and on top of walls, they create a softening effect.

When choosing ground covers, think about how their different textures and colors can enhance your landscape. Some, such as *Ajuga* (BUGLEWEED) • *Lamium* (DEAD NETTLE) • and *Viola* (VIOLETS), have the added bonus of producing beautiful blooms. They spread prolifically with leaves that hug the ground. Their leaves and those of other ground covers can often provide year-round interest. *Lamium* has pale green leaves etched with silver. (*Aegopodium podagraria* 'Variegatum' [BISHOP'S WEED or GOUTWEED] has similar blue-green silver-etched leaves but is deciduous.) With variegated shades of green and bronze, burgundy and cream, and lavender and cream, the leafy rosettes of *Ajuga* surpass the beauty of its flowers. Planted in sun or shade, it will form a

PLANTING TUBS OF PANSIES IN THE AUTUMN

With their richly colored faces, pansies are everybody's favorite. These sturdy plants perform in full or partial sun, and in hot or cool weather. They bloom with frost on their faces in 20° weather.

One weekend in early autumn, pick up a few six-packs of pansies and plant them in your window boxes and tubs. You'll enjoy their blooms until the mercury plummets. If you live in Zone 6 or above, the pansies will sink into a few weeks of dormancy in the frigid temperatures of late December and January. When they do, cover the containers with

several inches of straw. In the warmer Zones of 7 and 8, they'll keep on blooming through most of the winter; mulch around them with 1 or 2 inches of shredded bark and water them periodically so the soil doesn't dry out. Remove faded flowers and forming seed heads to prolong the life of your pansies.

In hot climates or when planted in full sun, pansies need a lot of water and grow into leggy specimens. Pansies will last longer when planted in partial shade, and when the faded flowers and forming seed heads are removed.

dense cover. The glossy dark green, heart-shaped leaves of *ASARUM* (WILD GINGER) spread thickly in the deepest shade. Some herbs, such as THYME and OREGANO, spread rapidly in full sun to form carpets of tiny leaves that fill the air with fragrance. *SEDUMS* (STONECROP) form succulent mats of yellow-green (*S. KAMTSCHATICUM*), gray-green (*S. SPATHULIFOLIUM*), or red-green (*S. SPURIUM*) leaves. They will creep over dry earth and rock, but also thrive in moist areas. However, they do not withstand foot traffic. Other ground covers grow into silvery, feathery mounds, such as the deciduous foot-tall *ARTEMISIA SCHMIDTIANA* 'NANA' or 'SILVERMOUND'-ARTEMISIA (SAGEBRUSH), a good choice for softening the edges of a stone wall or pathway. *STACHYS BYZANTINA* 'HELEN VON STEIN' and *S. LANATA* 'SILVER CARPET' (LAMB'S-EARS) soften the straight lines of beds with their soft, fuzzy, silvery gray-green leaves.

Besides using ground covers to camouflage problem areas, think about using them to create a special, care-free rock garden. Choose a mix of deciduous and evergreen plants that thrive in sun and well-drained soil. For vivid color, plant low-growing *DELOSPERMA COOPERI* (ICE PLANT); its deep green, finely cut foliage is covered with 2-inch purple daisies throughout the summer. Another prolific bloomer that grows about 6 inches tall and spreads into large mats is *CERATOSTIGMA PLUMBAGINOIDES* (PLUMBAGO). In summer intensely blue flowers cover the green foliage, which turns burgundy in autumn. For the rock garden, any ground cover particularly drought tolerant will do well. Some of these include *FESTUCA OVINA* (DWARF FESCUE) • *SAPONARIA* (SOAPWORT) • *SAXIFRAGA* (ROCKFOIL) • *SEDUM SPURIUM* and *S. ACRE* (STONECROP) • *SEMPERVIVUM* (HENS-AND-

BEAUTIFYING A TREE STUMP

When the stump of a fallen tree remains, accept it as a gift from nature and beautify it with plantings.

If the stump is 8 to 10 feet high, bore a 1-inch-diameter hole about 10 inches below the top of the stump. This will entice downy, hairy, and red-bellied woodpeckers to continue to hollow it out for nesting accommodations. A trunk that is rotting will attract chickadees, who will peck out nesting holes.

Cultivate the soil at the bottom of the stump and plant with flowers that will grow in the available light. See Chapters 3, 5, and 6 for suggestions.

When the trunk has a wide diameter, is about 3 feet high, and is located in full sun, cover it with plastic netting used to grow pole beans or cucumbers. Plant around the base with climbing vegetables such as tomatoes, winter squash, and melons. Or seed around with flowering vines such as *PHASEOLUS COCCINEUS* (SCARLET RUNNER BEAN) • *IPOMOEA PURPUREA* (MORNING GLORY) • *THUNBERGIA GREGORII* (CLOCKVINE) • or PERENNIAL CLEMATIS.

If the inside of the stump is rotting, form a shallow hole and fill with garden soil or compost. Plant with PETUNIAS • *VIOLA X WITTROCKIANA* (PANSY) • *TAGETES* (FRENCH MARIGOLD) • *SAPONARIA* (SOAPWORT) • *TROPAEOLUM* (NASTURTIUM) • or other colorful flowers.

ABOVE: Pink-flowering stonecrop (Sedum spurium) *and creeping Jenny* (Lysimachia num-mularia) *spread rapidly to cover the well-drained soil of a rock garden.*

CHICKENS) • *POTENTILLA* (CINQUEFOIL) • and *PHLOX SUBULATA* (MOSS or MOUN-TAIN PINK).

Some ground covers are more suitable for a woodland setting where plants of varying heights, textures, and colors can fill in beneath deciduous and evergreen trees. Such shade-loving, spreading plants include low-growing *GALIUM ODORATUM* (SWEET WOODRUFF), whose 6-inch-tall whorls of fine, narrow, bright green leaves are covered with dainty white flowers in May and June. *MAZUS REPTANS* is a beautiful plant with ragged bright green leaves and violet and white flowers. It spreads vigorously into low-growing, large mats when planted in moist soil and partial shade. A taller ground cover at 6 to 10 inches, *TIARELLA CORDIFOLIA* (FOAMFLOWER) puts on a show of erect clusters of white flowers above a dense growth of leaves. *HOSTAS* (PLAINTAIN LILIES) will grow into dense stands when planted in groupings. Their leaf colors range from pale green to blue green and from variegated white and green to yellow and green. Many varieties grow 20 inches to 2 feet tall by

2½ to 3 feet wide. They love light shade and moist soil, and need no fertilizing, spraying, or watering.

The best low-maintenance ground covers are perennials that hug the ground and send out strong runners. These include shrubs such as *JUNIPERUS PROCUMBENS* (PROSTRATE JUNIPER) • *COTONEASTER SALICIFOLIUS* (CREEPING COTONEASTER) • *EUONYMUS FORTUNEI* (WINTERCREEPER) • *GAULTHERIA PROCUM-BENS* (WINTERGREEN) • *CORNUS CANADENSIS* (MINIATURE DOGWOOD) • and DWARF AZA-LEAS. There are woody-stemmed vines that will tame a slope and control erosion but should not be planted with flowers and shrubs. These include *LONICERA JAPONICA* (HONEYSUCKLE) • VIRGINIA CREEPER • and *HEDERA HELIX* (ENGLISH IVY). Also, taller plant varieties such as FERNS • HOSTAS • *HEMEROCALLIS* (DAYLILIES) • and *HEUCHERA SANGUINEA* (CORALBELLS) multiply in clumps and, once established, spread densely.

Wherever you decide to plant a ground cover, match it to the conditions of your site, or you will be wasting your time, effort, and money. If chosen carefully, and once established, it will save you time because it won't need mowing and may never need weeding, fertilizing, or watering.

LOW-CARE GROUND COVERS

Here is a list of perennial evergreen ground covers well suited for the weekend garden. Plant them on a slope, under trees, or wherever it is difficult to mow or grass won't grow.

AJUGA REPTANS (BUGLEWEED)

AJUGA wins first prize for fast growth, beauty, and year-round color. Many varieties are available with varicolored foliage: deep green, bronze-purple, and cream with deep pink. The leaves form a dense tapestry of variegated rosettes, while the flowers grow 4 to 6 inches high and have blooms in pink, white, bright blue, and purple-blue. *AJUGA* prefers well-drained soil and grows in sun or shade but spreads faster and produces better blooms when it is in partial shade. An ideal choice for filling in large spaces, bugleweed forms a colorful spreading carpet and soon crowds out weeds with its creeping stems.

OPPOSITE PAGE: *Once it takes off, ivy creates a dense ground cover. Algerian ivy (Hedera canariensis) is particularly rampant and grows rapidly in sunny locations.*

ANACYCLUS DEPRESSUS (MT. ATLAS DAISY)

This 3-inch-tall plant has dark green narrow foliage that spreads from 1 to 1½ feet wide and produces white daisies with bright yellow centers. MT. ATLAS DAISY tolerates dry conditions and will grow in well-drained soil in full sun.

ARCTOSTAPHYLOS UVA-URSI (BEARBERRY)

'MASSACHUSETTS' BEARBERRY is an exceptionally hardy ground cover. Its tiny pale pink flowers are followed by a flush of red berries, food for birds and small mammals. The tiny leaves of this dense, spreading evergreen turn a beautiful rich bronze during the colder months. A vigorous grower even in poor and sandy soil, it thrives in full sun or partial shade.

ASARUM (WILD GINGER)

WILD GINGER is an excellent ground cover for the shady woodland garden. It spreads by creeping rhizomes and, depending on the variety, the evergreen heart-shaped leaves grow from 2 to 7 inches. Leaves of *A. CAUDATUM* • *A. ARIFOLIUM* • *A. EUROPAEUM* • and *A. VIRGINICUM* are glossy and hardy to minus 15 to minus 25°F. *A. CANADENSE* (CANADIAN WILD GINGER) is deciduous, with edible roots. Wild ginger prefers a shady location with rich, moist soil.

CHRYSANTHEMUM PACIFICUM 'GOLD-AND-SILVER'

Green leaves edged with white form dense 4-inch rosettes topped with showy clusters of yellow flowers in fall. Spreading but not invasive, this plant crowds out weeds as it grows to its 1-foot height. *C. PACIFICUM* loves full sun and well-drained soil.

CHRYSOGONUM VIRGINIANUM (GOLDEN STAR)

This rapidly spreading ground-hugging plant has dark green leaves and bright golden yellow flowers. Although it tolerates a few hours of full sun, it blooms from spring to autumn when planted in partial shade.

EUONYMUS FORTUNEI (WINTERCREEPER)

This trailing evergreen vine is a rampant grower, making a dense mat of dark green or variegated leaves. It grows 2 inches to 2 feet tall. It covers flat ground rapidly and climbs up walls and over shrubs. One plant will spread several feet in sun or shade. It grows in most soil conditions and is excellent for erosion control.

HEDERA (IVY)

HEDERA HELIX (ENGLISH IVY) cultivars are the most widely grown of the many varieties of ivy. Although tolerant of deep shade and full sun, ivy is a fast-growing evergreen that forms a dense 6-inch-high carpet when planted in partial shade. It likes loamy, well-drained soil and provides superb erosion control. Ivy will climb trees or other rough, vertical surfaces and has a tendency to smother all but the most persistent perennials. No strict maintenance is necessary, but ivy should be cut back in the spring using the highest setting on your mower to control density.

JUNIPERUS (JUNIPER)

Creeping JUNIPERS are tough, evergreen ground covers ideal for taming a slope and preventing erosion. Growing 6 to 20 inches high and spreading quickly once established, many varieties are available. JUNIPER likes full sun and well-drained soil. Don't plant it too close together—some plants will spread to 6 feet.

LAMIUM MACULATUM (DEAD NETTLE)

'BEACON SILVER' and 'WHITE NANCY' are two attractive varieties of LAMIUM with green leaves edged in silver or white. LAMIUM can be grown in full shade or full sun, but performs best in partial shade. The pink or white flowers bloom from April to November on 6-inch stems. L. GALEOBDOLON 'FLORENTIUM' (YELLOW ARCHANGEL) puts on a show of yellow flowers. LAMIUM tends to be a rampant spreader, and it transplants easily.

PACHYSANDRA (JAPANESE SPURGE)

Both the green-leaved and the silver-edged varieties of PACHYSANDRA are hardy evergreens and spread easily into a dense cover to crowd out weeds. Basically trouble free, PACHYSANDRA grows well in most soils, although it does best in loamy soil. It prefers shade or partial shade, but grows into sunny areas.

LEFT: Lady's-mantle and dead nettle make a pretty team of ground covers for sun or partial shade. The lady's-mantle forms large clumps, while dead nettle spreads by sending out long runners.

OPPOSITE PAGE: A few plants of mountain pink quickly spread and merge to form a dense ground cover.

this tiny-leaved evergreen grows 1 to 4 inches high and likes well-drained soil and full sun.

VINCA MINOR (PERIWINKLE OR TRAILING MYRTLE)

PERIWINKLE is a very hardy evergreen whose trailing glossy leaves spread in sun or shade. With its bright blue flowers, it provides early spring color. VINCA MINOR also is available with white or pink flowers. Its tendency to climb can make it a nuisance when planted around shrubs.

VIOLA (VIOLET)

This family of VIOLETS • VIOLAS • and PANSIES contains as many as 400 species, including several good ground covers. The dark green leaves grow in 6- to 8-inch-tall tufts and spread profusely. VIOLA ODORATA (SWEET VIOLET) produces small violet-like ½ - to 1-inch flowers in solid colors of purple, lavender, pink, yellow, and white. VIOLA CORNUTA (HORNED VIOLET) varieties have 1½ - to 2-inch pansylike flowers in varie-gated shades of cream, purple, yellow, and ruby. Violets like moist, loamy soil and will grow in sun or shade but prefer partial shade.

PHLOX SUBULATA (MOSS OR MOUNTAIN PINK OR CREEPING PHLOX)

This hardy ground cover of spreading PHLOX may bear flowers that poke 4 inches above the evergreen leaves in shades of purple, violet, pink, white, and candy-stripe. PHLOX SUBULATA grows quickly and spreads into dense, weed-smothering mats when it is planted in well-drained soil and exposed to full sun. Another variety, PHLOX DOUGLASII (DOUGLAS' PHLOX), produces pink blooms from spring to autumn. Drought and cold toler-ant, PHLOX is an excellent choice for planting on a steep slope or on top of a wall.

SAGINA SUBULATA (PEARLWORT)

PEARLWORT spreads into dense bright green evergreen mats that are even more beautiful when covered with lit-tle white flowers during the summer months. It will grow in sun or partial shade, but likes moist, well-drained soil wherever its location.

THYMUS PRAECOX (CREEPING THYME)

Several varieties of THYME form thick, rapidly spreading carpets of color. The red blooms of some varieties obscure the dark green foliage all summer. Other varieties have pale lavender blooms on silver or varie-gated foliage. Hardy to foot traffic,

Above: A bed composed of foolproof annuals such as scarlet sage, verbena, lobelia, dahlias, and marigolds will fill the garden with a rich tapestry of blooms from late spring until a hard frost in autumn.

WALDSTEINIA (BARREN STRAWBERRY)

Inedible tiny red berries and lots of little yellow flowers set off the toothed, three-leaflet dark green leaves of *WALDSTEINIA*. Whether in sun or shade, it spreads into a thick 3-inch-high invasive evergreen carpet. BARREN STRAWBERRY likes moist, well-drained soil.

Foolproof Annuals

Whether grown from seed or purchased as bedding plants, annuals are the perfect weekend garden plant. By Mother's Day, garden centers and nurseries across the country are selling flats of colorful GERANIUMS • PETUNIAS • BEGONIAS • SALVIAS • IMPATIENS • MARIGOLDS • LOBELIA • and other varieties. In just one weekend, you can fill a bare garden with promise, a superb show that will continue until the first hard frost.

Use colorful annuals to perk up a shady spot, add height at the back of the flower bed, or soften the edges of a sunny border. Most low and medium-high varieties are particularly effective when planted densely. Others can be grouped in varying heights in tubs and window boxes to show off textures, shapes, and colors. Some favorite varieties for tubs and boxes include

PELARGONIUM PELTATUM (TRAILING IVY GERANIUM) • *P. X HORTORUM* (COMMON GERANIUM) • *PETUNIA HYBRIDA* (PETUNIA) • *TROPAEOLUM* (NASTURTIUM) • *BROWALLIA* (AMETHYST FLOWER) • *SALVIA SPLENDENS* (SCARLET SAGE) • *CENTAUREA CINERARIA* (DUSTY-MILLER) • *TAGETES PATULA* (FRENCH MARIGOLD) • *LOBELIA ERINUS* (LOBELIA) • *VINCA* or *CATHARANTHUS ROSEA* (MADAGASCAR PERIWINKLE) • and *VIOLA X WITTROCKIANA* (PANSY).

Use annuals to establish your garden's different moods. Provide a splash of welcoming color by the front entry with IMPATIENS • *ZINNIA ELEGANS* (ZINNIA) • NASTURTIUM • *CALENDULA OFFICINALIS* (POT MARIGOLD) • *BEGONIA SEMPERFLORENS-CULTORUM* (WAX BEGONIA) • GERANIUM • *SALVIA SPLENDENS* (SCARLET SAGE) • *CELOSIA ARGENTEA* (COCKSCOMB)• and *ANTIRRHINUM MAJUS* (SNAPDRAGON). Or plant *HELIANTHUS* (SUNFLOWER) • *TAGETES*

PATULA (FRENCH MARIGOLD) • or *RUDBECKIA HIRTA* (GLORIOSA DAISIES). Choose a cool color combination, such as pink and lavender, blue and purple, or white, gray, and silver, to relax the viewer in the back garden. Some annuals that offer a good range of cool colors include *NICOTIANA* (ORNAMENTAL or FLOWERING TOBACCO) • IMPATIENS • PETUNIA • *LIMONIUM* (STATICE) • *EUSTOMA* (*LISIANTHUS*) • *LATHYRUS ODORATUS* (SWEET PEA) • COSMOS • *DIANTHUS CHINENSIS* (CHINA PINK) • *CLEOME* (SPIDER FLOWER) • *GYPSOPHILA* (BABY'S-BREATH) • *HELIOTROPIUM* (HELIOTROPE) • and DUSTY-MILLER.

To ensure nonstop blooms, most annuals need to be deadheaded regularly, which is time-consuming. To simplify and speed up this chore, shear off the heads after the first flush of bloom is over. Those that respond particularly well to this method include PETUNIA • *TAGETES* (MARIGOLD) • *IBERIS* (CANDYTUFT) • *LOBULARIA MARITIMA* (SWEET ALYSSUM) • and LOBELIA. Cut them back before you go on vacation so the plants will be thick with flowers by the time you return. Plants that respond well to an occasional pinching back include WAX BEGONIA • GERANIUM • SNAPDRAGON • POT MARIGOLD • and VINCA. Pinch back above a set of leaves so new, stronger branches will form. IMPATIENS is a good choice for the weekend gardener because they don't need pinching back and have a unique way of self-heading: The fading flowers drop off instead of drying on the stem.

WEEKEND PROJECT #11

BUILDING EASY TRELLISES AND ARBORS

Lattice is attractive, long-lasting, and a perfect support for sweet peas, clematis, morning glories, pole beans, rambling roses, and other lightweight vining plants. However, it is not strong enough to support thick-wooded perennial vines such as trumpet vine and wisteria.

You might want to install three or more sections of lattice as a trellis screen on a deck, or put up a fence of lattice around a swimming pool, the vegetable garden, or a propane gas tank. It comes in ¼- and ½-inch thicknesses, and 2 X 8-foot and 4 X 8-foot sections (ask the lumberyard to cut it into 4-foot-high pieces if that is what you need).

To construct an arbor, you will need two 2 X 8-foot sections of ½-inch lattice for the side pieces and a 2 X 4-foot piece for the top. Support the lattice with four pressure-treated 4 X 4-inch posts sunk 1 foot into the ground. Attach the side piece to the poles and the top to the side pieces with nails.

PLANTS FOR LATTICE ARBORS
Ornamental: *ARISTOLOCHIA DURIOR* (DUTCHMAN'S PIPE) • CLEMATIS • *PARTHENOCISSUS QUINQUEFOLIA* (VIRGINIA CREEPER) • *LATHYRUS LATIFOLIUS* (PERENNIAL SWEET PEA) • *L. ODORATUS* (SWEET PEA) • *IPOMOEA* (MORNING GLORY) • *CALONYCTION* (MOONFLOWER) • and *PHASEOLUS COCCINEUS* (SCARLET RUNNER BEAN—ornamental and edible).

Edible: POLE BEANS • CUCUMBERS • MELONS • PEAS • and TOMATOES.

PLANTING POINTERS

To get annuals off to a good start, make sure your soil is loose and enriched. To encourage repeat blooms, work a fertilizer high in phosphorus into the soil. Use a 5-10-5 fertilizer or a finely ground organic rock phosphate (a natural form of phosphorus) at the rate of 10 pounds per 100 square feet. Compost enriched with fish meal, although high in natural phosphates, has a strong odor; you may prefer to apply diluted fish emulsion directly to the garden bed. Sprinkle fertilizers over the ground, then work them into the top inch of soil. When you are ready to plant, spray the bed with water but don't saturate it.

FROM SEED: To cut costs, grow a few annual varieties from seed. Because some annuals do not respond well to thinning and transplanting, such as SWEET ALYSSUM • NASTURTIUM • LOBELIA • *IPOMOEA* (MORNING GLORY) • SWEET PEA • and *ESCHSCHOLZIA CALIFORNICA* (CALIFORNIA POPPY), sow the seeds in their final location. Depending on your region, you can start annual seeds outdoors anytime from April to June.

If your soil contains more clay than is recommended for sowing seeds, help germination by filling moist furrows with a trickle of vermiculite; spray to dampen. Sow seeds thinly to the recommended depth and in rows spaced about 1 foot apart. If the soil is clayey, cover seeds with a thin layer of vermiculite before topping off with a thin layer of soil. Gently tamp down with your palm or a hoe. Water lightly.

Keep the soil moist with a layer of wet newspaper, a covering of plastic, or a board laid over the top (most seeds germinate in the dark; refer to the packet or other source if you are in doubt) until the seeds sprout. This can take anywhere from 10 to 20 days; check the packet for germination time. Thin the seedlings when they reach 2 to 3 inches high and have developed at least one full set of true leaves. If they are not overcrowded, wait until they have two or three sets of leaves and the plants are sturdy. Thin by removing the seedling or young transplant with a clump of soil around its

LEFT: Give them full sun and these annuals will thrive in the smallest bed. Here, cosmos, sunflowers, and zinnias add vibrant color to a bed containing perennial purple coneflowers and feverfew. All are prolific self-seeders.

roots. Transplant at the same level, and space according to packet directions.

Tiny seedlings need watering regularly. Set the timer on your watering system for a daily five-minute soaking until they are a few inches high.

TRANSPLANTING ESTABLISHED BEDDING PLANTS: Most commercially grown annual bedding plants are ready for purchase from the end of April to Mother's Day, the second Sunday in May. Buy when there is a choice selection, but wait until after the last spring frost to plant in the garden. If there's danger of frost after you've planted, cover the plants with lightweight plastic, hot caps, or landscape fabric. Plants can remain under an opaque cover for up to three days without suffering light deprivation. If you need to cover them any longer to protect against a sudden dip in temperature, choose a lightweight row cover fabric that allows air, rain, and filtered light to pass through. If there is an unusual heat spell before you get the plants in, wait until the sun has gone down to set out the plants. This will prevent wilting.

Depending on the spread of the foliage, space annuals approximately 8 inches to 1 foot apart. For a dramatically lush effect, some smaller edging varieties, such as WAX BEGONIA • LOBELIA • SWEET ALYSSUM • and CANDYTUFT, can be planted 6 to 8 inches apart. Pansies can be planted in clumps or six-packs. Just be sure to carefully open any roots bound together by thick fibers—a common problem with cell packs. Cover roots with soil and tamp down.

Water transplants, then mulch to conserve moisture and control weeds. Annuals have shallow roots, and during a hot, dry spell, those in full sun may need an inch of water a week. A thick layer of mulch will prevent them from becoming too thirsty, however.

Don't overfertilize—no more than a ½ teaspoon per gallon jug of water per plant every four weeks. Otherwise, you will have lush leaves and few flowers. You won't need to fertilize at all if your soil has been enriched with composted organic matter.

Most annual varieties need six to eight hours of sun to grow to full maturity. Some sun-loving plants that need only four to six hours of sun will tolerate partial shade, especially in the South where the sun is strongest. Some annuals, however, must grow in shade or they will fade very quickly. To ensure that your annuals have the greatest success, plant them in appropriate light.

A FAIL-SAFE TRICK TO PROPAGATE SHRUBS

There is a very easy, fail-safe way to propagate AZALEAS • RHODODENDRONS • FORSYTHIA • RASPBERRIES • GOOSEBERRIES • ROSES • WOODY HERBS • and other SHRUBS—and it can be done anytime.

When you're working in the garden and notice a long branch growing near the ground, tuck the end or an "elbow" into loosened soil. Add enriched soil on top, and peg the branch into the soil with a metal plant name tag or a stone.

After several months, new growth will start to sprout from the partially buried branch, indicating that it has developed a root system and is ready to be transplanted to another location. Sever the new shoot by cutting between the parent plant and where it was pegged down. Plant in enriched soil, tamp down, and water thoroughly.

ANNUAL GARDEN

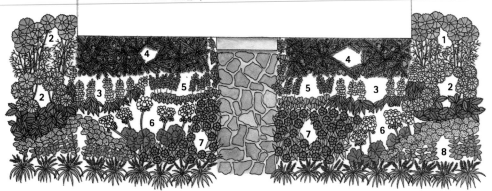

KEY	QTY	NAME
1	6	*Cosmos sulphureus* (cosmos)
2	12	*Dahlia* (dahlia)
3	10	*Antirrhinum majus* (snapdragon)
4	8	*Taxus cuspidata* 'Nana' ('Brown's' dwarf yew)
5	6	*Salvia splendens* (scarlet sage)

KEY	QTY	NAME
6	12	*Pelargonium* X *hortorum* (common geranium, white)
7	14	*Dianthus chinensis* (rainbow)
8	12	*Sedum spectabile* 'Autumn Joy' (showy stonecrop)
9	26	*Muscari liriope* 'Big Blue' (lilyturf)
10	1	Stone pathway

ANNUALS FOR SHADE

BEGONIA SEMPERFLORENS (WAX BEGONIA) • BROWALLIA (BUSH VIOLET) • COLEUS (FLAME NETTLE) • CALADIUM (ANGEL-WINGS) • IMPATIENS WALLERANA (BUSY LIZZY) • NIEREMBERGIA (CUPFLOWER) • and VIOLA X WITTROCKIANA (PANSY).

ANNUALS FOR PARTIAL SHADE

AGERATUM HOUSTONIANUM (AGERATUM or FLOSSFLOWER) • LOBULARIA MARITIMA (SWEET ALYSSUM) • IMPATIENS BALSAMINA (BALSAM) • BEGONIA SEMPERFLORENS-CULTORUM (WAX BEGONIA) • CYNOGLOSSUM AMABILE (CHINESE FORGET-ME-NOT) • LUNARIA ANNUA (HONESTY) • LOBELIA ERINUS (LOBELIA) • MIMULUS (MONKEY FLOWER) • NICOTIANA (ORNAMENTAL or FLOWERING TOBACCO) • VIOLA X WIT-TROCKIANA (PANSY) • and SALVIA SPLENDENS (SCARLET SAGE).

ANNUALS FOR SUN

AGERATUM HOUSTONIANUM (AGERATUM or FLOSSFLOWER) • ALTHAEA or ALCEA ROSEA (HOLLYHOCK 'MARJORETTE'—a biennial) • LOBULARIA MARITIMA (SWEET ALYSSUM) • ANEMONE CORONARIA (FLORIST'S ANEMONE) • CALENDULA OFFICINALIS (POT MARIGOLD) • CELOSIA (COCKSCOMB) • CLEOME (SPIDER FLOWER) • CENTAUREA CYANUS (CORN-FLOWER or BACHELOR'S-BUTTON) • CONVOLVULUS TRICOLOR (DWARF MORNING GLORY) • IBERIS AMARA (CANDYTUFT) • COSMOS SULPHUREUS (COSMOS) • HIBISCUS MOSCHEUTOS (HIBISCUS or ROSE MALLOW) • DOROTHEANTHUS BELLIDI-FORMIS (LIVINGSTON DAISY) • DAHLIA (DAHLIA) • DIANTHUS CHINENSIS (CHINA PINK) • ESCHSCHOLZIA CALIFORNICA (CALIFORNIA POPPY) • SENECIO CINERARIA (DUSTY-MILLER) • EUPHORBIA MARGINATA (SNOW-ON-THE-MOUNTAIN) • EUPHORBIA HETEROPHYLLA (MEXICAN FIRE PLANT) • LAVATERA TRIMESTRIS (TREE MALLOW) • MIRABILIS (FOUR-O'CLOCK) • GAILLARDIA (BLANKETFLOWER) • GOMPHRENA GLOBOSA (GLOBE AMARANTH) • PELARGONIUM HORTORUM (GERANIUM) • LOBELIA ERINUS (LOBELIA) • TAGETES PATULA (FRENCH MARIGOLD) • IPOMOEA (MORNING GLORY) • TROPAEOLUM (NASTURTIUM) • NICOTIANA (ORNAMENTAL or FLOWERING TOBACCO) • VIOLA X WITTROCKIANA (PANSY—needs water in full sun; low maintenance in semishade) • OENOTHERA (EVENING PRIMROSE) • PETUNIA HYBRIDA (PETUNIA) • PAPAVER RHOEAS (SHIRLEY POPPY) • PHLOX DRUM-MONDII (ANNUAL PHLOX) • PORTULACA (MOSS ROSE) • RUDBECKIA HIRTA (GLO-RIOSA DAISY) • SALVIA SPLENDENS (SCARLET SAGE) • ANTIRRHINUM (SNAP-DRAGON) • MALCOMIA MARITIMA (VIRGINIA STOCK) • HELIANTHUS (SUN-FLOWER) • VERBENA (VERBENA) • VINCA or CATHARANTHUS ROSEA (MADAGASCAR PERIWINKLE) • and ZINNIA ELEGANS (COMMON ZINNIA).

Prolific Self-Seeders

If you want to save time and money, buy annuals and perennials that self-seed. In fact, don't even bother to buy plants. Depending on plant requirements, prepare a bed in full sun or partial shade and sow seeds from a few varieties discussed in this section. In the North, sow perennial seeds in the spring; if you live in milder climates, you can sow them in the early fall, too. Seeds of perennials will get established before winter temperatures stop all growth. In the spring they will be hardy little plants, ready to grow quickly with the first warm temperatures. Sow seeds of annuals in April or May. Some annuals will reseed, and the seeds will lie dormant through autumn and winter and germinate in late spring.

How can you help the self-seeding process? After the plants—annuals and perennials—have their first flush of flowers, shear off the faded heads to encourage more blooms. Let the second flush of blooms dry on the plants and allow the fully ripened, dried seed heads to burst open or fall onto the bed. If your soil is loose and crumbly or covered with an organic, humus-rich mulch, you don't need to cover the seed heads with soil or water them. Nature will take care of them. You also can gather the dried seed heads, but this takes a watchful eye: Remove them when they have dried and before they burst. (This step is necessary to save the seeds of hollyhock and delphinium, which are not voluntary reseeders.) After the seed heads have ripened to a nut brown, remove them, pop them open, and sprinkle the seeds where you want plants to grow. Gardeners in cold northern climates should place the thoroughly dried seed heads in a

ABOVE, LEFT: Plant dahlias in full sun. If you want to save them for the next year, dig up the tubers in autumn before a hard frost kills them.

ABOVE, MIDDLE: Nicotiana (ornamental or flowering tobacco), which is available in a range of colors including fuschia, white, and lime green, will grow in sun or partial shade.

ABOVE, RIGHT: Plant spider flower in full sun and it will grow tall and reseed itself prolifically.

PLANTING HANGING BASKETS

Hanging baskets brighten up doorways, porches, decks, patios, balconies, and garage entrances during the warmer months. At the end of summer, you can trim back leggy growth and bring them indoors where they'll sprout new growth and blooms throughout the winter.

The most attractive hanging baskets are made from wire, lined with sphagnum moss, and filled with a variety of plants in such a way that they resemble large floral balls. Achieve this look by using colorful combinations of flowers and foliage in varying heights and textures.

To make your own hanging arrangement, pick up a wire basket, a package of sphagnum moss, a 5-pound bag of potting soil, and several six-packs of annual flowers, including upright, bushy, and trailing varieties. Plant brilliant red *TROPAEOLUM* (NASTURTIUM) • deep blue LOBELIA • and *CENTAUREA CINERARIA* (SILVERY DUSTY-MILLER). For a patriotic twist, combine red *PELARGONIUM X HORTORUM* (HOUSE GERANIUM) • trailing white-flowered *PELARGONIUM PELTATUM* (IVY GERANIUM) • and blue LOBELIA. For a softer look, pot up FUCHSIA with *ALYSSUM* (MADWORT), or try white and blue BELLFLOWERS. Grow a miniature garden of different varieties of THYMES; add AGERATUM as a complement to the silver-and-green THYMES.

Always plant varieties together that have the same water and light requirements. If you can only water on the weekend, choose plants that prefer partial shade (no more than four hours of sun a day) and hang them out of direct sun during the week. On the weekends, bring them into a slightly sunnier area if they look a little peaked.

Make simple baskets by using a single plant variety, such as IMPATIENS • PETUNIA • or *VIOLA X WITTROCKIANA* (PANSY). For an exceptionally stunning display, plant more than one color of IMPATIENS. Choose shades ranging from the palest pink to mauve to the deepest red, and offset with white. Or you can try a mix of bronze, orange, and salmon.

PETUNIAS are now available in so many colors that you can fill several baskets

ABOVE: Hanging baskets can be planted with annual flowers and herbs. Trailing varieties, such as ivy geranium, petunia, and French marigolds, will add vertical form and color.

before exhausting all the choices. PANSIES are also excellent for hanging baskets. They come in many deep and vibrant colors, and stand upright if trimmed but cascade when allowed to grow longer. They are hardy annuals, so you can find them in the garden centers as early as March and in autumn.

STEP-BY-STEP INSTRUCTIONS FOR PLANTING A WIRE BASKET

1. Set the wire basket on a bucket, flower-pot, or other container. Line the inside with sphagnum moss that has been soaked in water, pressing it to the sides so that it pokes through and disguises the wires. Line the moss with a piece of plastic (this will help to retain moisture) and puncture it in several places to allow for good drainage.

2. Fill the basket with compost-enriched potting soil or enriched top soil. A loamy soil retains more moisture and, with the plastic lining, will prevent the basket from drying out too quickly. However, if the basket hangs in full sun, prevent it from drying out by adding hydrogel moisture crystals to the soil. They absorb water, then release it slowly.

3. To get a flower-ball effect, fill one-third of the basket with soil. Cut slits in the moss and the plastic on the bottom and up the sides of the basket. Gently push the roots of the trailing plants through the outside of the basket and into the soil. Pull the moss and plastic slits back together around the plants so that soil doesn't seep out. Add another layer of soil until the basket is two-thirds full.

4. Position the upright and bushy plants in the center of the basket and push more trailing plants through the sides of moss and plastic into the basket. Add more soil to cover the plant roots, tamp down, and water thoroughly. As the soil settles, add more soil until it is 1 inch below the top of the basket and moss. Tamp down and water again.

5. If a ball effect is not desired, fill the basket two-thirds full with potting soil, and plant trailing varieties around the perimeter, and uprights and bushy plants in the center. Add more soil, tamp down, and water thoroughly.

6. Feed basket plantings twice a month with diluted 10-10-10 fertilizer, or use slow-release stick fertilizers pushed into the soil near the roots.

7. Pinch new growth occasionally to force branching and more buds. Cut off spent blooms and developing seedpods regularly to stimulate more flowers.

screw-top jar and store it in a cool garage until it's time to sow seeds the following late spring or early summer.

When seedlings push up in the spring, thin them, if necessary; transplant excess plants to another bed when they are 4 to 6 inches tall and after the weather is consistently mild. Invasive seeders such as *CLEOME* (SPIDER FLOWER) • *CHRYSANTHEMUM PARTHENIUM* (FEVERFEW) • *ECHINACEA PURPUREA* (PURPLE CONEFLOWER) • *ASCLEPIAS TUBEROSA* (BUTTERFLY WEED) • *LYCHNIS* (CAMPION) • and *DIGITALIS* (FOXGLOVE) produce crowded seedlings that should be thinned and transplanted or put into the compost pile. (See "Planting Pointers" on page 62.)

Here are some of the best self-seeding varieties for the weekend gardener:

SELF-SEEDING ANNUALS

BROWALLIA (BUSH VIOLET) • *CALENDULA* SPECIES (FIELD or POT MARIGOLDS) • *CENTAUREA CYANUS* (CORNFLOWER) • *CLEOME* (SPIDER FLOWER—can become invasive seeder) • *COSMOS* (COSMOS) • *ESCHSCHOLZIA CALIFORNICA* (CALIFORNIA POPPY) • *EUPHORBIA MARGINATA* (SNOW-ON-THE-MOUNTAIN) • *LINARIA* (TOADFLAX) • *MIRABILIS JALAPA* (FOUR-O'CLOCK) • *MYOSOTIS* (FORGET-ME-NOT) •

OENOTHERA (EVENING PRIMROSE) • *PAPAVER RHOEAS* (SHIRLEY POPPY) • *PORTULACA* (MOSS ROSE) • *TROPAEOLUM* (NASTURTIUM) • *NICOTIANA* (ORNAMENTAL or FLOWERING TOBACCO) • *NIEREMBERGIA* (CUPFLOWER) • *VIOLA PEDUNCULATA* (JOHNNY-JUMP-UP) • *LOBULARIA MARITA* (SWEET ALYSSUM) • *GAILLARDIA* (BLANKET-FLOWER) • *RUDBECKIA HIRTA* (GLORIOSA DAISY) • *DIANTHUS BARBATUS* (SWEET WILLIAM) • and *D. CHINENSIS* (CHINA PINK).

SELF-SEEDING PERENNIALS

ACHILLEA (YARROW) • *ASTER* (MICHAELMAS DAILY—can become invasive seeder) • *ASCLEPIAS TUBEROSA* (BUTTERFLY WEED—can become invasive seeder) • *AQUILEGIA* (COLUMBINE) • *MELISSA OFFICINALIS* (LEMON BALM—can become invasive seeder) • *ORIGANUM* (invasive seeder) • *DICENTRA EXIMIA* (FRINGED or WILD BLEEDING-HEART) • *CHRYSANTHEMUM MAXIMUM* (DAISY CHRYSANTHEMUM) • *COREOPSIS* (PERENNIAL TICKSEED) • *ECHINACEA PURPUREA* (PURPLE CONEFLOWER—can become invasive seeder) • *PHLOX DIVARICATA* (WOODLAND or BLUE PHLOX) • *SOLIDAGO* (GOLDENROD—can become invasive seeder) • *LYCHNIS* (CAMPION) • and *DIGITALIS* (FOXGLOVE—can become invasive seeder).

Rampant Rooters

The root systems of some perennials reach out, which can be a boon to the weekend gardener. Some are easy to control with occasional yanking; others, however, are so rampant that once they get a foothold in a flower bed, they are hard to eradicate. They should be used only to tame a slope or fill a space where nothing else will grow. Choose spreading plants carefully so they don't overrun your garden and fill your weekend with upkeep.

EASY-TO-CONTROL SPREADERS

ACHILLEA (YARROW) • *MONARDA* (BEE BALM) • *ALCHEMILLA MOLLIS* (LADY'S-MANTLE) • *ARTEMISIA* 'SILVER KING' (SAGEBRUSH) • *SANTOLINA* • *BERGENIA* • *BRUNNERA MACROPHYLLA* (SIBERIAN BUGLOSS) • *OENOTHERA* (EVENING PRIMROSE) • *PHLOX SUBULATA* (MOSS PINK) • *P. STOLONIFERA* (CREEPING PHLOX) • *IRIS CRISTATA* (CRESTED IRIS) • *I. ENSATA* (JAPANESE IRIS) • *HEMEROCALLIS* (DAYLILIES) • *STACHYS* (LAMB'S-EARS) • *AJUGA* (BUGLEWEED) • *ASTILBE* (SPIRAEA) • *RUDBECKIA* (CONEFLOWER) • and *SEDUM* (STONECROP).

INVASIVE SPREADERS

SOLIDAGO (GOLDENROD) • *PHYSOSTEGIA* (FALSE DRAGONHEAD) • *LYSIMACHIA CLETHROIDES* (GOOSENECK) • MINTS • *WALDSTEINIA* (BARREN STRAWBERRY) • and *VINCA MINOR* (PERIWINKLE).

OPPOSITE PAGE: The flowers in this bed (sweet William, fireweed, yarrow, and false lupine) comprise a self-perpetuating garden in the sun. Where sweet William is a self-seeding biennial, fireweed, yarrow, and false lupine spread by rootstock. Fireweed (Epilobium) is a rampant spreader when planted in moist soil.

LEFT: The well-drained soil in the raised bed encourages California poppy to produce many blooms over a long period. Excellent reseeders, these poppies are available in a variety of colors, some with double and semidouble flowers.

WEEKEND PROJECT **#14**

PLANTING A WINDOW BOX WITH SHADE- OR SUN-LOVERS

After you have built your window boxes (see Weekend Project #5), plant them with a colorful variety of flowers.

When you can only water your window boxes on the weekends, place them in a shady location and plant with shade-tolerant varieties such as *CALADIUM* (ANGEL-WINGS) • BEGONIA • *SALVIA* (SAGE) • *BROWALLIA* (FLAME NETTLE) • *IMPATIENS* (BALSAM) • *VIOLA* (VIOLET) • *CENTAUREA CINERARIA* (SILVERY DUSTY-MILLER) • LOBELIA • *PRIMULA* (PRIMROSE) • and *ADIANTUM TRICHOMANES* (MAIDENHAIR SPLEENWORT FERN).

Window boxes used to brighten the front of the house or a sunny patio should be planted with sun-loving, drought-tolerant plants like *ALYSSUM* (MADWORT) • *TROPAEOLUM* (NASTURTIUM) •

PETUNIA • *GAZANIA* • AGERATUM • *PORTULACA* (MOSS ROSE) • VERBENA • *TAGETES PATULA* (FRENCH MARIGOLD) • *CELOSIA* (WOOLFLOWER) • ZINNIA • *PELARGONIUM* (GERANIUM) • *STACHYS* (LAMB'S-EARS) • *SEDUM MORGANIANUM* (BURRO TAIL) • *SEMPERVIVUM TECTORUM* (HENS-AND-CHICKENS) • and *HELICHRYSUM BRACTEATUM* (STRAWFLOWER).

TIPS FOR SHADE-LOVING WINDOW BOXES

Boxes located in the shade need especially good drainage, so layer broken pottery shards over the drainage holes, then add a 1-inch layer of pebbles or gravel. Fill the container with an equal amount of topsoil, coarse builders' sand,

and compost. Or mix two parts potting soil with one part perlite. Space plants 4 to 6 inches apart. Plant the box as described in Weekend Project #5.

TIPS FOR SUN-LOVING WINDOW BOXES

Cover drainage holes of an 8-inch-deep plastic container with a layer of broken pottery. Fill with an equal mix of potting soil and leaf mold or compost. Aid water retention by adding hydrogel crystals to the soil. Space plants 4 to 6 inches apart. Mulch with a 1-inch layer of pebbles, which will not rob moisture from the soil. Water until saturated once a week—ideally before the soil dries more than 1 inch below the surface.

Water-Thrifty Plants

If you live in an area with sporadic rainfall, forgo trying to grow a lush landscape full of water-loving plants. Instead, plant varieties native to your area or those that don't mind going dry for a few days. In fact, if you mulch heavily, occasional rainfall will provide all the moisture these plants need.

To make watering easier, group plants with similar water needs in the same area. That way, when you must water them, they can be watered with the same drip-irrigation or soaker system—operated manually on the weekend or with a timer during your absence.

WATER-THRIFTY ANNUALS

AGERATUM • *ESCHSCHOLZIA CALIFORNICA* (CALIFORNIA POPPY) • CELOSIA • *CLEOME* (SPIDER FLOWER) • *CENTAUREA CYANUS* (CORNFLOWER) • COSMOS • *ANTHEMIS* (CHAMOMILE) • *PELARGONIUM* X *HORTO-RUM* (GERANIUM) • *MESEMBRYANTHEMUM CRYSTALLINUM* (ICE PLANT) • *VINCA* or *CATHARANTHUS ROSEA* (MADAGASCAR PERIWINKLE) • *CALENDULA* (POT or FIELD MARIGOLD) • *CHRYSANTHEMUM PARTHE-NIUM* (FEVERFEW) • *NICOTIANA* (FLOWERING TOBACCO) • *NIEREMBERGIA* (CUPFLOWER) • *OENOTHERA* (EVENING PRIMROSE) • *PORTULACA* (MOSS ROSE) •

RANUNCULUS (a tender bulb) • *HELIPTERUM* (STRAWFLOWER) • *HELIA-NTHUS* (SUNFLOWER) • *LOBULARIA MAR-ITIMA* (SWEET ALYSSUM) • and ZINNIA.

WATER-THRIFTY PERENNIALS

ARMERIA MARITIMA (SEA THRIFT) • *ASTER* (MICHAELMAS DAISY) • *AURINIA SAXATILIS* (BASKET-OF-GOLD) • *GYPSOPHILA* (BABY'S-BREATH) • *ASCLEPIAS TUBEROSA* (BUTTERFLY WEED) • *RUDBECKIA* (BLACK-EYED SUSAN) • *RUTA GRAVEOLENS* (BLUE RUE) • *MONARDA* (BEE BALM) • *IBERIS* (CANDYTUFT) • *COREOPSIS* (TICKSEED or THREADLEAF) • *DIANTHUS PLUMARIUS* (COTTAGE PINK) • *HEMEROCALLIS* (DAYLILY) • *OENOTHERA* (EVENING PRIMROSE) • *EUPHORBIA COROLLATA* (WHITE-FLOWERING SPURGE) • *E. POLYCHROMA* (YELLOW-FLOWERING SPURGE) • *GAZANIA* • *GAILLARDIA* (BLANKETFLOWER) • *LIATRIS* (GAY-FEATHER) • *ECHINOPS* (GLOBE THISTLE) • *ERYNGIUM MARITIMUM* (SEA HOLLY) •

SOLIDAGO (GOLDENROD) • *GERANIUM ENDRESSII* (CRANESBILL GERANIUM) • *STACHYS* (LAMB'S-EARS) • *LIMONIUM LATIFOLIUM* (SEA LAVENDER STATICE) • *LAVANDULA ANGUSTIFOLIA* (LAVENDER) • *LIRIOPE* (LILYTURF) • *ECHINACEA PUR-PUREA* (PURPLE CONEFLOWER) • *KNIPHOFIA* (RED-HOT-POKER) • *SALVIA AZUREA* (BLUE SALVIA or AZURE SAGE) • *SANTOLINA* • *SAPONARIA* (SOAPWORT) • *SEDUM* (STONECROP) • and *CERASTIUM TOMENTOSUM* (SNOW-IN-SUMMER).

WATER-THRIFTY SHRUBS

BERBERIS (BARBERRY) • *KOLKWITZIA* (BEAUTY BUSH) • *BUDDLEIA* (BUTTERFLY BUSH) • *CYTISUS* (BROOM) • *ARONIA* (CHOKEBERRY) • COTONEASTER • *EUONYMUS* (SPINDLE TREE) • JUNIPER • *FOTHERGILLA* • *PINUS MUGO* (MOUNTAIN PINE) • *NERIUM* (OLEANDER) • *LIGUSTRUM* (PRIVET) • *POTENTILLA* (CINQUEFOIL) • and *ROSA RUGOSA* (JAPANESE ROSE).

OPPOSITE PAGE: The ruffled blooms of Ranunculus hybrids are water-thrifty tender bulbs in the North, where they are planted in the spring. They are winter hardy in the South, where they will multiply rapidly.

ABOVE: Hardy crocus spread by bulbous roots and also reseed prolifically to provide masses of early spring color.

Bulbs for Year-Round Blooms

Mass plantings of bulbs are an inexpensive, effective, and reliable way to have colorful blooms from early spring into autumn. Hardy bulbs are perennials that bloom year after year. They multiply or replace themselves readily and require little maintenance, which makes them ideal plantings for the weekend garden.

Spend a few hours planting bulbs over a weekend or two in autumn, and you will be rewarded for many months each year with masses of colorful blooms.

With their brilliant colors and dramatic shapes and textures, flowering bulbs can turn your garden into a spectacular show. For a dramatic effect, create a river of color along the driveway. Don't be afraid to mix colors and varieties, especially when planting spring bloomers. A heady mixture of vivid reds, yellows, or oranges with pinks and blues offers a brilliant contrast after months of monochromatic winter landscape. For example, interplant red tulips with low-growing, vivid blue grape hyacinths. When space is limited, cluster a dozen or more bulbs for pockets of color. This is an easy way to brighten up a bleak corner, bring a perennial bed to life, or inject color into a woodland garden.

Use the small, early-blooming bulbs, such as GALANTHUS NIVALIS (SNOWDROP) • CROCUS • ERANTHIS HYEMALIS (WINTER ACONITE) • ANEMONE BLANDA (WIND-FLOWER) • MUSCARI BOTRYOIDES (GRAPE HYACINTH) • SCILLA SIBIRICA (BLUE SQUILL) • IRIS RETICULATA (DWARF BULBOUS IRIS) • PUSCHKINIA SCILLOIDES (PUSCHKINIA) • and CHIONODOXA (GLORY-OF-THE-SNOW), to fill in bare spots under deciduous trees and shrubs. Because these bulbs start to bloom as early as February, they can take advantage of the light that falls through the naked branches and, by the time leaves appear on the trees in early May, they will have finished flowering. Use these miniature blooms to pretty up a rock garden or to poke through low-growing ground covers such as THYMUS (THYME) • SEDUM SPURIUM 'RUBY GLOW' (DRAGON'S BLOOD STONECROP) • and VINCA MINOR (PERIWINKLE).

The taller and brighter bulbs of NARCISSUS (DAFFODIL) and TULIPA (TULIP) are especially suited to planting in swathes and clumps to soften the hard lines of a wall, hedge, or pathway. (Plant DAFFODILS behind taller perennials with lush foliage so the daffodil leaves are camouflaged during their long decaying process.) The 6- to 8-inch-tall HYACINTHUS ORIENTALIS (DUTCH HYACINTH) are pretty when used as an edging along a bed or border. With their huge blooms, sturdy stems, and medium size, they also are suitable for planting in containers.

All spring bulbs are perfect for containers and window boxes because they require planting from 5 to 9 inches deep and they don't have huge spreading root systems. They also provide blooms when other flowering plants are dormant. Place containers filled with a colorful mixture beside the front door, on the patio, and outside the dining room window. If the location is unprotected, choose short-stemmed varieties that won't get whipped by the wind. If your containers are large and deep, plant in layers, as you would in the yard, for blooms all spring. (See Weekend Project #15.)

Depending on your climate, FRITILLAR-IAS bloom in midspring to early summer. These showy bulbs produce pendulous flowers in bright primary colors or muted solid or checkered shades. FRITILLARIA MELEAGRIS (CHECKERED LILY) is one of the few bulbs that can be planted in soil with poor drainage or along the edges of a stream or pond where it will

SEASONAL BULB GARDEN

KEY	QTY	NAME
1	20	*Tulipa fosterana*
2	20	*Crocus*
3	20	*Galanthus* (snowdrop)
4	24	*Muscari* (grape hyacinth)
5	20	*Anemone blanda* (windflower)
6	8	*Dahlia*
7	16	*Narcissus* 'Minnow' (daffodil)
8	3	*Begonia* x *tuberhybrida* (begonia)
9	3	*Ranunculus* (buttercup)
10	10	*Lilium zantedeschia* (calla lily)
11	5	*Iris siberica* (Siberian Iris)
12	6	*Liatris* Blazing-Star (gay-feather)
13	6	*Lilium orientale* (Oriental lilies)
14	10	*Gladiolus*
15	3	*Allium aflatunense* (ornamental onion)

Left: The dainty bells of Siberian squills add their charm to the early spring garden. They naturalize readily in sun or partial shade.

naturalize. Most other bulbs rot in water-logged soil.

Several varieties of ALLIUMS or ORNAMENTAL ONION provide staggered blooms from midspring into midsummer. The big fluffy pom-pon heads come in varying shades of pink and purple and, set on top of 2½-foot-tall stalks, they add attractive and early blooms to a meadow, wild garden, or back of a perennial bed.

ASIATIC and ORIENTAL LILIES are also good choices for the back of a bed or border. They come in a range of colors, including yellow, orange, tangerine-red, copper, and pale pink. Some, such as the deep rose *LILIUM SPECIOSUM UCHIDA* (SHOWY LILY), are speckled and edged with white or cream. They are all stun-ningly beautiful and put on a spectacular mid- to late-summer show.

SCILLA HISPANICA (SPANISH SQUILLS or WOOD HYACINTHS) are particularly well suited to woodland gardens. Also called *ENDYMION HISPANICUS* (SPANISH HYACINTHS), they and *E. NON-SCRIPTUS* (WOODLAND BLUE-BELLS) resemble British bluebells and are available in bright pink and white, as well as rich blue. Like their British name-sakes, they bloom in April and spread prolifically. Their foliage is a glossy deep green, and when grown in partial shade the foliage remains attractive throughout the growing season. Another member of the family is *SCILLA SIBIRICA* (BLUE SQUILL), which is a dwarf bluebell look-alike that blooms two to three weeks earlier.

WEEKEND PROJECT #15

PLANTING BULBS IN CRITTERPROOF CONTAINERS

Chipmunks, squirrels, and other rodents consider tulip and crocus bulbs a delicacy. Even though chipmunks and voles burrow to get at them, squirrels simply dig them up. Your best defense is to line your planting hole with fine-mesh chicken wire. After placing the bulbs inside, cover with several inches of soil and tamp it down. Cover with more chicken wire and top with 1 inch of soil. The final depth of the soil above the bulbs should be three times the depth of the bulb. For example, if a tulip bulb measures 2 inches, plant it in a 6-inch-deep hole.

Bulbs that are not eaten by rodents include DAFFODILS • SCILLAS • and SNOW-DROPS.

MIDWINTER- AND SPRING-BLOOMING BULBS

The delicate blossoms of SNOWDROPS • CROCUS • SCILLAS • and WINTER ACONITE burst through the snow in midwinter, and these beauties bring more promise of spring than even the groundhog. After that *ALLIUM* (ORNAMENTAL ONION) • DUTCH IRISES • HYACINTHS • smaller NARCISSUS • as well as TULIPS and DAFFODILS are the classic bulbs, and you will want to have many or all of these favorites in your garden.

You will find that the life span of tulips is not as long as that of daffodils, which is a drawback for the weekend gardener. However, if you carefully choose tulip bulbs, you will be wasting neither your planting time nor your money. Although the Dutch and hybrid tulips put on a spectacular show, most of them are not repeat bloomers. For tulips you can count on, look for the hardy species varieties, the cultivated, star-shaped tulips that originated in the steppe regions of Turkey and central Asia. Also known as botanical tulips, these hardy flowers will provide at least five years of repeat blooms. Species varieties include *TULIPA PULCHELLA* 'VIOLACEA' • *T. GREIGII* • *T. DASYSTEMON* • *T. PRAESTANS* • *T. FOSTERANA* • *T. BAKERI* • and *T. KAUFMANNIANA*.

For tulips you can count on, buy from reputable nurseries and mail-order specialists that refrigerate their bulbs. Improperly stored tulip bulbs produce smaller flowers and have a shortened life span. It is possible to prolong the life of species tulips by feeding them a high-nitrogen fertilizer when you plant the bulbs and again when the leaves emerge in the spring.

SUMMER AND FALL BULBS

For the longest season of continuous color, select a mix of bulbs with staggered bloom times. As the midwinter and early-spring varieties finish blooming, a late-spring show of DAFFODILS and TULIPS will commence. This, in turn, will be followed by a glorious parade of early-summer color by *ALLIUM AFLATUNENSE* (ORNAMENTAL ONION) • *SCILLA HISPANICA* (SPANISH SQUILLS) • *ORNITHOGALUM UMBELLATUM* (STAR-OF-BETHLEHEM) • *LEUCOJUM AESTIVUM* (SUMMER SNOWFLAKE) • *CONVALLARIA MAJALIS* (LILY-OF-THE-VALLEY) • *CAMASSIA ESCULENTA* (INDIAN LILY) • *ERYTHRONIUM* (TROUT LILY) • *FRITILLARIA MELEAGRIS* (CHECKERED FRITILLARY) • and *F. IMPERIALIS* (CROWN IMPERIAL).

As these beauties fade, the show continues with midsummer-blooming bulbs, including *ALLIUM GIGANTEUM* (GIANT ORNAMENTAL ONION) • *CROCOSMIA* (MONTEBRETIA) • *EREMURUS* (DESERT-CANDLE) • *GLADIOLI* (HARDY GLADIOLUS) • and *LIATRIS* (BLAZING-STAR).

Varieties of *LILIUM* (LILIES) adorn the garden from early to late summer, while *LYCORIS SQUAMIGERA* (HARDY AMARYLLIS or MAGIC LILY) • *CYCLAMEN* (HARDY CYCLAMEN) • *CROCUS SPECIOSUS* (AUTUMN CROCUS) • and *COLCHICUM AUTUMNALE* (MEADOW SAFFRON) grace the fall garden.

Although IRISES are rhizomes and not true bulbs, some varieties, such as *IRIS ENSATA* (JAPANESE) • *I. SIBIRICA* (SIBERIAN or RUSSIAN) • and *I. FULVALA* (LOUISIANA), deserve consideration. They produce blooms in a wide range of colors—blue, lilac, burgundy, bronze, and yellow, for two weeks in June. Then, after the flowers die, their long, slender foliage slowly

turns a beautiful bronze and cascades into large mounds that last through the winter. JAPANESE IRIS is particularly good for planting alongside a stream or in the moist soil next to a pond, where it will spread prolifically.

Some spectacular summer-blooming bulbs, such as CALADIUM • *ZANTEDESCHIA* (CALLA LILY) • *CANNA* (CANNA LILY) • DAHLIA • *BEGONIA TUBERHYBRIDA* (TUBEROUS BEGONIA) • and *RANUNCULUS*, will not make it through winters north of Zone 8. These stunning plants can fit into the weekend garden, however, if they are treated as annuals and allowed to die off. Gardeners with more time should dig

the bulbs or tubers after the foliage has been killed by frost, then place them in a paper bag in a dry cupboard or cellar for the winter months. Another solution is to plant these bulbs in containers and let them flourish in the sun on a deck or patio. At the end of the summer, bring them indoors to overwinter.

Summer-blooming, multicolored florist's ANEMONES can be grown as perennial bulbs from Zone 7 into the southern states, or grown as annuals in Zones 3 to 6. Some varieties produce single flowers; others are double, with colors ranging from intense red, blue, and purple to softer shades of pink and white.

OPPOSITE PAGE: A carefully planned garden can be filled with the colorful blooms of spring-flowering bulbs.

ABOVE, LEFT: Hardy cyclamen carpets the ground beneath bare branches, where it will continue to bloom long after the trees have leafed out. The foliage will provide a ground cover after the blooms are gone.

ABOVE, RIGHT: Cultivars of the small-flowered Gladiolus byzantium are winter hardy and available in reds, pinks, whites, oranges, and bicolors.

ABOVE, TOP: To transplant daylilies, dig up in early spring before growth takes off, or in late summer after they have bloomed. Gently pull the individual plants apart and plant 4 to 6 inches deep to accommodate the long roots. Space 12 to 24 inches apart. Tamp down and water thoroughly.

ABOVE, BOTTOM: When planting bulbs in a new bed, sprinkle bonemeal to mark positions of different varieties.

OPPOSITE PAGE: Daffodils are vigorous naturalizers. Here they share space with mountain pink in a rock garden.

PLANTING POINTERS

Spring-blooming bulbs need cold to trigger the growth of a root system, so plant them in autumn or early winter. Gardeners in the northern zones and high-mountain regions should plant in September so the bulbs can develop strong roots before the ground freezes.

If you live in the South, Southwest, or West, forget varieties that burst into bloom when snow or frost is on the ground. The ground in these states doesn't get cold enough to trigger the root growth of SNOWDROPS • CROCUS • SCILLAS • and WINTER ACONITE. Those varieties that bloom late in the North, such as ORNAMENTAL ONION • DUTCH IRISES • HYACINTHS • SMALLER NARCISSUS • and midseason TULIPS, will receive adequate chilling, especially if placed in the refrigerator for a few weeks before planting. Any bulbs planted in the warmer regions need to be grown in partial shade; bulb flowers mature and die quickly when planted in intense heat or sun. Because the ground doesn't freeze in these regions, bulbs can be planted from late November through January.

When planting bulbs, choose a site with well-drained soil with a pH of 6.0 to 6.8. If you need to improve the drainage, loosen the top 1 foot of the ground and work in coarse builders' sand, peat moss, leaf mold, or compost. For earliest bloom, choose a sheltered site that faces south. Most bulbs prefer full sun or partial shade. If your region typically experiences cool springs, full sun is ideal. Where temperatures start to soar in April or May, bulbs will last longer when planted in partial shade.

Plant the larger bulbs of DAFFODILS • TULIPS • and DUTCH HYACINTHS 3 inches apart at a depth of 6 to 8 inches. Plant the smaller bulbs such as SNOWDROPS • SQUILL • and CROCUS so they are almost touching each other and 3 to 4 inches deep. For a drift effect, plant bulbs in groups of 12 or more, especially the smaller varieties.

To protect bulbs from moles, chipmunks, and squirrels, bury them in chicken-wire baskets (see Weekend Project #47). To protect foliage and buds from deer and rabbits, construct a deer fence (see Weekend Project #51).

Bulbs planted in soil enriched with compost won't need special feeding. If the soil is not fertile, feed bulbs annually in autumn with a slow-release 9-9-6 granular fertilizer (especially recommended to extend the life of tulips), or a liquid phosphorus fertilizer when foliage first appears and before buds form.

Water bulbs thoroughly after planting. Bulbs that bloom in late spring or summer may need watering once a week during dry spells. This will prolong their bloom time.

After blooms have finished, let bulb foliage die back naturally, which takes about six weeks. The leaves provide food for next year's blooms.

DAFFODILS that once flourished but begin to look puny may need dividing, a process that you'll need to go through rarely more than every 10 years. If you think that it's time to divide your daffodils, carefully dig up the clumps as soon as you notice the leaves are dying. Separate the offsets from the mature bulbs and replant immediately in compost-enriched soil.

NATURALIZING BULBS

When naturalizing a lawn or a grassy bank with GRAPE HYACINTHS • CROCUSES • DAFFODILS • SQUILLS • SNOWDROPS • and ANEMONES, scatter a handful or two and plant them where they land. When planting in lawns, use a bulb planter to remove a plug of turf and soil or cut out a square of turf, then dig a hole with a trowel or narrow spade. Loosen the soil if it's rock-hard, pop in the bulb, and tamp the grass plug back in place. The fastest way to plant bulbs is with an auger attached to a power drill. It will bore 6 inches deep and loosen the soil at the same time.

OPPOSITE PAGE: *This garden is alive with color from late spring into early summer. The pendulous lavender-blue panicles of wisteria intermingle with the golden laburnum and create a backdrop for the flowering bulb varieties of the deep pink ornamental onion and the yellow foxtail lily and hosta.*

Perennial Bulbs Bloom Information

BOTANICAL NAME	BLOOM TIME	HEIGHT/COLOR
ALLIUM AFLATUNENSE	May–June	3 feet/purple
ALLIUM GIGANTEUM	June–July	4 feet/purple
ANEMONE BLANDA	April–May	9 inches/multi
CHIONODOXA	April	6 inches/blue, white
COLCHICUM AUTUMNALE	September	12 inches/pink
CROCUS HYBRIDS	April	6 inches/multi
CROCUS SPECIES	March	5 inches/multi
CROCUS SPECIOSUS	September–October	6 inches/lavender
CYCLAMEN	September–October	5 inches/red, pink, white
ERANTHIS HYEMALIS	March–April	4 inches/yellow
EREMURUS	June–August	4 feet/yellow, white
ERYTHRONIUM	April–May	8 inches/yellow, white
FRITILLARIA IMPERIALIS	April–May	3 feet/yellow, red
FRITILLARIA MELEAGRIS	April–May	9 inches/white, mauve
GALANTHUS	February–March	5 inches/white
HYACINTHUS ORIENTALIS	April	1 foot/multi
IRIS RETICULATA	March–April	6 inches/blue, lavender
LEUCOJUM AESTIVUM	April–May	1¼ feet/white
LILIUM (ASIATIC/ORIENTAL)	June–August	2–4 feet/pink, red, yellow, orange, white
LYCORIS SQUAMIGERA	August	2½ feet/pink
MUSCARI BOTRYOIDES	April–May	6 inches/blue
NARCISSUS	April–May	1–1½ feet/yellow, orange, lemon, white
ORNITHOGALUM UMBELLATUM	May–June	9 inches/white
PUSCHKINIA SCILLOIDES	April	6 inches/blue, white
SCILLA HISPANICA	May–June	1¼–1½ feet/blue, white, pink
SCILLA SIBIRICA	April	5 inches/blue, white
TULIPA HYBRIDS	April–May	1–2 feet/multi
TULIPA SPECIES	April–May	4–20 inches/red, white, orange, pink, yellow

ORNAMENTAL GRASS GARDEN

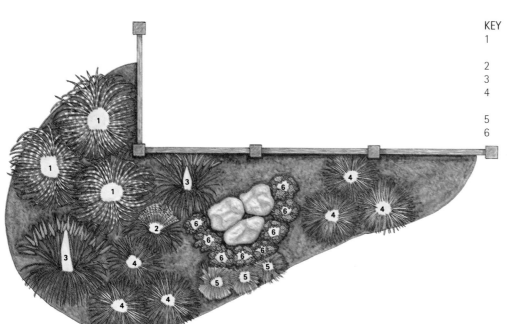

KEY	QTY	NAME
1	3	*Miscanthus sinensis* 'Zebrinus' (variegated Japanese zebra grass)
2	1	*Eragrostis* (annual love grass)
3	2	*Pennisetum alopecuroides* (fountain grass)
4	6	*Carex morrowii* 'Aura Variegata' (variegated Japanese sedge)
5	3	*Festuca ovina* var. *glauca* (blue fescue)
6	8	*Sedum spectabile* 'Autumn Joy' (showy stonecrop)

OPPOSITE PAGE: Graceful ornamental grasses, such as plumed, variegated Japanese silver grass 'Morning Light' and the shorter 'Arabesque', add interest to a fence or property line.

Ornamental Grasses for Year-Round Beauty

Ornamental grasses are perfect for the weekend garden. So many varieties exist, it's possible to landscape an entire yard with them. They add form, color, and texture year-round, and the foliage and plumes add a striking element to the muted tones of autumn and the barrenness of winter. For all their beauty and grace, ornamental grasses are easy to cultivate, undemanding, and virtually maintenance free. Dig a hole, plant and water the grasses, then leave them alone until it is time to cut off the dried foliage the following spring. They don't need watering or feeding, don't suffer from diseases, and are not attacked by insects.

Ranging in height from 6 inches to 15 feet, some varieties are short and tufted, while others are small and mounded. Some grasses tower tall and straight; some droop gracefully and sway in the breeze. The leaf textures of grasses range from smooth to stiff to saw-edged. Flowers may be nothing more than long, whiskered seed heads or soft, nodding silken plumes. Different varieties produce plumes resembling ostrich feathers, rabbit tails, or silken beadlike threads. Colors range from ivory, rose, and silver to golden brown or purple.

With such a variety of heights, colors, and textures, you'll have no trouble finding plenty of grasses to enhance any part of your garden or solve any problem. Use them to fill in gaps or add a striking element to a boring corner. Because tall ornamental grasses have a bold, sculptural effect, you can use them as a focal point. Or plant them in a row and use them to screen your yard from a neighbor's or a busy street. Shorter varieties can be put to great use—they can secure a bank, deter weeds, or provide a low-growing ground cover. Use ornamental grasses to soften corners and accent a perennial island or border. Plant the smaller varieties in half-barrels and set them in sunny or lightly shaded corners on a balcony, porch, patio, or deck.

PLANTING POINTERS

Plant ornamental grasses anytime from spring to autumn. Although some grasses will grow in the shade and some don't mind having their feet wet, most prefer a sunny location in well-drained soil. When including grasses in a perennial flower bed, choose clumping varieties— they spread more slowly.

- Dig a hole wider and deeper than the root ball. Loosen the soil and improve drainage by adding peat moss. Add organic matter if the texture needs improving. Although grasses will tolerate poor soil, they grow and spread faster in fertile soil that has a pH of 6 to 7.

- Remove the plant from the container by tapping the rim of the pot on a hard surface such as a rock or a wheelbarrow. Pull the roots apart and set them in the hole so the base of the grass clump is at soil level. Backfill with soil and tamp down with your palms, then water thoroughly. Fill the hole with more soil until you reach the base of the clump. Tamp down, water thoroughly, and then add 2 inches of shredded bark or wood chips.

- Resist any urge to plant grasses too close together—most grasses grow into wide, spreading specimens very quickly. The usual recommendation is to plant them almost as far apart as they are tall. Mail-order plants will be smaller than container-grown plants and will not grow as quickly during the first year. Once established, however, they will catch up.

- During a dry spell, water the newly planted grasses once a week for one month, until their roots are established. After that, grasses are very drought tolerant.

- In early spring, before new growth starts showing, cut off the old growth to within 6 inches of the ground. If new growth is already above 6 inches, prune just above it.

- Grass clumps may die in the center when not cut back annually. If this happens, dig up the remaining center. Cut off any vigorous roots and discard the dead parts. Remove some of the young outer shoots; then, after amending the soil with organic matter or a commercial fertilizer, replant with the dug up shoots. Sidedress with leaf mold or compost.

ANNUAL GRASSES

Annuals such as QUAKING GRASS • CLOUD GRASS • HARE'S-TAIL GRASS • SQUIRREL-TAIL GRASS • FEATHERTOP GRASS • FOXTAIL GRASS • and LOVE GRASS are easy to grow from seed in all zones. Sow in full sun in the spring. These grasses have interesting seed heads that add beauty and drama to the cutting garden and are ideal for dried arrangements.

ANDROPOGON NEBULOSA (**CLOUD GRASS**) Grows to 1 to 1½ feet tall with 2- to 3-inch-long delicate, flat seed heads.

BRIZA MINIMA; B. MAXIMA (**QUAKING GRASS**) Grows to 2 feet tall with drooping panicle seed heads supported on thin stalks.

ERAGROSTIS (**LOVE GRASS**) Grows to 2 feet tall with large fluffy seed heads tinged with purple.

HORDEUM JUBATUM (**SQUIRRELTAIL GRASS**) Grows to 1½ feet tall with 3-inch-long silky silver-gray seed heads.

LAGURUS OVATUS (**HARE'S-TAIL GRASS**) Grows to 1½ feet tall with 1½-inch narrow, furry seed heads.

PENNISETUM VILLOSUM (**FEATHERTOP GRASS**) Grows to 2 feet tall with 5- to 6-inch plumes supported on even taller stems.

SETARIA ITALICA (**FOXTAIL GRASS**) Grows to 3 feet tall with 5- to 6-inch cylindrical golden red, furry seed heads.

PERENNIAL GRASSES

Although it's possible to start perennial grasses from seed, it may take three to five years before they develop into mature plants. For faster results, buy container plants. If the choice at your local nursery is limited, check mail-ordercatalogs for a larger selection. If you already have established clumps growing in the garden, split off some of the outer shoots and plant those in the new location.

PLUMED GRASSES (7 TO 14 FEET TALL)

Use tall grasses as hedges, screens, focal points, specimen plantings, and additions to the back of the perennial border. The spread of most grasses is two-thirds of their height.

CORTADERIA SELLOANA 'RENDATLERI' (**ROSE-PINK PAMPAS GRASS**) Grows to 10 feet tall in full sun in Zones 7 to 10.

CORTADERIA SELLOANA 'SUNNINGDALE' (**SILVER PAMPAS GRASS**) Grows to 10 feet tall in full sun in Zones 7 to 10.

MISCANTHUS SINENSIS (**EULALIA GRASS**)
Grows to 10 feet tall in full sun in Zones 4 to 9.

MISCANTHUS SINENSIS 'ZEBRINUS' (**VARIE-GATED JAPANESE ZEBRA GRASS**)
Grows to 7 feet tall in Zones 5 to 9. Likes full sun and will grow in moist soil.

MISCANTHUS SINENSIS 'CABARET' (**VARIEGATED JAPANESE PLUME GRASS**)
Grows to 6 to 8 feet tall in full sun in Zones 7 to 10.

EIRANTHUS RAVENNAE (**RAVENNA PLUME GRASS**)
Grows to 10 to 14 feet tall in full sun in Zones 5 to 9.

PLUMED GRASSES (3 TO 6 FEET TALL)

PENNISETUM ALOPECUROIDES (**ROSE FOUNTAIN GRASS**)
Grows to 3 to 4 feet tall in full sun in Zones 5 to 9.

CALAMAGROSTIS ACUTIFLORA STRICTA (**FEATHER REED GRASS**)
Grows to 3 to 4 feet tall in full sun in Zones 5 to 9.

CORTADERIA SELLOANA 'PUMILA' (**DWARF PAMPAS GRASS**)
Grows to 4 to 6 feet tall in full sun in Zones 6 to 10.

MISCANTHUS SINENSIS 'PURPURASCENS' (**JAPANESE FLAME GRASS**)
Grows to 4 to 5 feet tall in full sun in Zones 5 to 9.

MISCANTHUS SINENSIS 'MORNING LIGHT' (**VARIEGATED JAPANESE SILVER GRASS**)
Grows to 5 to 6 feet tall in full sun in Zones 6 to 9.

MISCANTHUS SINENSIS 'GRACILLIMUS' (**MAIDEN GRASS**)
Grows to 5 to 6 feet tall in full sun in Zones 4 to 9.

GRASSES (6 INCHES TO 2 FEET TALL)

OPHIOPOGON PLANISCAPUS 'NIGRESCENS' (**BLACK MONDO GRASS**)
Grows to 6 inches tall and forms thick year-round cover. Will grow in full sun

OPPOSITE PAGE, LEFT: The drooping seed heads of annual quaking grass (Briza maxima) add texture and form to dried arrangements.

OPPOSITE PAGE, RIGHT: Clumps of Japanese plume grasses soften the approach to the straight lines of the stone steps. The single planting of Japanese flame grass in the forefront will eventually reach a height of 4 feet.

ABOVE: With its long feathery plumes, dwarf pampas grass (Cortaderia selloana 'Pumila') adds a striking note to the landscape.

but prefers partial shade and moist soil; grows in Zones 6 to 10.

FESTUCA OVINA GLAUCA (**BLUE FESCUE**)
Grows to 6 inches to 1 foot tall in full sun in Zones 4 to 9.

FESTUCA AMETHYSTINA (**LARGE BLUE FESCUE**)
Grows to 1 to 1½ feet tall in full sun in Zones 2 to 9.

ARRHENATHERUM ELATIUS BULBOSUM (**BULBOUS OAT GRASS**)
Grows to 1½ to 2 feet tall in full sun or partial shade in Zones 5 to 9.

IMPERATA CYLINDRICA 'RED BARON' (**JAPANESE BLOOD GRASS**)
Grows to 1½ to 2 feet tall in full sun in Zones 5 to 10.

HAKONACHLOA MACRA 'AURELA' (**VARIEGATED GOLDEN HAKONE GRASS**)
Grows to 1 foot tall in shade and moist soil in Zones 5 to 9.

MOLINIA CAERULEA (**VARIEGATED PURPLE MOOR GRASS**)
Grows to 2 to 3 feet tall in full sun in moist soil in Zones 5 to 9.

CAREX STRICTA 'BOWLES GOLDEN' (**BOWLES GOLDEN SEDGE**)
Grows to 2 feet tall in Zones 5 to 9. Likes full sun in cooler climes, partial where hot. Plant in moist or wet soil.

CAREX MORROWII 'AUREA-VARIEGATA' (**VARIEGATED JAPANESE SEDGE**)
Grows to 1 foot tall in full sun in Zones 5 to 9.

GRASSES TO CONTROL EROSION

SPARTINA PECTINATA 'AUREO-MARGINATA' (**VARIEGATED CORD GRASS**)
Grows to 6 feet tall in sandy or other soils in Zones 5 to 9. Spreads by sending out rhizomes.

ELYMUS ARENARIUS (**BLUE or SEA LYME GRASS**)
Grows to 2 to 3 feet tall in full sun in Zones 4 to 9. Likes well-drained soil and spreads with rhizomes.

UNIOLA LATIFOLIUM (**NORTHERN SEA OATS**)
Grows to 4 feet tall in partial shade or sun in moist soil in Zones 6 to 10.

PHALARIS ARUNDINACEA (**RIBBON GRASS**)
Grows to 3 feet tall in a wide range of soil

and light conditions in Zones 2 to 9. It is most vigorous in loamy, well-drained soil and spreads with an invasive rhizome system. Wet or dry soils slow growth.

PANICUM VIRGATUM (**SWITCH-GRASS**)
Grows 4 to 6 feet tall in full sun or partial shade, in a variety of soils in Zones 5 to 9.

ARUNDO DONAX (**GIANT REED GRASS**)
Grows to 15 to 20 feet tall in full sun in Zones 6 to 10. Likes moist soil and is very invasive.

MISCANTHUS SACCARIFLORUS (**SILVER BANNER GRASS**)
Grows to 8 to 10 feet tall in full sun in varied soil conditions in Zones 5 to 9. Spreads with rhizomes and is invasive in sandy soils.

OPPOSITE PAGE, LEFT: Short Korean grass edges a timbered moss carpeted pathway.

OPPOSITE PAGE, RIGHT: Japanese blood grass is a good choice for edging a bed or using with low-growing perennial flowers and ground covers. Here, it grows next to lamb's-ears.

LEFT: This mixed border is an excellent example of using richly colored and variegated foliage to create year-round interest. In late summer, the border is still bursting with the blooms of asters, mullein, goldenrod, roses, and hydrangeas. The colorful planting of pinkish red geraniums in the urn will continue to add interest into late autumn, until nipped by a hard frost.

Care-Free Lawns

According to the Professional Lawn Care Association of America, U.S. lawns cover more than 25 million acres and Americans spend an astounding one billion hours on lawn care every year. If you are like most homeowners, however, you use only a small area of your lawn space. You walk on it to get to the flower and vegetable beds or other areas of the garden. It seldom is used for recreation, and only rarely is it a source of enjoyment. Rather, it is a source of constant work.

TIPS FOR EASY-CARE LAWNS

The way to cut down on lawn maintenance is to reduce the size of the lawn by replacing its less-used areas with low-care plantings such as a grouping of sun-loving shrubs—*SPIRAEA JAPONICA* 'SHIBORI' and *S. JAPONICA* 'GOLDFLAME' (JAPANESE SPIRAEA) • *STEPHANANDRA INCISA* 'CRISPA' • *FORSYTHIA* 'MEADOWLARK' • *KOLKWITZIA AMABILIS* (BEAUTY BUSH) • *ILEX CORNUTA* 'CHINA BOY' and *I. CORNUTA* 'CHINA GIRL' (CORNUTA HOLLY) • *VIBURNUM OPULUS* 'COMPACTUM' (DWARF CRANBERRY BUSH) • *ACANTHOPANAX SIEBOLDIANUS* 'VARIEGATUS' • and *EUONYMUS ALATUS* 'COMPACTUS' (DWARF FLAME EUONYMUS). Or add clumps of ornamental grasses (see page 80), hardy evergreen ground covers (see

page 52), and a small meadow of wildflowers (see Weekend Project #3). Or convert part of the lawn into a pond that will attract wildlife and give you hours of pleasure with no work (see Weekend Projects #1 and #2).

Another way you can enjoy a low-maintenance lawn is to plant or reseed it with varieties of grass that grow slowly and need little or no watering. Any variety you choose, however, should be the best for your climate.

Although many American backyards are planted with KENTUCKY BLUEGRASS, this is the least efficient of the cool-weather grasses. If you live in the cool North, grow low-maintenance FESCUE (fine, tall, red, and meadow) • PERENNIAL RYEGRASS • CREEPING BENTGRASS • or COLO-

NIAL BENTGRASS. The tall and meadow FESCUES also do well in the South. In very dry conditions, however, southern gardeners will have an easier time if they plant warm-season grasses. These include BERMUDA GRASS • BUFFALO GRASS • CENTIPEDE GRASS • ZOYSIA GRASS • CARPET GRASS • ST. AUGUSTINE GRASS • BAHIA GRASS • MEADOW FESCUE • and TALL FESCUE. These varieties are drought tolerant and stay green during the dry heat of summer. In the winter, they turn brown and go dormant. For a shady garden, in the North or the South, choose fine FESCUES and shade-tolerant varieties of KENTUCKY BLUEGRASS.

No matter what kind of grass you have, save yourself a lot of work by following these recommendations:

OPPOSITE PAGE: *Warm-season grasses perform better in hot, dry climates. This lawn, in Santa Fe, New Mexico, is planted with drought-resistant buffalo grass.*

LEFT: Perennial ryegrass is a good choice for lawns in the North when grown in sun or partial shade. Lined with rhododendrons and azaleas, this pathway of ryegrass receives dappled sunlight.

- Grass needs a soaking only when footprints leave a grayish imprint.

- During an extended dry spell or drought, whether you live in the North or the South, don't water the lawn; allow it to go dormant. The roots will revive once the cooler, wetter autumn weather sets in. If you feel you must water during a dry spell, give your lawn a 1-inch-deep soaking once a week—longer if your soil is sandy and doesn't retain water.

- Don't mow your lawn when it's wet; the grass will tear and clump.

- Never cut the grass too short; this causes the roots to dry out. Different grasses demand different mowing heights. In general, set the lawn-mower blades at 2½ to 3 inches, but as high as 4 inches for tall FESCUES.

- Allow grass clippings to remain on the lawn as a mulch and organic nitrogen fertilizer. Lawns that are top-dressed with organic matter suffer from fewer diseases.

- Don't use a high-nitrogen fertilizer in late spring on cool-weather grasses or you'll spend all summer behind the mower. Spring fertilization stimulates excessive blade growth at the expense of root growth and makes the grass particularly vulnerable to drought conditions. It is better to fertilize cool-weather grasses in the autumn and/or the early spring as it breaks dormancy. Use a fertilizer that releases nitrogen and other nutrients slowly, preferably one that includes potassium, which builds resistance to turf diseases.

- Lightly fertilize grasses that grow in regions with hot summers and mild winters in April, May, and June. Use 1 pound of quickly available nitrogen per 1,000 square feet. Don't fertilize warm-weather varieties when they are dormant in autumn and winter.

If you decide to replace part of your lawn with ground covers or a meadow of wildflowers, spring is the best time. By summer, the plantings or seeds are able to flourish. If you want to reseed your lawn with better grass varieties, sow seeds in early spring or in autumn.

CHAPTER FOUR

THE WEEKEND VEGETABLE GARDEN

Nothing is more delicious than fresh-picked vegetables from your own garden. Gathered at their peak, they burst with unequaled flavor. Weekend gardeners may not be able to catch every tomato at its ripest and may harvest only one or two large zucchinis, but they'll still have the freshest and tastiest vegetables possible.

You may think that a vegetable garden is too much work for a weekend gardener. It doesn't have to be. Spend a weekend preparing the bed, then seed and plant in stages—an hour here, an hour there—on weekends from spring to autumn. Keep watering and weeding to a minimum by installing an automated irrigation system and covering the bed with mulch. Harvesting takes time, but that's why you plant a vegetable garden.

LEFT: Reaping the rewards of homegrown vegetables is probably one of the most enjoyable tasks the gardener faces. Late summer brings a bountiful harvest of eggplants, beans, peppers, winter and summer squashes, cabbages, and chrysanthemums.

VEGETABLE GARDEN

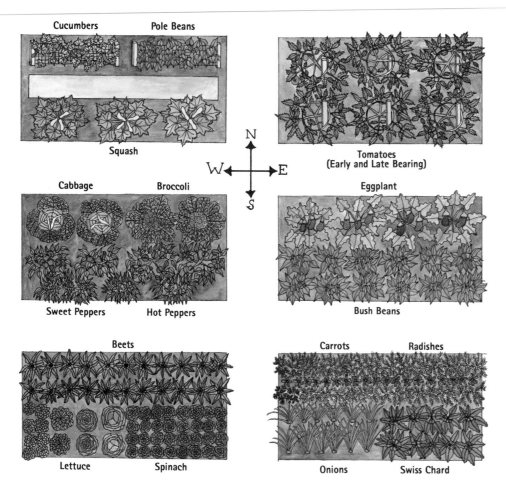

ABOVE: *The size and shape of your garden will reflect the number of people you intend to feed and whether you plan to grow flowers in the beds. Each mounded bed in this garden plan measures 4 X 8 feet. The plan is composed of six such beds separated by 2-foot-wide pathways, creating an overall size of 16 X 18 feet.*

To avoid compressing the ground when harvesting vertical crops such as cucumbers and pole beans, lay a plank on top of the soil to take your weight. The other crops can be harvested from either side of the narrow beds.

Location and Design

The first step to a weekend vegetable garden is choosing a site that gets at least six hours of full sun (eight to grow tomatoes) each day. If your backyard is mostly woodland, consider installing your vegetable garden elsewhere—in the front yard, perhaps. Surrounded by a low picket fence and perennial herbs and flowers, it can be an attractive part of your welcoming landscape.

No matter what hardiness zone you live in, your garden will have its own microclimate. For example, a south-facing slope will be warmer than a flat yard with few trees to block the wind. A stone or brick wall also creates a warm environment because it traps and radiates heat to plants growing nearby. Put your microclimates to best use.

Analyze your site's special conditions and decide how you will deal with them before installing your garden. For instance, if your best site is an open area exposed to prevailing winds, it will be colder than the rest of the garden, the soil will dry out more quickly, and the plants will lose moisture faster through their leaves. Shelter the beds with a windbreak, such as a hedge of *TAXUS* (YEW) • *THUJA* (ARBORVITAE) • *LIGUSTRUM* (PRIVET) • *ILEX* 'FOSTER' or 'NELLIE STEVENS' (narrow varieties of holly) • or any of the tall ornamental grasses. Plant the windbreak close enough to block wind but far enough away so it doesn't block the sun. Or install a 6-foot-high basket-weave or picket fence. Lattice can be used if planted with a fast-growing perennial vine such as CLEMATIS • WISTERIA • or *PYROSTEGIA* (FLAME VINE).

Once you choose the location, decide on the size and shape. Size depends on

LEFT: A garden composed of several raised beds makes efficient use of space. Metal frames attached to wood frames of raised beds can be covered with plastic or floating row covers to start the growing season earlier in the spring and extend it into autumn.

how many people you will feed and whether the bed will contain herbs and flowers as well as vegetables. You can grow enough vegetables in a bed of 800 to 1,000 square feet to feed a family of four from spring until frost. A garden this size will take about two hours of maintenance a week, excluding planting and harvesting.

Make the design of the beds rectangular, square, or pie-shaped—whatever works best for your space and suits your landscape. It is important to keep the beds narrow enough that you can reach the middle from either side; 4 feet is a good width for most people. If you want to plant a lot of vegetables but don't have one large space, grow crops more intensively in raised beds (see page 44).

If you don't have space for a designated vegetable bed, plant a border of lettuce in the flower bed. Grow herbs by the back or front door. Train tomatoes up a wall of the house or garage. Grow PEPPER PLANTS along the paths, and let CUCUMBERS • POLE BEANS • and other vining crops grow up the latticework below the deck. Just be sure to enrich the soil in these small spaces and see that the vegetable plants get at least six hours of sun each day.

THE CHEATER'S GUIDE TO GROWING LEEKS

If you forgot to mail-order leek seeds, you probably won't find any packets in your local hardware or garden store if it's late in the season. However, when you see leeks at the supermarket or produce store in the spring or autumn, pick up two or three bunches of the smallest you can find. Cut off the root ends and save them.

Dig a trench in your flower or vegetable bed where the earth is rich with composted material, and set the roots 6 to 9 inches apart. As the stems grow, mound soil around each plant to blanch the lower stem. When the green foliage is about 8 inches long, the white root will be about 1½ inches in diameter. Leeks mature in the autumn but can be left in the ground throughout the winter and pulled as you want them.

Preparing the Beds

When making beds, use a rototiller to break the surface or turn the earth over one shovel deep. The age-old method of double-digging—removing the topsoil the depth of a shovel, loosening the earth beneath to a depth of 9 inches, and replacing the top shovel of soil—creates excellent aeration and drainage, and allows plant roots to grow down. This is an especially good method to use if your major crops are carrots, parsnips, and other long-root vegetables. For other crops, including tomatoes, single-digging is adequate if you enrich the soil with regular additions of composted organic material. When dressing a vegetable garden with organic matter, also incorporate rotted manure and aged shredded leaves to add nitrogen.

If the location for your vegetable garden is covered with weeds or lawn, make mounded beds or build raised beds. (See Chapter 2 for information on raised beds.) This will eliminate the time and hard labor involved in removing sod. If you plan on ground-level beds, remove the sod; otherwise, rototilling or digging the sod into the soil allows the roots to keep sprouting and invites weeds. If you are making traditional ground-level beds over previously prepared ground, you still need to break up the earth by digging or rototilling. Make the individual beds 4 feet wide and as long as you want. Leave a 2- to 3-foot space between the beds for a path wide enough for a garden cart (or wider if the gardener is in a wheelchair). Break up the clods and incorporate several inches of organic materials, including composted plants, rotted manure (or commercial dehydrated manure), peat moss, and aged shredded leaves

ABOVE: These neat rows contain a mix of edibles and ornamentals.

(leaf mold). If you don't have any compost, add organic fertilizer by watering the beds with diluted liquid seaweed or fish emulsion, or sprinkle the beds with a slow-release, high-nitrogen fertilizer and rake it into the surface.

Vegetables won't grow in wet, poorly drained soil. If your site retains too much moisture, amend the soil with composted organic materials and raise the bed by mounding more compost-enriched soil on top.

When not seeding or planting right away, cover the beds with black plastic, landscaping fabric, or several inches of straw to keep weeds from growing.

Planning—Spring Through Autumn

Before you buy plants or seeds, put your planting ideas down on paper. Make a plan for each season so you can chart plantings and when they finish. Keep your plans as a reference for next year so you can rotate your crops properly. By planting members of different plant families in different places each year, you'll help control the spread of soil-borne diseases and insect infestations. For example, tomatoes and eggplants belong to the same family, so don't follow one with the other.

SUCCESSION PLANTINGS

Double your garden's yield with succession planting. Start early vegetables such as CABBAGES • LETTUCES • SPINACH • ONIONS • PEAS • and RADISHES before the last killing frost. Reseed three to four weeks later. When a variety stops producing and the temperatures are too hot to reseed, plant or seed the area with a later variety of vegetable, such as BEETS • CARROTS • PARSNIP • and BASIL. BEANS are fast producers, too, and, like LETTUCES, can be reseeded every month for a never-ending supply.

ABOVE: Sturdy trellises can be used to support tomatoes as well as vining crops such as beans, cucumbers, melons, Malabar spinach, and sweet peas.

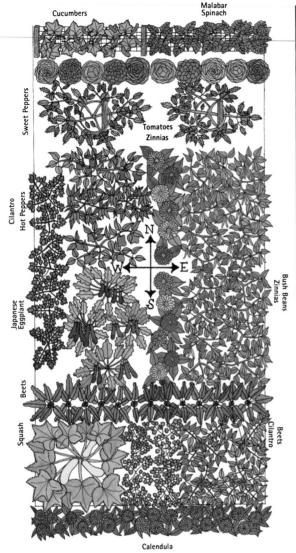

Cucumbers   Malabar
                   Spinach

Sweet Peppers

Tomatoes
Zinnias

Cilantro

Hot Peppers

N
W   E
S

Japanese
Eggplant

Bush Beans
Zinnias

Beets

Squash

Beets
Cilantro

Calendula

*ABOVE, LEFT: This 4 X 8-foot raised-bed
plan shows an intensively planted summer garden. Cucumbers and Malabar
spinach grow up a trellis. Lettuce is shaded by two tomato plants. Four plants of
peppers grow between parsley and dwarf
zinnias, which flanks bush beans. Beets
will be harvested as the dwarf squash
plant spreads into its 2-foot-square space.
Make succession sowings of cilantro and
basil throughout the summer.*

*ABOVE, RIGHT: Raised beds can be inten-
sively planted. These zucchinis and
onions will provide a prolific harvest.*

Varieties for the Weekend Garden

A disease-free garden means less work.
To protect your garden, only buy plants
or seeds that are resistant to diseases
and viruses. A plant labeled VFFNTA,
for instance, means the plant is resistant
to: verticillium wilt (a fungal disease),
two fusarium wilts (a soil-borne disease),
nematodes (tiny parasitic worms), tobacco mosaic virus, and alternaria or crown
wilt. Wilts and viruses can be transmit-
ted through infected soil or carried
from plant to plant by insects and gardeners. Choosing disease-resistant plants
will reduce these problems as well.

Some disease-resistant varieties give a
high yield, too. They produce a prodi-
gious quantity of fruits and vegetables
for a long time, a benefit that reduces

ripping out and reseeding or replanting.
High-yield vegetables also save space;
they have been bred to put more energy
into producing fruits than growing tall
and wide.

When selecting high-yield varieties,
check their maturity dates. Some of the
more compact, smaller-fruited, high-
yield plants take a long time to mature,
so make sure your growing season is
long enough for them.

You'll get a good yield of tomatoes if
you choose varieties that mature at different times. Plant fast-maturing early
determinate varieties at the beginning
of June and eat vine-ripened tomatoes
before the end of July as far north as
Zone 5. Determinates produce a big
crop of fruit in a short time, then die.
Indeterminate tomato varieties take

GROWING A WHEELBARROW OF SALAD GREENS

Placing soil in a wheelbarrow means you can prolong the growing season because the soil warms up earlier in the spring and doesn't freeze as early in autumn. In less than an hour, you can sow lettuce and herb seeds and get a jump on spring. Or, do this one morning in late summer and prolong the growing cycle after the first hard frost that autumn.

STEP-BY-STEP INSTRUCTIONS FOR CONSTRUCTING A WHEELBARROW OF SALAD GREENS

1. Create good drainage by spreading 1 to 2 inches of pebbles across the bottom of the wheelbarrow. If you can, drill several holes in the bottom to further improve drainage.

2. Top with 8 inches of garden or potting soil enriched with leaf mold, peat moss, or composted organic matter. Or use a nutrient-rich, soilless planting mix.

3. Moisten the soil before broadcasting seeds thinly over the surface. Mix a few seeds together from different varieties of loose-leaf LETTUCE; reserve a section to sprinkle with seeds of SPINACH • PARSLEY • and CILANTRO (all these seeds will germinate in the cooler spring and autumn temperatures). Cover your seeds with a light sprinkling of soil, and gently pat the soil down.

4. You don't want the soil to dry out or get waterlogged after a heavy rainfall. Protect the seeds by covering the wheelbarrow with clear plastic; you'll keep the soil moist and warm, as well as speed germination.

5. If you seed your wheelbarrow at the end of August, the temperatures will still be warm enough for basil to germinate. Sow a few basil seeds 6 to 8 inches apart and ¼ inch deep. When the seedlings are 6 to 8 inches tall, thin them out (use the thinnings to flavor a meal) and leave just three plants to grow big and bushy. Pinch off branches and flower heads to flavor stir-fries, rice, salads, and pasta.

From late summer into early autumn, you can keep the wheelbarrow outdoors in a sunny, protected location where it won't be flooded in a heavy rainstorm. Wheel it into the garage when the temperatures start to drop into the low 40s and keep it by a window so it will receive several hours of sun.

longer to produce fruit but do so over several months. By planting early, mid-season, and late determinate and inde-terminate varieties you'll have an abun-dance of tomatoes all summer long—from July into September in the North, and through October in central and some southern states. (For the small gar-den or to save space, select compact semi-indeterminate and dwarf varieties.)

When choosing transplants, avoid buying plants in bloom or those that have already fruited. These plants have diverted all their strength into maturing the developing fruits instead of putting out healthy vegetative growth. The result is small plants with low yields. If you do buy them, remove any flowers or fruits before transplanting to encourage stronger plant growth.

PERENNIAL VEGETABLES AND FOOLPROOF RESEEDERS

One way to keep your vegetable garden productive without much work is to plant perennials and foolproof reseed-ing annuals, which will give you a steady supply of vegetables and greens year after year. Perennial vegetables include ASPARAGUS • EGYPTIAN ONIONS (ALLIUM CEPA—PROLIFERUM GROUP) • JERUSALEM ARTICHOKES • LOVAGE • POTATOES (in moderate climates) • SORREL • and SCAL-LIONS. When scallions or Welch onions are left in the ground, the slender white bulbs become tough and inedible, but they continue to send up large, juicy green leaves that can be harvested for up to 10 months. In zones where temperatures never drop below 0°F, potatoes that are left in the ground will sprout into healthy flowering plants by

WEEKEND PROJECT #18

GROWING A TEPEE OF BEANS

When you're planting beans one week-end in May, take an extra 20 minutes to erect a tepee. It will provide the vertical support your climbing beans will need and allow more space for ground-hug-ging crops.

Arrange six 8-foot-long bamboo poles or skinny, straight branches about 8 inches apart. Secure them at the top with twine. Choose a place in full sun where the soil is enriched with compost and easy to work. Fork over the soil and break up the lumps. Rake smooth and push the poles 10 to 12 inches into the ground.

Plant two to three seeds outside each pole (to attract hummingbirds, seed with Scarlet Emperor runner beans). When the plants are 2 to 3 inches high, cut off the weakest seedling, then tie the remaining ones loosely to the poles with string. After this initial support, the plants will climb the poles by themselves. To keep the soil moist and weed-free, mulch inside and outside the tepee with several inches of straw. Water deeply once a week after the pods form.

Try to pick the beans frequently when they're no more than 8 inches long and less than 1 inch wide (they can grow to more than 12 inches, but will be tough). If you're only harvesting once or twice a week, pick them while they're small to keep up with the growth.

GROWING STRAWBERRIES IN MESH CYLINDERS

Plant everbearing strawberries in a sunny spot in May, and you will have bowlfuls of luscious, ripe-red fruits the same summer. If you do not have space in the garden, grow them in a container on a balcony, patio, deck, or porch that gets six hours of sun a day.

Before you go shopping for strawberry plants, prepare strawberry containers in less than an hour. That way, you'll be able to plant them right away when you get home.

Use 4-foot-wide, plastic-coated wire with a 2- to 4-inch mesh. Form a 3-foot length into a circle by hooking the two sides together. Line it with a heavy-duty plastic garbage bag with several holes punched in the bottom for drainage. Set the cylinder on a large planter saucer with a drainage hole in the middle. Fill the bag with an equal mixture of garden soil (or potting soil) and peat moss.

Starting 6 to 8 inches from the bottom, cut slits in the plastic at 6- to 8-inch intervals up the sides of the cylinder. Gently push the strawberry roots through the plastic and tuck them into the soil, but don't cover the crowns. When the planting is complete, water thoroughly to eliminate air pockets. After the soil has settled, top the container with a layer of mulch. Water thoroughly once a week if there has been no rainfall, and add water-soluble fertilizer once a month. Remove the runners as they form. In November, cover the top with a layer of straw and drape the cylinder with landscape fabric. Tie loosely with string to keep it in place.

June, and just one month later they'll be ready to harvest.

Let prolific reseeders such as BASIL • CILANTRO • MÂCHE • and DILL go to seed in a permanent bed. Don't pull the ONIONS and LEEKS either; let them form a large round seed head, then scatter the seeds over the ground. Allow annual herbs to dry thoroughly before pulling the plants, then sprinkle the seed on top of the soil. A light covering of straw will protect your herbs, and they'll germinate in late spring to early summer. Where temperatures don't drop below 0°F, some perennial herbs such as THYME • OREGANO • and *ROSMARINUS* 'ARP' (ROSEMARY) don't die back completely. Help them stay green by mulching them with several inches of freshly shredded leaves or straw.

Perennial small fruits also are worth considering as care-free plantings. These include RHUBARB • BLUEBERRIES • GOOSEBERRIES • and RASPBERRIES. Homegrown strawberries taste great, but they need too much attention. Furthermore, they stop performing after three years, and they're an easy target for slugs and crows. Leave them to commercial growers or see Weekend Project #19.

SCARECROWS THAT FLUTTER AND RUSTLE

Scarecrows—they're fun to make and they add character to your garden. But do they work to scare crows and other creatures? The static scarecrows don't; the ones that rustle and flutter probably will.

Making a scarecrow is a fun project to do with the kids one afternoon in late autumn or winter. That's also a good time to put out a scarecrow if your plantings are being eaten by deer.

To build a great scarecrow you need: two poles—one 6- to 8-feet long, the other 3 feet long; some straw, newspapers, or a large ball for the head; twine; a large black plastic leaf bag; a 13-gallon white plastic garbage bag; and a red or yellow plastic shopping bag. If you would like your scarecrow to make more rustling sounds, thread several aluminum muffin tins on a length of twine and attach to the cross arm poles.

STEP-BY-STEP INSTRUCTIONS FOR CONSTRUCTING A SCARECROW

1. Take one large black plastic leaf bag and stuff a head-size wad of straw, scrunched-up newspapers, or a large ball into the closed end. Wrap twine around an imaginary neck to enclose the head.

2. Slip the 6-foot pole up into the head area and secure tightly by encircling the neck area with twine.

3. Lift the black bag up toward the neck and use twine to lash a 3-foot pole horizontally to the 6-foot pole at shoulder height. Pull down the bag and make the necessary holes to allow the arms to protrude.

4. Take a white 13-gallon plastic garbage bag and slip it over the head. Slip a red or yellow plastic shopping bag over the top and cut a circle out of this colored bag to create a face shape. Shred the area at the top of the colored bag to create banglike strips. Tie twine around the neck. Shred the portion of the red or yellow bag that falls below the neck into strips to imitate hair.

5. Make holes in the white garbage bag for the horizontal arm pole. Shred 12 inches at the bottom of the white and the black garbage bags to form long strips that will move and flutter in the wind.

6. If desired, string several (disposable) aluminum muffin cups together and attach them to the ends of the pole arms. These will move and jangle in the breeze.

Planting

Before planting, check to make sure your soil is not too wet. Squeeze a handful into a ball. If it is crumbly or falls apart when you drop it to the ground, it's ready for planting; if it sticks together, it's too wet. You'll get the best results if your soil is broken up to look like small crumbs—but not powdery—so crush any clods and remove any stones before seeding and transplanting.

SPACING

When space is limited, plant vegetables in wide rows instead of single, narrow rows. When you plant intensively in wide rows, the plant leaves cover most of the bed, creating shade that helps keep the soil cool and free of most weeds.

Another space-efficient method is to interplant varieties that mature at different times. For example, seed between rows of tomato transplants with lettuce, spinach, and other small, fast-growing greens. The greens will mature before the tomato plants create too much shade. Plant squash next to maturing peas. As the peas finish producing, the squash will spread into their space. Or plant radishes and squash together. Do this with any of your favorite vegetables when one variety matures earlier, leaving room for the other to continue growing and spreading.

Another way to gain space is to use fences, lattices, trellises, and pole tepees to support climbing varieties such as CUCUMBERS • PUMPKINS • MELONS • RUNNER BEANS • LIMA BEANS • SWEET POTATOES • PEAS • and other vining fruits, vegetables, and flowers.

SEEDS

In the early spring, sow PEAS • ONIONS • BEETS • CARROTS • TURNIPS • PARSNIPS • RADISHES • and a variety of greens directly in the vegetable beds. Seed them in neat rows ¼ inch deep or scatter them in blocks. Cover the seeds with a light sprinkling of soil, then pat the soil with your hand or the back of a hoe. Gently spray the soil with water. Scatter a thin layer of straw over the top to keep the

ABOVE: This beautiful garden is overflowing with tender vegetables.

ABOVE, TOP: A-frame trellises are easy to construct and can be used to support tomatoes and vining crops.

ABOVE, BOTTOM: Decorative bottle gourds, soon to be turned into bird houses and feeders, grow up a tepee.

soil moist and water the area again. You can speed germination by covering the straw with clear plastic to create a warmer bed; remove the plastic when the seeds sprout through the straw. In early spring, when the soil naturally is damp, watering the seeded area on the weekends is enough. During warmer weather, seeds must be watered daily, so set your automated timer and sprinkler to water for 15 minutes every day.

TRANSPLANTS

Whether you are using plants you started indoors (see Weekend Project #6) or transplants you've purchased, choose only the strongest and sturdiest. Discard any that look spindly.

Before moving tender young plants into the garden, harden them off. Place them outdoors in a sheltered spot during the day and take them into the garage at night. Each day move them into a less-sheltered spot with more sun and wind to toughen them up. Hardening off usually takes about 10 days. However, when you are away from your garden all week, your plants must be hardened off in two to three days. When placed in permanent beds after such a short period, they will need protection from harsh winds and frost.

Cover your plants with row-cover fabric or commercial hot caps. Or cut the tops off plastic soda bottles, then stick the soda bottles upside down an inch into the soil around the individual plants. This also provides protection against cutworm.

Transplant vegetables after the sun has gone down or on a cloudy day. If you must plant them on a hot day, provide shade and wind protection until evening. Water the seedlings or plants, remove them from their pots (if they've been grown in flats, cut them apart with a sharp knife), and set them in holes that are a little wider than the root system and deep enough to come to where the stem begins.

Tomatoes and peppers respond best to deep planting. Remove two to four of the lower leaves and sink the plants in the soil. They'll send out a root system from the stem. If the tomato plants are leggy, set them on their sides in a trench so only the top leaves are above the soil. As they grow, pinch off the suckers, which grow between the main branches, to keep fruit production high.

Plant peat pots with the plant. Water heavily, then sink the pots into the soil until the rim is below ground. If necessary, break away some of the rim. If

BOXING AND CORRALING YOUR PLANTS

Some plants need no more than a single stake to support their foliage. Others, such as tomatoes, bell peppers, and peonies, grow better in cages, boxes, and corrals. If you can not stack cages at the end of the season, use stakes and twine to form rectangular box-type supports or corrals. No matter how you plan to support your plants, hammer in the stakes at the time of planting so you don't damage growing root systems later.

Count on about 15 minutes to install each box or corral (the rectangular box method will take a little longer). Whether you will need to spend a half-day or almost all weekend depends on the size of your garden and the number of plants that need supporting.

BOXES: To box three tomato plants you will need ten 6-foot X 2-inch X 2-inch stakes. Using a mallet, hammer each 1 foot into the ground, 18 to 24 inches apart, to form a rectangular box. Position a stake 1 foot in front and 1 foot behind each tomato plant so that you have a straight line on either side. Tie twine onto the end stack, 8 to 12 inches off the ground, and wind it around the stakes according to the dia-

gram. As the plants grow, add layers of twine as needed, 8 to 12 inches up from the last layer.

CORRALS: Corrals, used to support individual plants such as peonies, daisies, and chrysanthemums, are constructed in a similar manner but with a different configuration. Hammer five 3-foot X 1-inch X 1-inch stakes, poles, or

thin metal rods 6 to 8 inches into the ground in a pentagon shape. Keep the stakes about 6 inches away from the plants so as not to damage the roots. Tie twine to one stake, 8 to 12 inches up from the ground, then weave from stake to stake in star design as shown. The plants will grow up through the twine and hide the stakes.

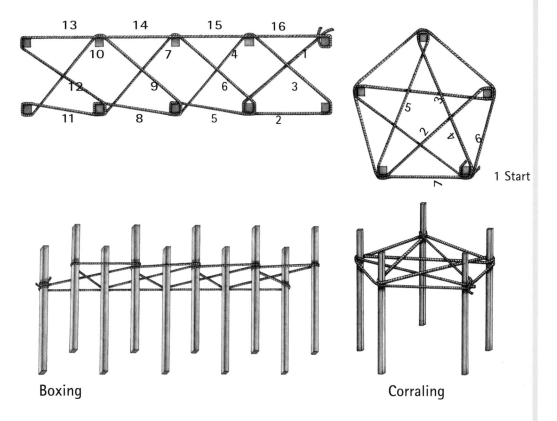

Boxing

Corraling

RIGHT: This method of trellising scarlet runner beans is neat and efficient and leaves room for plantings of flowers or crops of herbs and salad greens.

OPPOSITE PAGE, LEFT: Tomato 'Sweet 100' bears clusters of delicious cherry-size fruits that explode with sweetness and flavor. They're so easy to pop in the mouth right off the vine that they may never make it to the dinner table.

OPPOSITE PAGE, RIGHT: A transplant of tomato 'Fantastic' will have its shape confined by a galvanized metal cage.

exposed to air and sun, peat pots will dry out and draw moisture from the plant roots.

Supporting

Crops with large fruits such as tomatoes, peppers, and eggplants need supporting with stakes or a combination of stakes and cages. (See Weekend Project #21 and "Staking Systems for Flowers and Vegetables" at right.) If using stakes, drive them into the ground when you plant—it's easier to work with small plants, and you don't run the risk of damaging roots that have spread out. Depending on the different varieties, tomato plants require stakes 5 to 6 feet high. Pepper plants also need support,

especially the bushy varieties bearing large, sweet bell-shaped fruits. However, even the smaller, hot pepper varieties need a short stake.

If you plan to grow melons and pumpkins on a vertical frame, you'll need to support fruits with some form of sling. Hosiery is strong, soft, and stretchy—ideal for looping around the growing fruits and tying to a support.

STAKING SYSTEMS FOR FLOWERS AND VEGETABLES

Plants with huge blossom heads, heavy fruit yields, and tall and top-heavy form all require staking. No one method is the best or the easiest; it all depends on the plant that needs supporting. You'll

also want to consider the look of the stake system and its cost.

Before you stake, look carefully at the plant. If it's a perennial, check to see whether it would grow bushier and sturdier if divided or cut back.

For a wide array of stake system designs, thumb through garden catalogs. You will find designs in all kinds of shapes, from metal rings to linking squares, circles, and towers. They'll last for years, and all you have to do is push them into the ground at planting time.

A less costly option is to buy a few wooden or metal stakes, bamboo poles, and some plastic-coated 6-inch-wide mesh wire. With these materials, any of the following supports are easy to erect.

ERECTING LONG-LASTING FRAMES

SINGLE STAKES

Using single stakes probably is the easiest, most common, and least costly method. Take a stake 5 feet tall and 1 inch in diameter—a broom handle, a thick bamboo branch, or a 1-inch square stick—and hammer or push it a foot into the soil when you plant. Loosely secure the plant to the stake with a strip of soft cloth, pantyhose, twine, or a twist tie. As the plant grows, continue to tie the main stem to the stake. This works well for eggplant. Tomato and bell pepper plants need two stakes, one on each side of the plant. Large indeterminate tomato plants will need three or four stakes. Twine can be wound around the outside to confine the plant within the framework of the stakes.

CAGES

Cages are easy to make and last for years. They offer one of the best supports for tomatoes and make harvesting easy. Buy a roll of 4-foot-wide plastic-coated or galvanized 6 X 4-inch mesh wire (you'll need to put your hand through the squares, so buy a wider mesh if you think you need it). Cut the wire into 4-foot-long lengths, curve each into a circle, and attach one end to the other by looping the wire together.

For shorter vegetable plants and perennials such as peonies, yarrow, and chrysanthemums, make 2-foot-high

If you need a frame for a trellis, plastic tunnel, or shade tent, take a trip to the garden center and buy lengths of PVC piping and three-way PVC elbows. When you get home, it will take just a few minutes to connect the lengths with the elbows and set the frames in the ground or in raised beds, or turn them into an arbor. No nails, screws, or glue is required. It's that simple.

Buy nylon trellis netting and tie it between two side lengths and an overhead connected with two elbows. For a season-extender tunnel or a summer shade tent, use four lengths as side pieces and two upper lengths connected with four three-way elbows. Drape with clear plastic or woven shade fabric. At the end of the season, leave in place in the garden or dismantle and store in a tool shed.

cages in whatever diameter is desired. Bell pepper plants develop a bushy form and are better surrounded by 3-foot-diameter cages.

Place the cages over the young plants and stabilize the cages by tying them to a pole or stake hammered into the ground on one side. This prevents the cage from being moved by the wind.

"PEA" BRANCHES

Of all the staking systems, the English method of supporting pea plants is the oldest and easiest. Gather a bunch of twiggy branches that are not too old or brittle, sharpen the bottoms, and push them into the ground around dwarf peas, peppers, eggplants, even perennial

flowers if needed, then tie the plants to the support. Ideally, the supports should be a little shorter than the plant when it's mature so the supports will be completely covered by foliage.

Watering

When you can tend your garden only on the weekends, you'll need to install an automatic watering device connected to a drip-irrigation system or soaker hoses so the vegetables can be watered during the week. A permanent watering system works best for the weekend gardener. It can be as elaborate as installing an underground pipe from the house down to a water faucet near the bed, or as easy as running a length of good-quality flex-

ible hose over the ground. Either can be hooked up to a drip-irrigation or soaker-hose system; the advantage of using the flexible hose is that you need not bury it. Within a few months the flexible hose will sink into the ground and serve well for many years. (See "Drop-by-Drop Watering Systems" on page 175.)

To prevent the soil from drying out quickly, layer several inches of straw or shredded leaves over the top of the drip or soaker hoses.

Weeds attract many insects so keep your beds and the edges of your plot weed free. When you see a few weeds poking through the mulch, pull them out before they go to seed. Pull or cut weeds off at ground level rather than use a hoe or other tool. Deep hoeing or cultivating the soil closely around plants could injure shallow roots. Keep the garden healthy by removing any small piles of pulled weeds. Harmful insects and bacterial and fungal infections often harbor in piles of weeds, which never get hot enough to kill off disease organisms. Instead, collect a big pile in a cage in the middle of your vegetable plot. It will get hot enough to kill bacterial diseases and be too hot to provide a breeding ground for insects. Best of all, you'll have compost at your fingertips.

Harvesting

Most vegetable plants benefit from constant harvesting—it stimulates further producing. Gardeners who can harvest only on the weekends will need to pick some vegetables when they are almost too small. This is better than leaving them on the plant, allowing them to grow too large and tough during the week. You still will enjoy the taste of many tender immature vegetables.

Pick squash when it is only 4 to 6 inches long. At this early stage, they have a creamy, firm texture and small seeds and are ideal for eating raw (grated, julienned, or sliced) in salads or in pita pockets. Cucumber are deliciously crunchy when they are picked small. For a real treat, briefly sauté sliced cucumbers in oil and garlic and serve as a side dish.

Pepper plants are prolific producers and often become weighed down with too many fruits. Start picking peppers when they're moderately small and use the darker green ones in salads and stir-fries. Peppers don't get tough or bitter when left unpicked, just sweeter and riper—which makes them an ideal vegetable for the weekend gardener, who can leave them for picking on another weekend.

That is not the case with okra, peas, and beans. Pick okra and snap peas when they are 1 to 2 inches long, before they get tough and stringy. Snap beans are best when no more than 6 inches long. You'll find them crisply tender and more flavorful when picked as "baby" vegetables. When growing arugula or spinach, cut off the heads or pick off the leaves. Don't pull the entire plant; it will keep producing. Use mature lettuces, arugula, or spinach in soups, spaghetti sauces, and stir-fries. Basil, cilantro, and dill can be snipped from the sides or the center to keep them from producing flower heads.

OPPOSITE PAGE: A metal A-frame strung with a nylon trellis supports a planting of peas. Orange daylilies add a colorful touch to the vegetable garden.

LEFT: Harvesting is easy when vegetables are planted in neatly arranged raised beds. If you are only able to harvest on the weekends, pick peas, beans, okra, and summer squash when they are small and tender. Enjoy them as baby vegetables before they get too big and tough.

Gardening with Herbs

Sweet scented and full of flavor, herbs are a delight for all the senses. They deliver flavor, fragrance, and foliage for cooking, potpourris, wreaths, and bouquets. Best of all, though, herbs are some of the easiest plants to grow. The weekend gardener will want to include them for their beauty, but also for their disease resistance and their pungent perfume, which deters bugs. They grow into succulent specimens when planted in soil loaded with organic matter, but they produce healthy foliage and lovely flowers when grown in any loose, well-drained soil. They don't need a lot of space either; you can cultivate them in window boxes, large pots, or half-barrels placed on the patio.

Many of the low-maintenance flowers found in perennial borders belong to

WEEKEND
PROJECT **#23**

DRYING AND FREEZING HERBS FROM THE GARDEN

Pick herbs at their peak, before the flowers open and when the leaves are tender and most flavorful. If your plants have already flowered, remove the deadheads and any damaged or tough leaves.

Pick your herbs in the morning so they are fresh and not wilted from the heat of the day. If you watered your garden or it rained recently, you won't need to wash them. If it is necessary to wash the leaves, do it gently, and blot dry with paper towels or spin them in a salad dryer.

Annuals such as basil, cilantro, dill, and parsley lose a lot of flavor when dried. A better way to preserve them is to freeze them. Use freshly harvested leaves. Wash, blot, or spin dry, then pack into self-lock freezer bags with all the air squeezed out. Freeze and use within three months.

Another method is to chop or puree the leaves and very soft stems with olive oil (2 cups of leaves to ⅓ to ½ cup oil). Freeze in ½-cup plastic containers or small glass jars. When combined with oil, frozen herbs will retain their flavor for 12 months. Or pack the puree into ice cube trays and freeze overnight. Remove cubes from the trays and place in plastic containers or freezer bags. To dry herbs, choose from the following methods:

In the microwave oven: lay leaves between two layers of paper towels and microwave for two to three minutes, until all moisture is removed. In a gas oven with pilot light on only: arrange herbs in a single layer on a cookie sheet and allow to dry for six to eight hours. In a home dehydrator: set thermostat at 90° to 100° for two to three hours.

Tie herbs in bunches and hang them in a dark, airy closet. Store dried herb leaves in jars away from light and heat.

HERB GARDEN

the herb family. Although gardeners include the showier herbs for their ornamental effect, many of them have valuable healing benefits as well. These include *Monarda didyma* (bee balm) • *Echinacea purpurea* (purple coneflowers) • *Lavendula* (lavender) • *Rosa* (rose) • *Paeonia* (peony) • *Digitalis* (foxglove) • *Salvia elegans* (pineapple sage) • *Tanacetum vulgare* (tansy) • and *Achillea* (yarrow).

Creating an Herb Garden

If you would like herbs to be a major component of your landscape, consider turning part of your front lawn into a classic European knot garden. While the original Elizabethan knot gardens were huge, a relatively modest 12-foot square can be just as pretty and productive. Plant it with edible and ornamental herbs contained by low hedges of dwarf *Buxus* (boxwood) • *Santolina virens* (green santolina) • or *Teucrium chamaedrys* (germander).

Create a decorative and functional herb garden from a circle divided into four quarters by a path of bricks, pebbles, or flagstones. Place a birdbath, sundial, or terra-cotta pot filled with rosemary in the center.

Including both edible and ornamental herbs gives you the widest range of colors, textures, and heights. The furry silvery-green leaves and purple flowers of *Stachys lanata* (lamb's-ears) will attract bees. Choose variegated sages such as *Salvia officinalis* 'Aurea' • *S. officinalis* 'Purpurea' • and *S. officinalis* 'Tricolor' for their leaves colored

Above: Create this beginner's herb garden in just one weekend. Although the brick pathway adds a lovely element to the design, you could use a thick layer of pebbles over black plastic. Either method will keep the paths weed free. A birdbath or sundial placed in the center will create an instant focal point.

Opposite page: Herbs are care-free plants that will grow in any well-drained area. While flowering herbs are commonly grown in perennial borders, many edible herbs such as parsley, basil, cilantro, dill, oregano, and thyme are pretty enough to include in a flower bed.

with pink, purple, cream, and yellow. Like *SALVIA OFFICINALIS* (COMMON SAGE) with gray-green leaves, they all bear long spires of deep mauve. Include *SALVIA ELE-GANS* (PINEAPPLE SAGE) for its deep-green scented leaves and scarlet flowers. Its leaves are delicious as a flavoring for iced teas, fruit salads, stuffings, and many other dishes. Another star bloomer is *ALLIUM SCHOENOPRASUM* (CHIVE); use its purple pom-pon heads in bouquets or to dress up a simple green salad. *TROPAEOLUM* (NASTURTIUM) adds vibrant orange and green to the garden and spicy edible leaves and flowers to the salad bowl. You can include *PELARGONIUM CAPITATUM* (SCENTED GERANI-UM) for its filigreed and fragrant foliage; flavor potpourris, desserts, and teas with its intense perfume of rose, lemon, apple, coconut, or nutmeg. For more beautiful fernlike foliage plants, choose *TANECETUM VULGARE* (TANSY). It bears deep yellow flower heads and repels most insects. It attracts lady bugs, however, which feed voraciously on aphids. Use *LAVENDULA SPICA* 'MUNSTEAD' (MUN-STEAD LAVENDER) as a low hedge; dry the perfumed heads for potpourri sachets.

Keep your herb garden simple by planting it in one or two 4 X 8-foot raised beds filled with amended soil (see

ABOVE: *A care-free combination of edible and ornamental herbs perfumes the air and pleases the eye.*

Chapter 2). If you have a low hedge or wall, especially one that faces south, plant herbs in front of it. If your driveway turns in front of the house, make the herb garden its focus and surround the bed with an aromatic hedge of *THYMUS HERBA-BARONA* (CARAWAY THYME) or *THYMUS X CITRIODORUS* (LEMON THYME) • *LAVENDULA SPICA* 'HIDCOTE' (DWARF HID-COTE LAVENDER) • or *ARTEMISIA ARBROTANUM* (SOUTHERNWOOD).

A wooden ladder with 12 or more rungs provides an attractive and easy frame for a small herb garden. Treat the

ladder with a wood-preserving liquid recommended for use near vegetables. Lay the treated ladder on top of the bed and fill the rungs with soil. Plant perennial herbs between the rungs and fill in here and there with annuals. If you don't have a ladder, make the same design with bricks or roof tiles. Or use a row of construction blocks filled with soil. Camouflage the outside edge of the blocks with white paint (to reflect the sun), or plant along the outside with *SANTOLINA VIRENS* (EVERGREEN SAN-TOLINA). Plant a narrow border of

ALLIUM SCHOENOPRASM (CHIVES) • *THYMUS VULGARIS* (COMMON THYME) • *SALVIA OFFICINALIS* (COMMON SAGE) • *PETROSELINUM* (PARSLEY) • *OCMUM BASILICUM* (BASIL) • *ANETHUM GRAVEOLENS* (DILL) • and *CORIANDRUM SATIVUM* (CILANTRO) outside the kitchen door so that your sauce and salad seasonings are conveniently close.

When you don't have space to create a separate herb garden, plant a variety of thymes and oreganos among the flowers along the path to your front door. Each time you or your visitors brush against them, they'll release their aromatic scent. Include *THYMUS* Χ *CITRIODOR-US* 'AUREUS' (VARIEGATED YELLOW and GREEN LEMON THYME) • *T.* Χ *CITRIODORUS* 'ARGENTEUS' (SILVER-EDGED THYME) • and *T. SERPYLLUM COCCINEUS* (MOTHER OF THYME) to form dense mats. *ORIGANUM* (OREGANO) will give a taller profile; if you plant GOLDEN ORIGANUM, you will be rewarded with its richly colored leaves of lime yellow.

Once you start planting herbs, you'll find all kinds of places to tuck them to bring their beauty, flavor, and fragrance to your yard.

Planning

Which herbs and how many of each kind you want to grow will determine the size of your herb garden. Sixty-four square feet of bed space is plenty of room for at least 15 varieties in a pleasing layout. Save yourself some work by having two small beds—one for perennial herbs and the other for reseeding annuals. This way the annual seeds can be left to come up where they fall to give you a free harvest, while the perennial bed is undisturbed.

HERBAL VINEGARS

WEEKEND
PROJECT **#24**

One way to save the essence of herbs all year is to preserve them in vinegars. Bottles of flavored vinegars can make great gifts—they're pretty and colorful, and they add delicious flavor. For the most flavor, pick herbs before they start flowering. Have bottles or pretty jars, and quarts of mellow vinegars on hand. It only takes an hour or so to mix up a few vinegars.

STEP-BY-STEP INSTRUCTIONS FOR MAKING HERBAL VINEGARS

1. Pick the herbs in the morning. Swish them gently in a bowl of cold water, then blot dry between paper towels (if you don't spray pesticides or herbicides around your garden, you don't need to wash your herbs if it rained recently).

2. Place some herbs in a screw-top jar and cover with 1 pint of vinegar. Screw the top on and let stand on a sunny windowsill for two weeks. Shake periodically.

3. After two weeks, strain the liquid into an attractive jar or bottle, and add one or two sprigs of the fresh herb. For a more pungent flavor, add several cloves of peeled garlic or shallots threaded on a wooden skewer. Or, as a decorative touch, insert long pieces of lemon peel, spikes of purple basil flowers, chive blossoms, and nasturtium leaves and flowers. For gifts, affix a pretty label indicating the contents and tie a little ribbon around the neck of the bottle or jar.

Planting

Although some herbs grow in partial shade, most need at least six to eight hours of sun to grow into luxuriously bushy plants. If your site gets only four hours of direct sun, plant *PETROSELINUM CRISPUM* (PARSLEY) • *MENTHA* (MINT) • *ALLIUM SCHOENOPRASM* (CHIVES) • CHERVIL • OREGANO • and *LEVISTICUM* (LOVAGE).

MELISSA OFFICINALIS (LEMON BALM) and *BORAGO* (BORAGE) will grow with even less sunlight, though they'll be leggy. When planted in full sun, lemon balm grows thick and bushy and reseeds prolifically.

Plant herbs in soil amended with compost containing aged shredded leaves, decayed organic matter or rotted manure, and peat moss. If your site is

MAKING AN HERB WREATH

A wreath made with fresh herbs goes together more easily and quickly than one made with dried herbs. It is so easy, in fact, that you will want to make several at a time. Buy a small wire circle or other shape, collect grapevines from the garden, or shape a thin coat hanger into a circle or a heart. You also will need thin, green wire and narrow, green floral tape, available from the florist or a hobby shop.

STEP-BY-STEP INSTRUCTIONS FOR MAKING AN HERB WREATH

1. Using a metal wreath form or a coat hanger, wrap it with green floral tape until it is totally covered. Cut perennial herbs, such as SAGE • ROSEMARY • LAVENDER • GOLDEN OREGANO • and TARRAGON into 8-inch lengths. Gather several stems to form a thin bunch and bind to the center of one side of the wreath with a piece of wire. Work down each side, overlapping the bunches so that the stem ends are hidden by the next bunch.

2. Add color and texture with round and spiky flower heads and tricolored leaves. Good choices include blossoms of SAGE (red pineapple sage and purple common sage) • the spikes and leaves of purple and dark-green BASIL • LAVENDER flowers • white or pale pink ROSEBUDS • the fuzzy, mauve flowers of OREGANO • and the little, rosy-red spikes of THYME.

3. To make the wreath last a few months, hang it on a wall that doesn't receive too much light until the herbs and flower heads have dried; then it can be moved to a well-lit wall. Do not hang the wreath near a fireplace (where it can be a fire hazard) or on a door where constant movement will cause the dried herbs to drop prematurely.

To train living, potted rosemary or ivy into a wreath shape, form a wire hanger into a circle, cover with green tape, then push the (uncovered) hook into the soil of the pot. As the rosemary or ivy grows, wrap the branches around the wreath. Prostrate rosemary is more pliable and easier to train than regular rosemary.

rocky or hard clay, plant in a raised bed filled with enriched soil.

Perennial herbs like a slightly acidic soil with a pH range of 6 to 6.5. Annuals will readily accept a sweeter soil that's a neutral 7 to 7.5. For good root growth, plant annual and perennial herbs in soil with good drainage—herbs rot quickly when planted in moisture-retentive soil. To improve drainage, add 1 inch of coarse builder's sand to the soil.

If you have not amended the soil with composted organic material, add a 1-inch-thick layer of rotted manure or sprinkle with synthetic, slow-release, high-nitrogen 10-5-5 or 10-6-4 fertilizer. Rake into the prepared bed. Another way to add nitrogen, which stimulates leaf growth, is to water the herbs with diluted liquid seaweed or fish emulsion.

Though many perennial herbs can be grown from seed, it takes most a long time to develop into good-size plants. The exceptions include mother of thyme and oregano. To get your garden off to a quick start, purchase plants of *SALVIA* (SAGE) • *ALLIUM SCHOENOPRASUM* (CHIVES) • *ORIGANUM* (OREGANO) • *THYMUS VULGARIS* (COMMON THYME) • *ARTEMISIA DRACUNCULUS* (TARRAGON) • and *ROSMARINUS* (ROSEMARY). Although you can find a good selection of herbs at nurseries and garden centers, it is very easy to grow annuals and biennials from seed. *OCIMUM BASILICUM* (BASIL) • *ANETHUM GRAVEOLENS* (DILL) • and *CORIANDRUM SATIVUM* (CILANTRO) germinate in 10 days and *PETROSELINUM CRISPUM* (PARSLEY) takes from 14 to 21 days. Seed them outdoors after the last

OPPOSITE PAGE: In mild climates, Rosemarinus officinalis (rosemary) will overwinter and can grow as tall as 6 feet.

ABOVE, LEFT: With its flat yellow flower head, Anethum graveolens (dill) makes a choice addition to the herb garden. Like parsley, it is a favorite of swallowtail butterfly caterpillars.

ABOVE, MIDDLE: The small, mauve flowers of Origanum X majoricum (Italian oregano) will attract honeybees. All oreganos are prolific self-seeders and root spreaders.

ABOVE, RIGHT: Salvia officinalis (sage) and Eremurus (foxtail lily) are happy bedfellows in well-drained soil.

frost or start seeds in trays on a sunny windowsill indoors in late March or early April.

Many annuals go to seed quickly, so do successive seedings throughout the summer to continue your harvest. For instance, seed basil, cilantro, and dill every three to four weeks. It is possible to eliminate successive seedings of basil if you harvest the leaves and flower buds weekly, encouraging the plants to grow bushy and to last all summer long.

If you are using a separate bed for annuals, allow some annuals to go to seed toward the end of the summer, then leave the plants in the ground through the winter. Or, when the seed heads have dried, pull the plants and shake or rub off the seeds and leave them on top of the ground. They'll reseed next spring when all danger of frost has passed, saving you the trouble of seeding annuals again. In extremely cold regions, mulch the bed with straw or seed-free hay after the ground freezes, then pull back the mulch in early spring to let the ground warm up.

When spacing perennial herbs such as *Salvia* (SAGE) • *Artemisia dracunculus* (TARRAGON) • *Levisticum* (LOVAGE) • *Origanum* (OREGANO) • or *Rosemarinus officinalis* 'ARP' (hardy to Zone 7), take their branch spread into consideration and plant them 1 foot apart. *Mentha* (MINT) will take over the bed; to contain its roots, plant it in a pot and sink the pot into the bed, or keep it in a pot by the back door.

To prevent your herbs from wilting, always try to plant on a cloudy day or in the evening, and be sure to water the bed thoroughly. Mulch with a 2-inch layer of shredded bark to deter weeds and retain moisture. Renew the mulch once a year or whenever you replace or add plants.

When the plants are well-established, snip off the tips of the branches to stimulate growth and prevent flowering.

PROPAGATING PERENNIAL HERBS

Propagate perennial herbs from cuttings. Using a sharp knife, cut a 3-inch tip or side shoot of new green growth from an established plant. Trim the lower leaves and place each cutting ½ to ¾ inch deep in a moistened soilless growing mix or half sand and half perlite. Use individual 2-inch plastic pots, or plant several of the cuttings together in a larger container without crowding. Water the pot until the soil is slightly moist, then place it in a plastic bag. Seal the bag and place it out of direct sunlight. The roots will develop in approximately three to four weeks. At that time, transplant the cuttings into individual 4-inch pots containing an equal mixture of potting soil and soilless growing mix.

If you are going to be gone during the week, moisten the soil in the 4-inch pots and place them in plastic bags out of direct sunlight. On the weekend, remove them from the plastic and set them on a sunny windowsill. Repeat this routine for about a month. When top growth is visible, discard the plastic bags. Keep them on a sunny windowsill and water them weekly until you are ready to plant them outdoors. When the cuttings are about 6 inches tall, pinch the center to encourage branching and sturdy development.

OPPOSITE PAGE: Neatly contained within the confines of a white picket fence, the herbs growing in these raised beds create a feast for the eye as well as the palate. By choosing herbs for their richly textured foliage and colorful flowers, it's possible to build a garden around the many varieties of culinary, medicinal, and ornamental herbs.

LEFT: Herbs are easy to grow in containers. If brought indoors, this pretty potted thyme can be harvested during the winter.

Growing Herbs in Pots

Growing herbs in pots is a good way to enjoy herbs year-round. The weekend gardener can start herbs earlier and prolong the harvest. You can take the pots indoors during the week when there is risk of frost. If you want to grow herbs through the winter, raise new plants indoors on a sunny windowsill or bring your outdoor pots inside.

Plastic pots, small wooden tubs, window boxes, hanging baskets—anything with drainage holes (or anything you can drill holes in) can be a container. Line wood, clay, and unglazed earthenware with plastic so that moisture isn't wicked from the soil into the container

itself (but you still need some water, so make sure there is a drainage hole at the bottom).

Fill the containers with two parts potting soil to one part soilless seed starter mix, vermiculite, or peat moss. Add hydrogel or polymer crystals as recommended. These crystals absorb water and keep plant roots moist. When away for longer than one week during the summer, top the containers with a capillary matting that wicks water from a dish or reservoir.

If you want to create a miniature garden, use a large container such as a wooden wine crate, a window box, or a 12-inch-diameter pot or hanging basket,

and plant with a selection of herbs spaced 4 to 6 inches apart. For example, plant a clump of *ALLIUM SCHOENOPRASUM* (CHIVES) • one *THYMUS X CITRIODORUS* (LEMON THYME) • one *OCIMUM BASILICUM* 'RUFFLES' (GREEN RUFFLES BASIL) • one *O. BASILICUM* 'PURPURASCENS' (DARK OPAL BASIL) • and one *ORIGANUM* 'GOLDEN' (GOLDEN OREGANO). Fill a hanging basket with *ROSMARINUS PROSTRATUM* (PROSTRATE ROSEMARY) and a selection of creeping thymes that will drape over the sides. Let variegated sage and prostrate rosemary spread down the sides of a container, accented with a few fast-peaking annuals such as CILANTRO • DILL • and

Because they have large root systems, TARRAGON • SAGE • and ROSEMARY need room to thrive. Plant each one in an 8- to 10-inch pot. BASIL and PARSLEY are slow growers that develop large root systems. Plant tender 6-inch seedlings or sow seeds directly into containers, 4 to 6 inches apart.

Fertilize herbs growing in pots monthly with liquid seaweed or fish emulsion diluted to half the recommended dose. Water them thoroughly when the soil feels dry ½ inch below the surface. Remove the saucer and allow the water to run out of the pot, then set it back onto the saucer. Don't let your herb pots sit in water, and don't let the soil dry out.

If you live in a region where perennial herbs such as chives and tarragon die back to the ground, allow them to go through a chilling process before you bring them indoors. Let the first frost kill off the foliage, then cut them back and bring them indoors. The warm environment will trigger new growth that will continue through the winter. Bring tender rosemary plants in before the first hard frost. Thyme and oregano remain evergreen in many areas of the country, so they can be brought indoors anytime—or mulched and left in the garden for continued harvesting through the winter.

Don't dig up mature annual plants; they will finish their cycle too quickly. It is better to sow seeds indoors for winter use.

15 Flavorful Herbs

The herbs in this list are foolproof additions for the weekend garden. You can plant them, then forget about them. Go away for a week or two and they'll still be growing, totally care-free. Only the annuals require any work at all and even that is just pinching off the flowerheads. When leaving on vacation, cut annuals back so they won't go into flower while you are away. They will be thick and bushy when you return.

A = ANNUAL

B = BIENNIAL

HA = HARDY ANNUAL

P = PERENNIAL

TP = TENDER PERENNIAL

PIMPINELLA ANISUM (**ANISE**) (**A**): Height: 2 feet. Leaves and seeds taste like licorice. Harvest the seeds when they are ripe in mid- to late summer and store in a screw-top jar. Use anise to flavor baked goods, teas, and soups.

OCIMUM BASILICUM (**BASIL**) (**A**): Height: 1 foot. Many varieties of basil are available, with flavors ranging from mild to pungent, sweet to spicy. Remove the leaves in early summer. Pinch back the flower buds and cut off tender stems in midsummer. Cut back in late summer. Chop fresh leaves for pesto. Simmer leaves in tomato sauces and soups. Shred leaves and add to breads, muffins, rice and grain dishes, and vegetables. To store, layer leaves in olive oil and store in the refrigerator, or freeze unwashed leaves in bags.

LAURIS NOBILIS (**BAY**) (**TP**): Height: Slow grower to 30 feet. Harvest leaves at any time. Bring indoors if winter temperatures drop below 15°F. Use fresh or dried leaves to flavor soups, sauces, and stuffings. Use leaves to repel insects in closets and pantry.

ALLIUM SCHOENOPRASUM (**CHIVES**) (**A**); *A. TUBEROSUM* (**GARLIC CHIVES**) (**P**): Height: 1 foot. Regular, tubular-leafed chives impart a mild onion flavor. The ¼-inch-wide, flat leaves of garlic chives are very pungent but are milder when grown (and blanched) under a flowerpot. Cultivation and harvesting are identical. Harvest a few leaves at a time by cutting them at soil level; this will stimulate new growth. Use fresh chopped leaves to sprinkle over mixed salads, cooked vegetables, pasta, and rice dishes. Cut off flower heads, pull apart, and add to salads or stir-fry with vegetables. Chop the leaves and freeze them in airtight plastic bags.

***CORIANDRUM SATIVUM* (CILANTRO/ CORIANDER) (HA):** Height: 18 inches. Also called Chinese Parsley. The parsley-like foliage, called cilantro, has a very distinctive aromatic flavor. The dried seeds, known as coriander, are sweetly perfumed. Cilantro and coriander are widely used in Chinese, Thai, Vietnamese, Hispanic, and Indian cooking. Use leaves sparingly in vegetable sauces so as not to overwhelm delicate flavors. Use to flavor pasta sauces, salsas, and bean dishes. Add crushed seeds to curries, soups, and fruit desserts. Harvest the foliage and remove flower buds often from early summer on. Chop the leaves and store in olive oil in the refrigerator or freeze whole leaves and tender stems in airtight bags. Store seeds in a screw-top jar or pepper grinder. Seeds that drop onto soil reseed prolifically during the summer and then overwinter to come up in early spring.

***ANETHUM GRAVELOENS* (DILL) (A):** Height: 2 to 3 feet. Seed in late spring and start harvesting in early summer to prevent formation of seed heads. Sow repeatedly all summer. The feathery foliage of dill has a strong flavor. Use

ABOVE: A garden planted with herbs is filled with texture, color, and fragrance. The edible flowers can be eaten in salads and used to garnish savories and desserts.

ABOVE: In this mixed bed of flowers and herbs, the feathery foliage of fennel (Foeniculum vulgare) is surrounded by drifts of calendula and the arching pink and white stems of Mexican bush sage (Salvia leucantha).

OPPOSITE PAGE, TOP LEFT: Curly French parsley makes an attractive edible edging plant.

OPPOSITE PAGE, TOP RIGHT: A tender perennial, ginger is grown for its spicy root.

OPPOSITE PAGE, BOTTOM RIGHT: With its dark green leaves, lovage is a handsome plant to grow at the back of an herb bed.

freshly snipped leaves (sparingly, then adjust to taste) in potato, macaroni, pasta, vegetable, and rice dishes, and salad dressings. Dried dill is not as flavorful as fresh and loses potency quickly. Freeze or dry foliage, and collect seeds or let them drop to the ground to sprout in the spring. When you do let the plants go to seed, the yellow flowers make a stunning bouquet.

FOENICULUM VULGARE (FENNEL) (P): Height: 3 feet. Harvest new-growth foliage all summer. Once gone to seed, cut plant to the ground to encourage new growth. The flavor is mildly anise-like, and tastes like the foliage of the sweet Florence fennel bulb (also called finocchio and anise). Use fennel foliage to flavor vegetable sauces and salads, and use the seeds to flavor teas and baked goods.

ZINGIBER OFFICINALE (GINGER) (TP): Height: 1 foot. Cultivated for its root, ginger is considered more spice than herb. Plant the rhizomes (pieces of ginger root with "eyes"). Harvest young shoots and cut pieces off the growing rhizome. Grate the fresh root into sauces, sesame-peanut dips, and stir-fry dishes. The sliced root can also be candied and used in pies and cakes. Store this pungently spicy root in the refrigerator vegetable drawer or slice and place in a jar covered with rice wine or sherry.

LEVISTICUM OFFICINALE (LOVAGE) (P): Height: 3 feet. Sow from seed or buy plants. One small plant will provide more lovage than most people need. The leaves and stems of lovage taste like celery. Start harvesting when the plant is young. Use leaves and stems in place of celery to flavor soups, spaghetti sauces, dips, stuffings, and potato salads. Freeze or dry the leaves.

ORIGANUM VULGARE SPP. HIRTUM (OREGANO) (P): Height: 4 inches to 2 feet, depending on variety. Oregano spreads quickly and prolifically by roots and seeds. Harvest the sprigs and pull

off the leaves. Chop to release the pungent oil; flavor varies from weak to strong. Use oregano to flavor soups, sauces, pasta dishes, most cooked vegetables, and salad dressings. Freeze or dry the leaves.

***PETROSELINUM CRISPUM* (PARSLEY) (B):** Height: 12 inches. Curly and flat-leafed varieties—some more pungent than others. Harvest frequently and don't allow to bloom, which causes almost immediate root termination. It overwinters (dies back in northernmost regions unless mulched with shredded leaves or a few inches of straw) and puts out new growth in early spring. Broadcast seeds in spring to keep the patch going. A rich source of vitamins A, B, and C, parsley is the best all-purpose herb. Add to sauces, soups, pasta, rice and grain dishes, salsas, stuffings, and breads. Loses flavor when dried. Chop leaves,

cover with oil, refrigerate, or freeze whole leaves and tender stems.

***ROSMARINUS OFFICINALIS* (ROSEMARY) (TP):** Height: 6 inches to 6 feet. Hardier cultivars can be coaxed into overwintering if they are in a protected area, mulched heavily, and the temperature doesn't drop much below 20°F. Growing rosemary in pots inside in the winter isn't easy if the air is too dry. It can be wintered more successfully in the southern window of a garage that doesn't drop below 32°F. The soil must not dry out. The wide or narrow, gray-green or dark green needlelike foliage has a wonderful flavor. Harvest by cutting a few of the tender, soft, green tips. Fresh rosemary can be used to flavor any dish; just don't let it dominate when you want other flavors to come through. The secret is to use a few leaves for a delicate flavor and two or more tablespoons for

a pungent kick. Experiment with rosemary in breads and biscuits, jellies, quiches, roasted potatoes and onions, chowders, and melon balls. To dry, pull up an entire plant and hang it upside down in a dark, dry closet.

SALVIA OFFICINALIS (SAGE) (P): Height: 2 feet tall and wide spreading. Long, soft, fuzzy leaves in silvery-green, golden, tricolor (green/white/purple), or purple, depending on cultivar. Plant these herbs, with their long sprays of purple flowers, in a perennial border. *SALVIA ELEGANS* (PINEAPPLE SAGE) has red blooms; *S. GUARANITICA* (VIOLET SAGE) has violet-blue flowers. Harvest the soft branch tips and remove the leaves. Use fresh, dried, or frozen—sparingly in

some dishes as the flavor is pungent. Chop fresh or crumble dried leaves into soups, beans, apple sauce, salads, potatoes, and stuffings.

ARTEMISIA DRACUNCULUS (FRENCH TARRAGON) (P): Height: 1 to 2 feet. Bright green, slender leaves are tender and taste of anise. Harvest when the stems are soft; the tips and leaves can be chopped. Harvest often to encourage new growth. Toward the end of the season when the stems are long and tough, clip sprigs and strip off the leaves. Use sparingly in sauces, mayonnaises, and fruit salads, or with parsnips, potatoes, squash, and savory dishes. Freeze tender stems of tarragon leaves in airtight plastic bags or submerge in vinegar or oil.

ARTEMISIA REDOWSKII (RUSSIAN TARRAGON) is a flavorless imitation.

THYMUS VULGARIS (COMMON THYME, FRENCH NARROWLEAF THYME, AND ENGLISH BROADLEAF THYME) (P): Height: 12 to 15 inches. Besides these three varieties of *T. VULGARIS*, other exceptionally good flavors include lemon thyme (*T. X CITRIODORUS* and *T. X CITRIODORUS* 'AGENTEUS', a lemon-flavored silver thyme); caraway or Corsican thyme (*T. HERBA-BARONA*); and winter thyme (*T. HYEMALIS*). All thymes make a wonderful addition to the landscape with their creeping forms; textured leaves; dark, light, or variegated leaves; and profuse pink to violet blooms. Use fresh, dried, or frozen leaves. The flavors vary but most are quite strong—use sparingly and adjust to taste. Like parsley, thyme can be used to flavor just about any dish, but is particularly good in soups, salad dressings, stuffings, rice dishes, and pasta sauces, or sprinkled on vegetables.

OPPOSITE PAGE: This herb and vegetable garden is based on a traditional English potager. To eliminate the need to trim the edging plants, use slow-growing plants such as coralbells (Heuchera sanguinea), Santolina, germander (Teucrium), or lamb's-ears (Stachys byzantium).

LEFT: True French tarragon (Artemisia dracunculus) is flavored with the distinctive taste of anise.

CHAPTER FIVE

GARDENING IN THE SHADE

Consider yourself a lucky weekend gardener if you have an area that gets more shade than sun. By choosing plants and shrubs that thrive in the shade, you can have a low-maintenance garden that offers fascinating foliage and bountiful blooms from early spring into late autumn. A shady garden stays cool and moist throughout summer, so blooms last longer. It requires little, if any, watering. It retains moisture even in a drought and is virtually weed free because most weeds prefer the sun. Raking is unnecessary; you can let garden leaves fall to form a natural mulch and enrich the soil.

This is the ideal setting for a woodland garden, where mosses and ground covers slowly creep together, where light-colored blooms and pale variegated foliage draw the eye deeper into the shade, and where the rich reds, vivid pinks, and brilliant oranges and yellows of spring and summer flowers, autumn leaves, and winter berries provide accents of intense color year-round.

LEFT: *In midwinter,* Helleborus *carpets the ground and brightens the shady garden.*

GROWING YOUR OWN MOSS

Mosses are fascinating plants that fill barren areas in the shade garden with texture and color.

Grow your own mosses by spraying the areas with natural molds. Make a thin paste from equal parts of ground-up moss and buttermilk, or ground-up moss, fresh bread, and water. English gardeners spread a thin paste of cooked oatmeal over shaded rocks because it grows mold very quickly. In most regions of North America, however, crows and raccoons eat the mixture before it has time to turn moldy and produce moss.

You also can make a bare space more inviting to moss already growing in the area by sprinkling the area with flowers of sulphur (use half the quantity recommended on the packet). It creates an acid environment that kills weeds and grass, and encourages the spread of existing mosses.

Shade also is perfect for a rich tapestry of textured foliage. Here, different species of ferns grow and spread, with varied leaves in hues of palest to darkest green. Taller varieties make a bold backdrop for other shade-loving plants bearing lacy fronds, delicate leaves, flowery spikes, and feathery plumes. Low-growing ferns nestle into rock crevices, and spill over onto ground covers that carpet the woodland floor.

Flowers are illuminated not by bright sun but by the dappled light that filters through an overhead canopy of deciduous trees. On a hot summer's day, the cool shade of this green oasis offers a seductive escape.

Plants that Love Shade

The secret to a successful shade garden is the right choice of shade-tolerant plants and well-drained, humus-rich soil.

Many shrubs and flowers thrive under the cool canopies of trees. Perennials, such as ASTILBE • *CONVALLARIA* (LILY OF THE VALLEY) • HOSTA • FERNS • *PHLOX DIVARICATA* (WILD BLUE PHLOX) • and *MERTENSIA VIRGINICA* (VIRGINIA BLUEBELLS), are at their best when planted in the shade. Bulbs, bringing the first flush of spring color, also do well there. Good choices include CROCUS • *SCILLA* (SQUILL)• *GALANTHUS* (SNOWDROP) • *NARCISSUS* (DAFFODIL) • and *ANEMONE BLANDA* (WINDFLOWER) because they naturalize easily through seeding and bulb multiplication. Ground covers such as *GALIUM ODERATUM* (SWEET WOODRUFF) • *EPIMEDIUM* (BARRENWORT) • *LAMIUM* (DEAD NETTLE) • *PHLOX STOLONIFERA* (CREEPING PHLOX) • *VIOLA ODERATUM* (VIOLET) • *ASARUM* (WILD GINGER) • *PACHYSANDRA* (SPURGE) • *HEDERA* (IVY) • and *VINCA* (PERIWINKLE) grow thick and luxuriant in shady surroundings. When the trees drop their leaves, the vase-shaped flowers of *COLCHICUM* (AUTUMN CROCUS) light up the early autumn garden in shades of pale pink, purple, and white.

Broadleaf evergreen shrubs such as *RHODODENDRON* • *KALMIA* (MOUNTAIN LAUREL) • *MAHONIA AQUIFOLIUM* (OREGON or MOUNTAIN GRAPE) • and *PIERIS JAPONICA* (JAPANESE ANDROMEDA) add color with their spring blooms. Midsize deciduous trees such as *ACER PALMATUM* (JAPANESE MAPLE) • *CERCIS* (REDBUD) • *AMELANCHIER* (SERVICEBERRY) • *CORNUS FLORIDA* (FLOWERING DOGWOOD) • and *ENKIANTHUS* and deciduous shrubs such as *MYRICA* (BAYBERRY) • *CORNUS MAS* (CORNELIAN CHERRY) • *FOTHERGILLA* • and *RHODODENDRON ARBORESCENS* (SWEET AZALEA) brighten up the shade in the autumn with their richly hued leaves in bronze, flame-pink, and purple.

If you want your shade garden splashed with color from June to frost, fill in with annuals. The paler varieties of *IMPATIENS* (BALSAM), as well as the purest white and candy-stripe varieties, will brighten shady nooks and corners. In fact, with its wide range of colors (pinks, lavenders, reds, oranges, and white) and low-maintenance characteristics (self-heading, spreads profusely, and blooms nonstop) *IMPATIENS* can be called the queen of the weekend shade garden. Other annuals that brighten a shade garden include *BROWALLIA* (BUSH VIOLET) • *IMPATIENS BALSAMINA* (GARDEN BALSAM) • *MYOSOTIS SYLVATICA* (GARDEN FORGET-ME-NOT) • *LOBULARIA MARITIMA* (SWEET ALYSSUM) • and *IBERIS* (CANDYTUFT). These, along with *LOBELIA ERINUS* (LOBELIA) and *VIOLA* X *WITTROCKIANA*

OPPOSITE PAGE: Replace a sparse lawn in a wooded garden and add brilliant color with flowering plants and woody ornamentals that love the shade. Orange azaleas and bluebells (Endymion) will thrive and spread in a shady spot.

ABOVE: Impatiens and ferns make a good plant combination for a shady bed. Ferns add height and texture; impatiens contributes delicate flowers from early summer until a hard frost in autumn.

(PANSY), will survive a few light frosts and provide the longest-lasting annual color. Also, look for plants with colorful foliage, such as *Coleus* and *Caladium*, whose leaves come in white, red, yellow, chartreuse, and green.

A way to select plants for your shade garden is to find what grows well in your area and when blooms occur. Check out gardens in your neighborhood, visit a park or arboretum, and consult with your county extension office.

What Kind of Shade Do You Have?

When planning a shade garden, you first need to determine which kind of shade you have. You can do this by simply looking at the kinds of trees that grow on your property. Heavy shade is found beneath evergreen trees; little will grow there. It also is found beneath deciduous trees that create a dense canopy during the growing season. When the lower branches of these trees are removed, more peripheral light reaches the ground, permitting a greater variety of plants to grow. Depending on the kind of plants growing in the shade garden, pruning lower branches also will be necessary as trees grow taller and branches reach out, throwing more shade over the garden. If pruning is impossible, plant varieties that prefer heavy shade.

Following the descriptions of the different kinds of shade are lists of plants that thrive in each condition. Keep in mind that these lists do not include all varieties, but highlight the most carefree and widely available plants. For complete information and descriptions, refer to books about shade gardens, contact plant societies, and ask the horticulturalist at your local nursery.

Left: A wooded walkway is flanked by a harmonious planting of red and pink azaleas. Azaleas tolerate sun in northern climates but need shade in the South.

GROWING SHRUBS AND SMALL TREES IN CONTAINERS

Growing shrubs and trees in containers is the perfect way to create mini gardens on the patio, deck, or porch. If you can only water on the weekends, however, choose varieties that prefer partial shade. During the summer, move them so that they will get indirect light (no direct sunlight). If you place the larger and heavier containers on a base fitted with wheels, they will be easier to move around.

Plant trees and shrubs in large, deep pots; the soil in small containers requires more frequent watering and fertilizing because the soil dries out quickly. Also, the roots of trees and shrubs planted in small pots are more likely to freeze in regions where winters are severe. For the plant to survive the winter, plant a dwarf maple, for example, in a pot no smaller than 18 inches in diameter with an 18-inch depth.

STEP-BY-STEP INSTRUCTIONS FOR PLANTING SMALL TREES AND SHRUBS IN CONTAINERS

1. Choose a container with drainage holes. Cover these with broken pottery and a 1-inch layer of pebbles.
2. Fill about one-third to one-half of the pot with garden topsoil enriched with shredded bark, compost, or peat moss. This creates a crumbly mixture that allows for root growth and good drainage.
3. Place the bare roots or loosened root ball on top of the soil, hold the plant upright, and backfill with the same mixture of soil. Tamp down firmly and fill the container to within 1 inch of the top.
4. Water thoroughly and mulch with shredded bark or wood chips.

WINTER PROTECTION FOR CONTAINER PLANTS

As soon as nighttime temperatures drop into the 20s, protect container plants from wind and cold. Move them to a sheltered location against the house or a brick or cement wall that retains the sun's heat. Or move them to an unheated garage, under a deck or porch, or closer to the front door.

Water them periodically during the winter so the soil doesn't dry out and keep them mulched with a thick layer of leaves (they don't need shredding), straw, or wood chips.

When it's impossible to move the containers out of prevailing winds, protect them with burlap or plastic wrapped around stakes, or chicken wire. In regions where the winters are frigid and night temperatures drop to 0°F, small evergreens should be completely covered. Surround the container and shrub with chicken wire, fill to the top with dry leaves or broken straw, and cover the entire structure with burlap or canvas. Secure by looping twine around the chicken-wire cage. Leave wrapped until nighttime temperatures consistently reach the high 30s.

RIGHT: The graceful foliage of maidenhair ferns and the delicate pastel colors of hardy tuberous begonia and wild blue phlox are pretty companions for light and partial shade.

OPPOSITE PAGE: Yellow columbines and purple bellflowers (Campanula persicifolia) make a complementary pairing for a garden that is partially shaded.

FULL/DEEP/DENSE/HEAVY SHADE

Full shade is found year-round under the branches of evergreens and during the summer beneath the canopy of thickly grown mature deciduous trees. This summer canopy keeps a good deal of rain from reaching the ground, but the soil retains the moisture it receives because it is rich from thick layers of decayed leaves. The soil beneath dense evergreen boughs basically is dry year-round (except in snow-laden regions of the country), which, coupled with a dense foliage that allows no light to penetrate, makes it an inhospitable area.

To open up areas of deep shade under mature deciduous trees, remove the lower branches to a height of about 20 feet. Or thin some of the upper branches to allow light to filter through to the ground below. This will not only improve the light but increase the air circulation, discourage fungal diseases, and allow rain to soak the earth below.

PLANTS THAT WILL GROW IN FULL SHADE

Perennials: *ARISAEMA* (JACK-IN-THE-PULPIT) • *POLEMONIUM* (JACOB'S-LADDER) • *BEGONIA GRANDIS* (HARDY TUBEROUS BEGONIA) • *SANGUINARIA CANADENSIS* (BLOODROOT or TETTERWORT) • *TRILLIUM* (WAKE-ROBIN) • *HEPATICA* (LIVERLEAF) • *PODOPHYLLUM PELTATUM* (MAYAPPLE) • *ANEMONELLA THALICTROIDES* (RUE ANEMONE) • *ERANTHIS* (WINTER ACONITE) • *POLYGONATUM* (SOLOMON'S-SEAL) • *BRUNNERA* (BUGLOSS) • some FERNS • *HOSTA* • and *SCILLA HISPANICA* (SPANISH BLUEBELL).

Ground Covers: *PACHYSANDRA* (SPURGE) • *GALIUM ODERATUM* (SWEET WOODRUFF) • *VIOLA* (VIOLET) • *HEDERA* (IVY) • *VINCA* (PERIWINKLE) • *AJUGA* (BUGLEWEED) • *ASARUM* (WILD GINGER) • *AEGOPODIUM* (GOUTWEED) • *EPIMEDIUM* (BARRENWORT) • *PHLOX STOLONIFERA* (CREEPING PHLOX) • *LAMIUM* (DEAD NETTLE) • and MOSSES.

Shrubs: *RHODODENDRON*

LIGHT/MEDIUM/FILTERED SHADE

This kind of shade is found under trees with tall trunks and higher branches more widely spaced than lower branches. Light filters through the branches creating a dappled effect. Plants below receive indirect or reflected light but no direct sun. To allow sun to reach the ground, thin out a few branches to open up the canopy.

PLANTS THAT WILL GROW IN LIGHT SHADE

All of the plants that grow in deep shade plus:

Perennials: *ACONITUM* (MONKSHOOD) • *ASTILBE* (SPIRAEA) • *HYPERICUM* (ST-JOHN'S-WORT) • *CENTRANTHUS* (VALERIAN) • *PELTIPHYLLUM* (UMBRELLA PLANT) • *PULMONARIA* (LUNGWORT) • *PRIMULA* (PRIMROSE) • *DIGITALIS* (FOXGLOVE) • *ARABIS* (ROCK CRESS) • *AQUILEGIA* (COLUMBINE) • *CIMICIFUGA* (BUGBANE or SNAKEROOT) • *BERGENIA* • *LOBELIA CARDINALIS* (CARDINAL FLOWER) • *LOBELIA SIPHILITICA* (GREAT BLUE LOBELIA) • *HEUCHERA* (CORALBELLS) • *MYOSOTIS SYLVATICA* (GARDEN FORGET-ME-NOT) • *HELLEBORUS NIGER* (CHRISTMAS ROSE) • *ORIENTALIS* (LENTEN ROSE) • *DORONICUM* (LEOPARD'S-BANE) • *CONVALLARIA* (LILY-OF-THE-VALLEY) • *TRADESCANTIA* (SPIDERWORT) • *MERTENSIA VIRGINICA* (VIRGINIA BLUEBELL) • *LIGULARIA* (GOLDEN-RAY) • and all spring bulbs except tulips.

Ground Covers: *EPIMEDIUM* • *LAMIUM* (DEAD NETTLE) • *LIRIOPE* (LILYTURF) • *PHLOX DIVARICATA* (WILD BLUE PHLOX or WILD SWEET WILLIAM) • and *TIARELLA* (FOAMFLOWER).

Annuals: BEGONIA • *COLEUS* (FLAME NETTLE) • *IMPATIENS* (BALSAM) • *MIMULUS* (MONKEY FLOWER) • and *TORENIA* (WISHBONE FLOWER).

Shrubs: *RHODODENDRON* • *PIERIS JAPONICA* (JAPANESE ANDROMEDA) • *MYRICA* (BAYBERRY) • *KALMIA* (MOUNTAIN LAUREL) • *VIBURNUM X BURKWOODII* (BURKWOOD VIBURNUM) • *VIBURNUM ACERIFOLIUM* (MAPLE-LEAVED VIBURNUM) • *FOTHERGILLA* • *CALYCANTHUS FLORIDUS* (CAROLINA ALLSPICE) • *MAHONIA AQUIFOLIUM* (OREGON or MOUNTAIN GRAPE) • and *GAULTHERIA* (WINTERGREEN).

Trees: *CORNUS FLORIDA* (FLOWERING DOGWOOD) • *ILEX OPACA* (AMERICAN HOLLY) • and *ILEX AQUIFOLIUM* (ENGLISH HOLLY).

PARTIAL/OPEN/HALF/SEMI-SHADE

Partial shade means the site receives three to four hours of direct sun, then is in shade. Morning sun is kinder to plants. The intensity of afternoon sun can shrivel plants that prefer a shady location. If your site gets afternoon sun, plant sun-loving perennials and annuals on the edges of the garden and keep the shade lovers back underneath the trees.

PUTTING PLANTS ON WHEELS

When you want to be able to move your container plants or small water garden from one end of the patio to the other, set them on wheels before you fill them. Although you can buy special planter saucers equipped with wheels, if you can't find the size you need, set the container in a wood or metal wagon. Or make your own, which you can build to the correct specifications.

No matter what size your cart is, you will need: two 1 X 4-inch redwood, cypress, or cedar boards for the bottom (leave a small space between them so that water can drain through) and two for the sides; two 2 X 2-inch boards that will go under the cart to hold the four small caster wheels; and eight ¼- X 1-inch screws to attach the casters and thirty 2-inch galvanized nails to hold the 1X4s and 2X4s together. It is also possible to find kits for mobile wooden planter trays at garden centers.

PLANTS THAT WILL GROW IN PARTIAL SHADE
All of the plantings that grow in light shade plus:

Perennials: *ANEMONE JAPONICA* (JAPANESE ANEMONE) • *MONARDA* (BEE BALM) • *ARUNCUS* (GOATSBEARD) • *TROLLIUS* (GLOBE-FLOWER) • *ASCLEPIAS TUBEROSA* (BUTTERFLY WEED) • PHLOX • *HEMEROCALLIS* (DAYLILY) • *ANCHUSA* (BUGLOSS) • ASTER • *BAPTISIA* (FALSE INDIGO) • *CAMPANULA* (BELLFLOWER) • *PAEONIA* (PEONY) • *PHYSOSTEGIA* (FALSE DRAGONHEAD) • *RANUNCULUS* • *GYPSOPHILA* (BABY'S-BREATH) • *GENTIANA* (GENTIAN) • GERANIUM • *LILIUM* (LILY) • IRIS • *LUPINUS* (LUPINE) • *THALICTRUM* (MEADOW RUE) • *FILIPENDULA* (MEADOWSWEET) • *ACONITUM* (MONKSHOOD) • *VERONICA* (SPEEDWELL) • VERBENA • *CHRYSANTHEMUM SUPERBUM* (SHASTA DAISY) • and *RUDBECKIA* (BLACK-EYED SUSAN).

Ground Covers: *ALCHEMILLA* (LADY'S-MANTLE) • *IRIS CRISTATA* (CRESTED IRIS) • and *POTENTILLA*.

Annuals: *AGERATUM* (FLOSSFLOWER) • *LOBULARIA MARITIMA* (SWEET ALYSSUM) • ASTER • BEGONIA • *CALENDULA OFFICINALIS* (POT MARIGOLD) • *CLARKIA* • *IBERIS* (CANDYTUFT) • *PELARGONIUM X HORTORUM* (GERANIUM) • *LOBELIA ERINUS* (LOBELIA) • *NICOTIANA* (ORNAMENTAL or FLOWERING TOBACCO) • *VIOLA X WITTROCKIANA* (PANSY) • PETUNIA • *SALVIA SPLENDENS* (SCARLET SAGE) • and *ANTIRRHINUM MAJUS* (SNAPDRAGON).

Shrubs: *HIBISCUS SYRIACUS* (ROSE-OF-SHARON) • *CAMELLIA* • COTONEASTER • *HAMAMELIS* (WITCH HAZEL) • *LIGUSTRUM* (PRIVET) • *ILEX GLABRA* (INKBERRY) • *BERBERIS* (BARBERRY) • and DAPHNE.

Trees: *CERCIS* (REDBUD) and *TAXUS* (YEW).

OPPOSITE PAGE: *Grown in full sun or partial shade, verbena and petunias add brilliant color to the garden.*

LEFT: *With its pinkish purple foliage that is washed with orange in the autumn, Japanese barberry (Berberis thunbergii) is a choice shrub for shade or sun. Here it creates an effective backdrop for a mass grouping of containers planted with dwarf aster, lobelia, and geranium.*

THE CORRECT WAY TO REMOVE A LARGE BRANCH

Pruning shade trees is usually unnecessary unless they have grown too large for their location or have dead branches, or you want to increase light in your garden. Plan to prune trees in late winter so you don't interrupt the growth spurt in spring. Although minor pruning can be done anytime, there is an added advantage to pruning deciduous trees now: The leaves have dropped so it is easier to see the true shape of the tree. When branches are more than 1½ inches in diameter, the easiest way to remove them is to make a three-way cut:

STEP-BY-STEP INSTRUCTIONS FOR REMOVING A LARGE BRANCH

1 Saw the bottom of the branch 6 to 12 inches from the trunk and about one-third of the way through the branch.

2 Make a second cut from the top about 3 inches farther out from the undercut. Angle it so that it meets the undercut and the branch falls away.

3 Cut back the stub to the collar of the branch.

Make sure you don't paint over a cut; painting can trap moisture and will encourage disease.

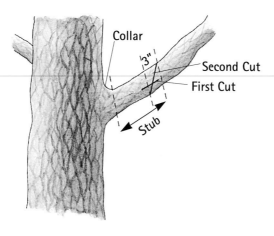

Collar

3"

Second Cut

First Cut

Stub

Preparing the Bed

If the site of your shade garden is under deciduous trees that have shed their leaves and enriched the soil beneath for years, you probably won't need to amend the soil before planting. If you do need to amend or loosen the soil, use a shovel and work around tree roots, removing them judiciously where you plan to plant a large shrub or small specimen tree. To improve texture, aeration, and drainage, work peat moss and composted organic matter containing

aged manure, leaves, or a mix of both into the soil. Most shade plants prefer a soil pH of 6.0; if your soil is closer to a pH of 4.5, plant RHODODENDRONS • AZALEAS • MOUNTAIN LAUREL • *ANDROMEDA* (BOG ROSEMARY) • and other BROADLEAF EVERGREENS that thrive in acidic conditions. See "Earthworks" on page 167 for directions on amending soil pH.

If you're creating an island shade garden under a tree on the lawn, you may need to add several inches of topsoil for an ideal planting medium. Don't mound soil or mulch right up to the tree trunk. This invites moisture-loving insects to enter the bark, allows rodents to gnaw at it unseen, and encourages moisture- and soil-borne fungal diseases. Also, add just enough soil for your shade plants to grow in; too much soil could suffocate the tree's roots and possibly kill the tree.

Depending on the maturity and variety of the trees, an island garden may receive light from all angles as the sun rises and sets. Plantings that prefer partial shade will do well in this setting. This type of shade garden also lends itself to the addition of large rocks, which will become footholds for small ferns, mosses, and ground covers that spread to create dense mats.

OPPOSITE PAGE: Mature plantings of cranesbill, daffodils, and other spring-blooming perennials add cheerful color to the edges of a paved pathway.

LEFT: Astilbe and lady's-mantle grow in lush profusion along the shaded banks of this water garden.

WEEKEND PROJECT **#30**

GROWING MUSHROOMS THE EASY WAY

If you have a shade garden or a woodlot, you can grow mushrooms. Tasty Asian shiitake mushrooms are the easiest to grow. Shiitake mushroom spawn is available from several mail-order companies, or check the yellow pages to see if it is grown at a local herb farm.

To start the mushrooms, drill holes every 4 to 6 inches in a few freshly cut oak logs. Insert the spawn into the holes and seal with softened wax (included in a mushroom-growing kit). Stack the logs in full or partial shade, and water them periodically during dry weather. The logs will begin to bear mushrooms in 6 to 12 months and will continue to produce four crops a year for many years to come.

WOODLAND SHADE GARDEN

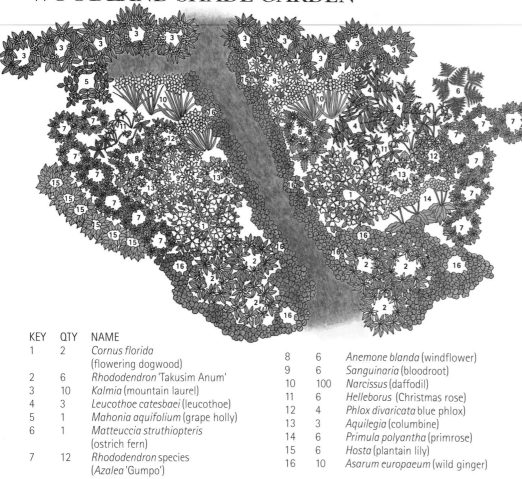

KEY	QTY	NAME
1	2	*Cornus florida* (flowering dogwood)
2	6	*Rhododendron* 'Takusim Anum'
3	10	*Kalmia* (mountain laurel)
4	3	*Leucothoe catesbaei* (leucothoe)
5	1	*Mahonia aquifolium* (grape holly)
6	1	*Matteuccia struthiopteris* (ostrich fern)
7	12	*Rhododendron* species (*Azalea* 'Gumpo')
8	6	*Anemone blanda* (windflower)
9	6	*Sanguinaria* (bloodroot)
10	100	*Narcissus* (daffodil)
11	6	*Helleborus* (Christmas rose)
12	4	*Phlox divaricata* blue phlox)
13	3	*Aquilegia* (columbine)
14	6	*Primula polyantha* (primrose)
15	6	*Hosta* (plantain lily)
16	10	*Asarum europaeum* (wild ginger)

A Woodland Garden

If your backyard is part woodland, clear out the shrubby undergrowth and plant a garden containing wildflowers, spring-blooming bulbs, and shade-loving (and shade-tolerant) perennials and shrubs. Lay a footpath that meanders through this moist, leafy grotto. Let ground covers fill in bare spaces and luxurious fern fronds hide the spent foliage of early blooming woodland flowers.

Include species that are native to woodlands. Choose varieties best suited to your region for a carefree garden. There are several good ground-cover choices. The heart-shaped, evergreen leaves of ginger grow in clumps and spread without being invasive. *ASARUM EUROPAEUM* (EUROPEAN WILD GINGER) has glossier leaves than most varieties and, like *A. CAUDATUM* (BRITISH COLUMBIA WILD GINGER), tolerates winters to minus 25°F.

The hardiest and the most common is *A. CANADENSE* (CANADIAN WILD GINGER), which withstands cold to minus 35°F. *A. ARIFOLIUM* and *A. VIRGINICUM* are native to the warmer southeastern states.

LENTEN ROSE is an exquisite blossom for the woodland garden. The different species vary in height from 10 inches to 2 feet. One of the prettiest is the smaller *HELLEBORUS ORIENTALIS*, with single, five-petaled pink, purple, or white roses and lobed evergreen leaves on 1-foot stems. A similar plant, *HELLEBORUS NIGER* (CHRISTMAS ROSE), blooms in the winter and early spring. This beauty perks up a lighted or partially shaded woodland site.

PHLOX DIVARICATA (BLUE PHLOX) and *P. STOLONIFERA* (CREEPING PHLOX) also belong in the woodland garden. *P. STOLONIFERA* is evergreen, and both form attractive ground covers and bloom for three weeks or longer in the spring. The dainty flowers range in color from sky blue and pinky-purple to white.

Another native ground-hugging plant is *SHORTIA GALACIFOLIA* (OCONEE-BELLS). This plant has little white bell-like flowers in the spring and glossy green leaves that take on a purple cast in the winter. Another creeper with attractive glossy leaves that turn purple in the cold weather is *GAULTHERIA PROCUMBENS* (WIN-

TERGREEN). It is covered with tiny red berries in winter, as is *MITCHELLA REPENS* (PARTRIDGEBERRY). The leaves of this spreading shrub are green with a central white vein.

For a really dense ground cover, plant *PACHYSANDRA*. The native species, *PACHYSANDRA PROCUMBENS* (ALLEGENY SPURGE), has light green leaves spotted with silver, and though they are not as hardy as the most commonly used JAPANESE PACHYSANDRA, they are evergreen.

SANGUINARIA (BLOODROOT) is a native wildflower that produces one large leaf and a multipetaled pink flower. Easily propagated by root division, it is a lovely spring plant for the woodland garden.

Combine some of these natives with FERNS • HOSTAS • *AQUILEGIA* (COLUMBINE) • *PRIMULA* (PRIMROSE) • *IRIS CRISTATA* (DWARF-CRESTED IRIS) • *ANEMONE BLANDA* (WINDFLOWER) • *RHODODENDRON* (AZALEA and RHODODENDRON) • *KALMIA* (MOUNTAIN LAUREL) • *CORNUS* (DOGWOOD) • and *CERCIS* (REDBUD). Include other shade-loving perennials and ornamentals, and you'll have a garden that stays beautiful and interesting without much effort.

LEFT, TOP: *A naturalized planting of tulips, miniature daffodils, and star flowers receive hours of sun in the spring before the trees leaf out.*

LEFT, BOTTOM: *Lenten roses (Helleborus orientalis) and snowdrops are among the first flowers to brighten the late winter landscape. Both plants self-sow and spread underground.*

A Fern and Foliage Garden

With their varying shades of green, ferns and foliage plants provide lushness in the shade garden, as well as a wide range of shapes, sizes, and textures. Include them to add contrast to an area planted with several varieties of ground covers, to act as a backdrop to flowering annuals and perennials, and to be a permanent year-round attraction. Many foliage plants, especially ferns, retain their fronds through most of the year and add graceful beauty to the garden during the winter. Foliage plants and ferns survive in low-light situations and will grow where few other plants will.

ABOVE: Christmas fern (Polystichum acrostichoides) *and blue phlox* (Phlox divaricata) *naturalize by clumping and seeding, and spread quickly when planted in light shade.*

EASY-CARE FERNS

Some ferns are easier than others to grow in a woodland setting. Ferns require well-drained, moist soil. They thrive best in light shade in compost-enriched, slightly acidic soil mulched with layers of shredded leaves.

Filtered light passes through the tall canopies of deep-rooted trees such as *QUERCUS* (OAK) • *ACER* (MAPLES) • *FAGUS* (BEECH) • *TILIA* (LINDEN) • and *CARYA* (HICKORY) to create the perfect habitat for ferns. Their deep roots don't wick the surface moisture required by ferns.

The halo-shaped *ADIANTUM PEDATUM* (MAIDENHAIR FERN) is a hardy native fern that spreads slowly into wide clumps. The delicate fronds, supported on black leaf stalks, are deciduous. *POLYSTICHUM ACROSTICHOIDES* (CHRISTMAS FERN) has tough evergreen fronds and spreads by clumping and seeding from spores that form in brown clusters at the tips of the fern fronds.

MATTEUCCIA STRUTHIOPTERIS (OSTRICH FERN) is famous for producing edible fiddleheads. The plumed fronds of this tall fern grow in a graceful vase shape and can reach a height of 5 feet. In autumn, the inner, spore-bearing fronds turn a rich brown. This fern will grow in light or partial shade and can be an aggressive grower with its running rootstock.

ATHYRIUM FILIX-FEMINA (LADY FERN), with its light green, lacy fronds, is a good choice for partial shade. Growing from a central crown and spreading by producing offshoots, it is invasive, so plant it where it has room to spread.

ATHYRIUM NIPPONICUM 'PICTUM' (JAPANESE PAINTED FERN) is one of the most exquisite ferns for the shade garden. Its variegated silver and green fronds are attached to 18-inch weeping burgundy stems. The silvery fronds stand out in the shade, making this fern a spectacular specimen to interplant with darker foliage plants.

ONOCLEA SENSIBILIS (SENSITIVE FERN) may crowd out other plantings but its advantage is that it will grow in sun or shade. Although not an evergreen (the triangular green fronds shrivel in late summer), its brown, beaded, fertile fronds remain visible all winter.

OSMUNDA REGALIS (ROYAL FERN) grows in sun or shade but needs moist soil to reach a height of 4 feet. The graceful fronds of this vase-shaped fern change from red in the spring to green to burnished gold in autumn.

Some compact ferns will grow well on tree stumps or in rock outcroppings. One is *POLYPODIUM VIRGINIANUM* (POLYPODY FERN), which forms mats of bright green, waxy leaves. Its leaves grow from the spreading roots that creep over a thin layer of soil in light shade. Another small fern is the delicate-looking but actually sturdy *CYSTOPTERIS FRAGILIS* (FRAGILE FERN). Its lacy pale green 6-inch fronds form clumps. Fragile fern requires rich soil and full to light shade.

MAKING A LARGE ROCK A FOCAL POINT

If you have a giant rock in your garden, use it as a focal point in a rock-garden design or construct a pond at the base and make it into a waterfall.

Or, position a big rock to draw attention to a single specimen tree, such as a *CORNUS FLORIDA RUBRA* (RED FLOWERING DOGWOOD) • *ACER PALMATUM* (JAPANESE MAPLE) • *BETULA PENDULA GRACILIS* (WEEPING BIRCH) • or *TSUGA CANADENSIS PENDULA* (WEEPING HEMLOCK). Such trees will arch over the front of the rock or boulder, and soften it. Around the front and the sides of the rock, plant a variety of bulbs, such as *GALANTHUS* (SNOWDROPS) • *ERANTHIS HYEMALIS* (WINTER ACONITE) • *CHIONODOXA* (GLORY-OF-THE-SNOW) • *SCILLA SIBERICA* (SIBERIAN SQUILL) • CROCUS • and DWARF *TULIPA* (TULIP). To provide year-round color, carpet over the bulbs with *PHLOX SUBULATA* (MOSS PINK) • *VINCA MINOR* (MYRTLE) • *ARCTOSTAPHYLOS UVA-URSI* (BEARBERRY) • or other evergreen ground covers (see "Great Ground Covers" on page 52). The bulbs will push through in the spring.

When the rock is craggy with fissures, fill the cracks with a little earth and plant with *SEMPERVIVUM TECTORUM* (HENS-AND-CHICKENS) • *AUBRIETA* (PURPLE ROCK CRESS) • *SEDUM CORTICOLUM* (STONECROP) • *DASYPHYLLUM* (STONECROP) • *THYMUS SERPYLLUM* (MOTHER-OF-THYME) • and *VERONICA LATIFOLIA PROSTRATA* (CREEPING SPEEDWELL). *PARTHENOCISSUS* (VIRGINIA CREEPER) will climb over the rock and add beautiful shades of red, purple, and orange as the leaves change color in the autumn. The shallow roots and thin vines are easy to control.

If your rock is in the shade, encourage mosses to grow in the cracks. To do this, fill the cracks with soil and take a little moss from another shady spot in your garden. It will grow and spread. Or, you can grow moss from a natural mold base (see Weekend Project #26). Plant around the base of the rock with shade perennials such as FERNS • HOSTAS • *GALIUM ODORATUM* (SWEET WOODRUFF) • *SANGUINARIA* (BLOODROOT) • and *DICENTRA* (BLEEDING-HEART). Add shrubs such as *RHODODENDRON* • *BERBERIS* (BARBERRY) • *KALMIA* (MOUNTAIN LAUREL) • or other plants that are recommended in this chapter.

FERN AND
FOLIAGE GARDEN

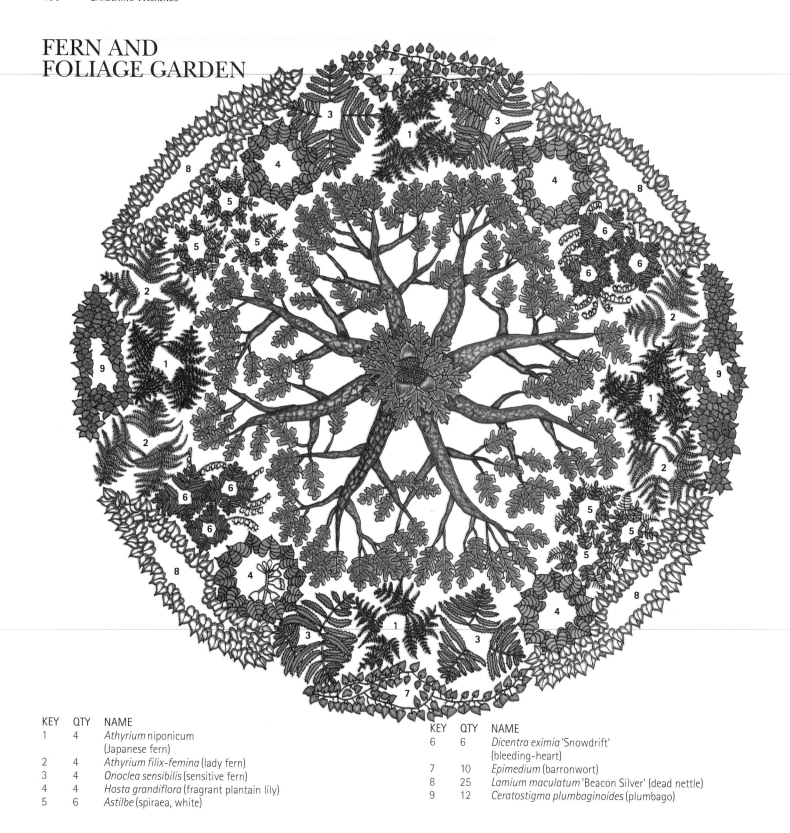

KEY	QTY	NAME
1	4	*Athyrium* niponicum (Japanese fern)
2	4	*Athyrium filix-femina* (lady fern)
3	4	*Onoclea sensibilis* (sensitive fern)
4	4	*Hosta grandiflora* (fragrant plantain lily)
5	6	*Astilbe* (spiraea, white)

KEY	QTY	NAME
6	6	*Dicentra eximia* 'Snowdrift' (bleeding-heart)
7	10	*Epimedium* (barronwort)
8	25	*Lamium maculatum* 'Beacon Silver' (dead nettle)
9	12	*Ceratostigma plumbaginoides* (plumbago)

LEFT: A ground cover of dead nettle (Lamium) *spreads its light green and silvery leaves under shade trees.*

and red-tipped flapper moss are all at home in damp, shady places.

The rounded snouts of *PODOPHYLLUM* (MAYAPPLE) poke through the earth in early spring and unfurl into 8-inch-wide umbrella-like leaves on stubby foot-high stems. Also known as American mandrake, mayapples quickly form a temporary ground cover bearing small, white cup-shaped flowers. The green leaves die back in midsummer and are soon covered by other woodland foliage.

Grown mostly for its delicate, fernlike foliage, *DICENTRA* X 'LUXURIANT' and *D. EXIMIA* 'SNOWDRIFT' are fringed bleeding hearts with a long bloom time. The red 'LUXURIANT' and white 'SNOWDRIFT' blossoms hang like bells on thin stems several inches above the 1-foot-tall blue-

EASY-CARE FOLIAGE PLANTS

To highlight a shady fern and foliage garden, choose plants with interesting leaf colors, richly textured foliage, and flowers forming plumes, spires, and bells. Wherever possible, choose flowers with intense colors such as *LOBELIA CARDINALIS* (CARDINAL FLOWER), bright red and hot pink astilbes mixed with the frothy plumes of white astilbes, and the lavender-blue flowers of *IRIS PALLIDA* (ORRIS), with their long-lasting variegated green leaves streaked with cream and white.

Creeping over moist soil and rotting logs are the rootless mosses—intricately patterned tapestries of the woodland floor. Feathery, treelike club moss, rosette star moss, rounded pincushion,

green foliage. For an attractive combination, plant *DICENTRA* (BLEEDING-HEART) at the foot of *BAPTISIA* (FALSE INDIGO). The dicentra contrasts nicely with baptisia's deep blue, brilliant yellow, or crisp white flowers on blue-gray foliage. In autumn, large black seed pods hang from the 3-foot-tall stems of baptisia.

HOSTAS, with their blue-green and variegated cream, yellow, and green leaves, are grown primarily for their stunning foliage. Grow *HOSTA PLANTAGINEA* 'GRANDIFLORA,' however, for its fragrant, 5-inch white flowers. *LIRIOPE* (LILYTURF), another plant grown for its tufts of leaves, has grasslike blades that vary in width and feature variegated green, yellow, and cream stripes. Depending on the species, flowers may be white, purple, or lilac. Its foliage may need cutting back in early spring. *LIRIOPE MUSCARI* (BIG BLUE LILYTURF) is a tough evergreen good for edging the foliage garden.

Choose ground covers for their mottled, spotted, striped, or edged leaves and let them highlight a tree trunk or a distant corner. *LAMIUM* (DEAD NETTLE) is a beautiful ground cover for the shade. *LAMIUM MACULATUM* 'BEACON SILVER' (SPOTTED DEAD NETTLE) has 6-inch-tall silver-striped green leaves that change to pinkish-purple in autumn. It also bears

purple flowers in the spring. Other cultivars have leaves splotched with yellow and send up yellow flowers.

EPIMEDIUM (BARRENWORT), although less spectacular than dead nettle, is easy to grow in light shade beneath ferns and other tall foliage. This ground cover dies back in late winter and sends up new pale green leaves dusted with pink in the spring. *MAHONIA REPENS* (CREEPING MAHONIA) grows about a foot tall and adds color and texture with its purple-green, hollylike leaves. The bright yellow flowers that decorate the plant in spring later turn into clusters of purple berries.

CERATOSTIGMA PLUMBAGINOIDES (DWARF PLUMBAGO) also grows easily in light shade and produces small, deep blue flowers that bloom from late summer well into autumn. The dark green 3-inch long leaves die back in winter in most regions but come back strong in the spring. Another deciduous ground cover is *TIARELLA* (FOAMFLOWER); its bright green, lobed leaves are a rich purple-red in the autumn and add color to the winter shade garden. However, foamflower is grown primarily for its showy flower spires, which come in various colors including pink, purple, red, and white. Or you can always depend on reliable favorites such as *PACHYSANDRA* (SPURGE) •

ASARUM (WILD GINGER) • *AJUGA* (BUGLE-WEED) • and *HEDERA* (IVY).

Flowering evergreen shrubs with glossy green, purple, or variegated foliage include RHODODENDRONS • *ANDROMEDA* (BOG ROSEMARY) • and, in mild areas, *CAMELLIA*. *FOTHERGILLA GARDENII* (WITCH ALDER) is a small shrub with dark green, leathery foliage that turns bright yellow and orange in autumn. These colors are more brilliant when *FOTHERGILLA* is planted at the edges of a shade garden, where it can receive several hours of sun a day.

Woodland gardens planted with ferns, trees, shrubs, wildflowers, and foliage plants are easy-care environments for the weekend gardener. Not only do they require little upkeep, they can remain a focal point of the garden year-round.

OPPOSITE PAGE: Dogwoods and narrow-leafed evergreens add height in the shade garden and create a canopy for ferns, rosemary, and numerous varieties of rhododendrons.

CHAPTER SIX

BURSTING WITH BLOOMS— SPRING THROUGH AUTUMN

I f you dream of a garden that blooms from early spring until the first hard frost, plant perennials—the backbone of the flower garden.

Beginning in February with the daintiest SNOWDROPS • WINTER ACONITE • SQUILLS • and CROCUS, perennials put on a show until autumn. Gracing the summer garden are long-blooming varieties such as *ACONITUM* (MONKSHOOD) • *ASCLEPIAS TUBEROSA* (BUTTERFLY WEED) • *SALVIA X SUPERBA* 'EAST FRIESLAND' (VIOLET SAGE) • PHLOX • *RUDBECKIA FULGIDA* 'GOLDSTURM STRAIN' (BLACK-EYED SUSAN) • *ECHINACEA PURPUREA* (PURPLE CONEFLOWER) •

LEFT: *This garden features a successful interplay of perennials that bloom in late summer and autumn. The rich yellows of black-eyed Susan and goldenrod mingle with the pinkish red heads of stonecrop 'Autumn Joy' as well as the deep purple asters. The drift of white asters adds a pleasing touch of coolness to the strong colors in this border.*

ABOVE: *Fast-growing climbing roses weave their way around the door and window of this charming cottage.*

ASTER X FRIKARTII 'MONCH' (HARDY ASTER) • LIATRIS (BLAZING STAR) • and ACHILLEA (YARROW). Then the garden winds down in September and October with a last blast of color from *HELENIUM AUTUMNALE* (SNEEZEWEED) • MONTAUK (NIPPON) DAISIES • *CHRYSANTHEMUM X MORIFOLIUM* (HARDY GARDEN CHRYSANTHEMUMS) • SEDUM SPECTABILE X 'AUTUMN JOY' and S. SPECTABILE 'BRILLIANT' (STONECROPS) • ACHILLEA 'GOLD PLATE' (FERNLEAF YARROW) • *HELIANTHUS RIGIDUS* (PERENNIAL SUNFLOWER) • SOLIDAGO X HYBRIDA (GOLDEN RODS) • and ASTER NOVAE-ANGLIAE (NEW ENGLAND ASTER).

Although some perennials bloom for just two to three weeks, most have attractive foliage that enhances the border for several months. These include *RUTA GRAVEOLENS* (BLUE RUE) • PEROVSKIA (RUSSIAN SAGE) • VERONICA (SPEEDWELL) • ASTILBE (SPIRAEA) • PAEONIA (PEONY) • IRIS SIBIRICA (SIBERIAN IRIS) • HEUCHERA (CORAL-BELLS) • IBERIS SEMPERVIRENS (CANDYTUFT) • YUCCA • and STACHYS (LAMB'S-EARS).

Though each bloom of *HEMEROCALLIS* (DAYLILY) lasts just one day, each plant produces many flowers over at least two weeks. Also, many varieties of daylilies have subsequent blooming times, so as one variety subsides, another bursts into bloom. When different varieties are massed together, the flowering season can stretch from early to late summer.

This effect is enhanced when longer-blooming, more compact varieties such as brilliant red 'PARDON ME' • yellow 'HAPPY RETURNS' • and 'SILOAM PINK GLOW' are intermingled in the bed. Whether planted in full sun or partial shade, daylilies will naturalize, spreading to form a colorful, care-free bed.

Choosing a Suitable Location

There is no fixed rule controlling the shape and size of a perennial bed. It can be as simple as a mass of long-blooming perennials on each side of the front or back door, or a narrow border along a garden path. Or it can be a large bed filled with a variety of complementary and contrasting plants.

If your garden is open with few shade trees, you'll have choice locations in full sun. If you have tall trees casting shade, your options will be different.

When filling in around foundation plantings or using perennials to minimize the height of a deck or porch, choose sun worshipers for the south and west sides and shade-tolerant varieties for the east and north.

If you have a long evergreen hedge or a stone wall, soften its stiff lines with a year-round display of color. A wall or hedge can offer the perfect perennial

PERENNIAL BORDER

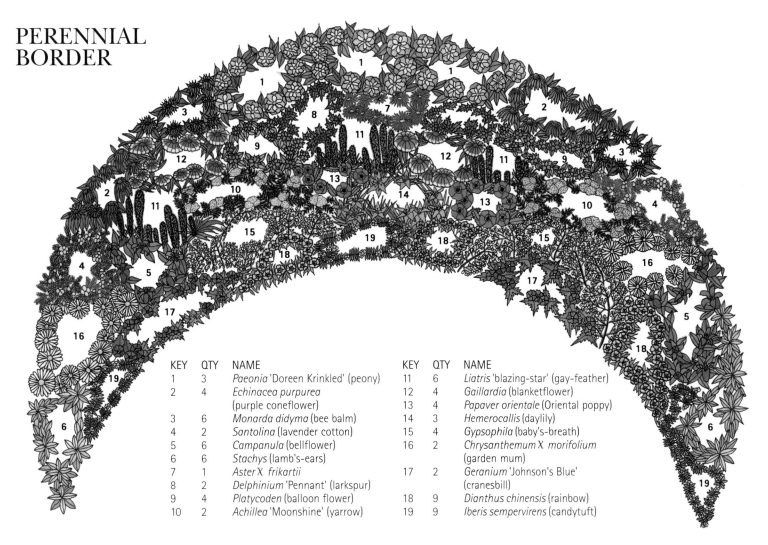

KEY	QTY	NAME	KEY	QTY	NAME
1	3	*Paeonia* 'Doreen Krinkled' (peony)	11	6	*Liatris* 'blazing-star' (gay-feather)
2	4	*Echinacea purpurea* (purple coneflower)	12	4	*Gaillardia* (blanketflower)
3	6	*Monarda didyma* (bee balm)	13	4	*Papaver orientale* (Oriental poppy)
4	2	*Santolina* (lavender cotton)	14	3	*Hemerocallis* (daylily)
5	6	*Campanula* (bellflower)	15	4	*Gypsophila* (baby's-breath)
6	6	*Stachys* (lamb's-ears)	16	2	*Chrysanthemum* X *morifolium* (garden mum)
7	1	*Aster* X *frikartii*	17	2	*Geranium* 'Johnson's Blue' (cranesbill)
8	2	*Delphinium* 'Pennant' (larkspur)	18	9	*Dianthus chinensis* (rainbow)
9	4	*Platycoden* (balloon flower)	19	9	*Iberis sempervirens* (candytuft)
10	2	*Achillea* 'Moonshine' (yarrow)			

setting, providing an attractive backdrop for flowers while holding heat and protecting plants from drying winds.

Most perennials prefer soil that drains quickly. To improve drainage and fertility, incorporate organic matter into at least the top 6 to 8 inches of soil. If the soil is permanently moist from underground water, create a bog garden with varieties that thrive in wet soil (see Weekend Project #34).

Planning a Perennial Border or Bed

A perennial bed is a long-term investment, so to avoid wasting time, money, and effort, first plan the garden on paper. Sketching in the different varieties will give you an idea of how many plants you should buy (remember, most plants will double in size in two years) and where the plants should be placed in the bed.

For beds viewed only from one side, position the tallest perennials at the back of the border and mingle different varieties of varying colors. For layers of blooms, decrease the height of the plantings so the middle rows drop from 2 feet to 18 inches. Continue to stagger plantings toward the front of the bed. Finally, line the edge with mounding 4- to 6-inch-tall plants that will spread to create a soft, harmonious edge.

A GARDEN FOR HUMMINGBIRDS

Your garden doesn't need to be big to attract hummingbirds. In just a few hours one weekend, you can plant a small patch or a raised bed with a colorful mix of the annuals and perennials listed here. Fill hanging baskets or window boxes with a selection of these flowers, and you will have the pleasure of watching hummingbirds up close.

Hummingbirds winter in tropical climates and arrive in northern regions in March and April. They will return year after year to the same patch of flowers or the same location where a feeder was hung. With needle-like bills and long, rough tongues, hummingbirds sip nectar from the deep recesses of tubular and cup-shaped flowers in their favorite colors of pink, red, orange, and yellow. If they reach your garden before it can provide them with a steady supply of flower nectar, augment their diet with sugar-water. Place feeders outside your window, on a deck, and in the flower bed, and watch them dart from feeder to feeder. To make nectar, use one part sugar (don't use honey; it ferments) to four parts water. Boil it until the sugar melts, let it cool, then pour it into the feeders. Most commercial hummingbird feeders are decorated with red plastic flowers. If yours isn't, attract the birds by adding a few drops of red artificial food coloring to the sugar water.

When planted to attract birds, butterflies, or insects, your garden should be kept free of pesticides. Either hand-pick or use a jet of water to remove unwanted creatures. Or let nature and your garden helpers take care of the invaders.

PLANTS FAVORED BY HUMMINGBIRDS

Annuals:

ANTIRRHINUM (SNAPDRAGON)

CUCURBITA (SQUASH)

DAHLIA

GLADIOLUS

HIBISCUS

IMPATIENS (BALSAM)

IPOMOEA (MORNINGGLORY)

JASMINUM (JASMINE)

LATHYRUS ODORATUS (SWEET PEA)

MIRABILIS (FOUR-O'CLOCK)

NICOTIANA (TOBACCO)

PELARGONIUM (GERANIUM)

PETUNIA

PHASEOLUS COCCINEUS (SCARLET RUNNER BEAN)

SALVIA RUTILANS (PINEAPPLE SAGE)

S. SPLENDENS (SCARLET SAGE)

TROPAEOLUM (NASTURTIUM)

Perennials:

ALTHAEA or *ALCEA ROSEA* (HOLLYHOCK)

AQUILEGIA (COLUMBINE)

DELPHINIUM

DIANTHUS BARBATUS (SWEET WILLIAM)

DICENTRA (BLEEDING-HEART)

DIGITALIS (FOXGLOVE)

HEMEROCALLIS (DAYLILY)

HEUCHERA (CORALBELLS)

KNIPHOFIA (RED-HOT-POKER)

LILIUM (LILY)

LOBELIA CARDINALIS (CARDINAL FLOWER)

MONARDA DIDYMA (BEE BALM)

PENSTEMON GLOXINIOIDES (PENSTEMON)

PHLOX

PHYSOSTEGIA VIRGINIANA (FALSE DRAGONHEAD)

PRIMULA

TULIPA (TULIP)

Shrubs:

ABELIA

AESCULUS (RED and FLAME BUCKEYE)

ALBIZIA (SILK TREE)

CAMPSIS RADICANS (TRUMPET VINE)

CERCIS (REDBUD)

FUCHSIA

KOLKWITZIA (BEAUTY BUSH)

LONICERA (HONEYSUCKLE)

RED CURRANT

RHODODENDRON (RHODODENDRON and AZALEA)

WEIGELA

WISTERIA

*OPPOSITE PAGE: In a garden in Palm
Springs, California, a Costa's hummingbird takes a sip of nectar from an ocotillo
plant* (Fouquieria splendens).

If the bed is against a wall or hedge, plant clumps of daffodils and tulips at the base and position tall, summer-blooming perennials directly in front of them. The summer foliage of the perennials will hide the dying leaves of the daffodils and tulips.

For a border that's a traffic-stopper from the beginning, overplant. If the plants you buy are small and bare-rooted, they will take about two years to grow lush; plant at least five of each variety in a grouping. Perennials in containers are two-year-old plants and already have mature growth; if cost is a consideration, you can achieve a pleasing effect by grouping just three of these.

For dramatic splashes of color, allow some varieties, such as *PHLOX PANICULATA* (GARDEN PHLOX) • *P. MACULATA* (WILD SWEET WILLIAM) • *MONARDA DIDYMA* (BEE BALM) • *COREOPSIS* (TICKSEED) • *ACHILLEA* (YARROW) • *CAMPANULA* (BELLFLOWER) • *OENOTHERA* (EVENING PRIMROSE) • *ECHINACEA PURPUREA* (PURPLE CONEFLOWER) • *GAILLARDIA* (BLANKET FLOWER) • *HELENIUM* (SNEEZEWEED) • and *RUDBECKIA* (BLACK-EYED SUSAN), to grow into large drifts. It will be about five years before these plants spread out of control; when they do, divide the plants or pull up runners and seedlings and plant in another site.

Taller plants, such as *ALTHAEA* or *ALCEA* (HOLLYHOCK) • *KNIPHOFIA* (RED-HOT-POKER) • YUCCA • and *ASTILBE* (SPIRAEA), are perfect accent plants in a border. Tuck spring-blooming bulbs into every available space. Once they have bloomed, their yellowing foliage will be hidden by summer- and autumn-blooming perennials. Until your perennials fill out to give an array of continuous color to the bed, plant annuals in between and at the front of the border.

If you're partial to a particular color—red, for instance—have a large splash of it in the border. Tone it down with other strong colors such as whites, blues, or a mix of pastels. Another pleasing effect is to mix varying shades of one color, such as purple, lavender, mauve, pink, and candy-stripe.

Choosing Low-Care Perennials

Once you've decided on the location of the perennial bed, follow the golden rules of easy-care plantings:

• Select varieties that will grow readily in the light available at the site. Many perennials need six to eight hours of sun, but some will grow with only three to four hours of sun, in dappled sunlight, or with no direct sunlight. If your

site is large, determine the amount of sun in each part; it may vary.

- Always choose varieties appropriate for your climate. Some plants don't like heat and humidity. Others can't survive a long winter. Know your planting zone and any microclimates in your yard so you can choose the appropriate plants.

- Keep your soil type in mind when selecting plants. If you want to grow plants that like a soil different from what's in your garden, amend it in the area they will grow.

- If your summers are hot and dry, choose drought-tolerant plants and mulch heavily.

- When you're not sure how a plant will grow in your area, check with your local arboretum, botanical garden, or county extension office for recommendations.

- Choose sturdy varieties that don't require staking. If you like tall flowers such as *DELPHINIUM* (LARKSPUR) • *ALTHAEA* or *ALCEA* (HOLLYHOCK) • *ACHILLEA* (YARROW) • ASTER • *PLATYCODEN* (BALLOON FLOWER), and PEONY, choose dwarf or compact cultivars so you don't have to spend time staking. For example, choose the

shorter *DELPHINIUM* 'PENNANT MIX' • *ASTER* X *FRIKARTII* 'WONDER OF STAFFA' and 'MONK' • *PLATYCODON GRANDI-FLORUS* 'DOUBLE BLUE' • *ACHILLEA* X 'MOONSHINE' • and *ALTHAEA* 'MAJORETTE.' Single and Japanese peonies are shorter cultivars with stronger stems and lighter heads. Look for *PAEONIA* 'DOREEN' • *P.* 'CORAL 'N' GOLD' • and *P.* 'KRINKLED WHITE'.

Here are some suggestions for the best easy-care plants:

PERENNIALS THAT GROW BEST IN FULL SUN

GAILLARDIA (BLANKETFLOWER) • *HELIANTHUS* (PERENNIAL SUNFLOWER) • GLADIOLUS • *EUPATORIUM PURPUREUM* (JOE-PYEWEED) • *ECHINACEA PURPUREA* (PURPLE CONEFLOWER) • *ECHINOPS* (GLOBE THISTLE) • *ACHILLEA* (YARROW) • *LILIUM* (LILIES) • *ARMERIA MARITIMA* (SEA PINK or THRIFT) • *ALTHAEA* or *ALCEA* (HOLLYHOCK) • *ARTEMISIA* (WORMWOOD) • *OENOTHERA* (EVENING PRIMROSE) • *LIATRIS* (BLAZING-STAR) • *PEROVSKIA* (RUSSIAN SAGE) • *PAPAVER ORIENTALE* (ORIENTAL POPPY) • *SOLIDAGO* (GOLDENROD) • *COREOPSIS* (TICK-SEED) • *DELPHINIUM* (LARKSPUR) • and *KNIPHOFIA* (RED-HOT-POKER).

PERENNIALS THAT BLOOM NON-STOP FROM JUNE TO SEPTEMBER

ACHILLEA 'MOONSHINE' (YARROW) • *A. MILLEFOLIUM* 'RED BEAUTY' • *CAMPANULA CARPATICA* (TUSSOCK BELLFLOWER) • *C. ROTUNDIFOLIA* (BLUEBELL) • *COREOPSIS*

LANCEOLATA (TICKSEED) • *C. VERTICILLATA* 'MOONBEAM' • *HEMEROCALLIS MIDDENDORIFII* (DAYLILY) • *H. ALTISSIMA* • *H.* 'HAPPY RETURNS' • *DIANTHUS* (GARDEN PINK) • *OENOTHERA TETRAGONA* 'YELLOW RIVER' (EVENING PRIMROSE) • *RUDBECKIA FULGIDA* 'GOLDSTURM' (BLACK-EYED SUSAN) • *ECHINACEA PURPUREA* 'BRIGHT STAR' and 'ROBERT BLOOM' (PURPLE CONEFLOWER) • *GAILLARDIA* Χ *GRANDIFLORA* 'BURGUNDY' and 'GOBLIN' (BLANKETFLOWER) • *SALVIA* Χ *SUPERBA* 'EAST FRIESLAND' and 'MAY KNIGHT' (SAGE) • *S. PATENS* 'CAMBRIDGE BLUE' • *ASTER* Χ *FRIKARTII* 'MONCH' and 'WONDER OF STAFFA' • *VERBENA CANADENSIS* (ROSE VERBENA) • *V. HASTATA* (BLUE VERVAIN) • *GERANIUM* Χ *OXONIANUM* 'CLARIDGE DRUCE' • *G. ENDRESSII* 'WARGRAVE PINK' • *G. SANGUINEUM* 'SHEPHERD'S WARNING' • *HELIOPSIS HELIANTHOIDES* (OXEYE) • *H. SCABRA INCOMPARABILIS* • *POTENTILLA NEPALENSIS* (CINQUEFOIL) • *P. FRUTICOSA* • *P. ATROSANGUINEA* • *GYPSOPHILA PANICULATA* 'COMPACTA PLENA' and 'PINK STAR' (BABY'S-BREATH) • *LIATRIS SPICATA* 'KOBOLD' and 'SILVER TIP' (BLAZING-STAR) • *PHLOX PANICULATA* (GARDEN PHLOX) • and *ROSA* (ROSE): 'THE FAIRY' • 'CAREFREE WONDER' • MEIDILAND VARIETIES: 'BONICA' • 'ALBA' • 'SCARLET' • and 'FUSCHIA' • and all climbing roses such as 'SPECTRA' • 'BLAZE' • and 'CLIMBING JOSEPH'S COAT'.

Preparing the Soil

If you are turning the ground in your perennial site for the first time, loosen the soil with a rototiller or with a shovel and a fork to a depth of 12 to 18 inches. Or, install raised beds (see page 40). One month before planting, cover the entire site with several inches of composted organic matter to increase nutrient content and improve tilth. If you don't have any compost or rotted leaves to enrich the soil, increase the nutrient

OPPOSITE PAGE: While not as tall as tender gladiolus, the more compact winter-hardy variety of Gladiolus byzantium *does not need staking. Like all gladiolus, it is a colorful prize in the cutting garden.*

*ABOVE: Clustered bellflower (*Campanula glomerata*) is a long-blooming summer showstopper. Its purple flowers are stunning when combined with the strong yellow blooms of yarrows (*Achillea Χ *'Moonshine' and* Achillea Χ *'Coronation Gold').*

A BUTTERFLY GARDEN

Plant a bed of colorful flowers in a sunny, protected area, and butterflies will flock to your garden. It doesn't have to be very big—a space 4 X 10 feet is ample, especially if you tuck a few annuals and perennials that butterflies love here and there in the rest of the garden. Even if starting from scratch you can plant a flower border in a weekend. See "Planting the Border" on page 149 for planting pointers.

Butterflies will sip nectar from many different flowers. However, they'll stay and lay their eggs only if you include plantings that are a source of food for their larvae and that offer overwintering places for eggs and pupae. Dill, fennel, parsley, and anise provide food for butterfly larvae. Make other areas of the garden inviting by providing woodpiles and leaf litter where adults as well as pupae can spend the winter. They also appreciate native trees and wildflowers, some flowering weeds, and grasses (see Weekend Project #3). Don't mow or scythe your meadow or wildflowers in the fall; wait until late spring after the butterfly eggs have hatched.

Add a shallow pool of water (a bird-bath will do) and a few flat stones where the butterflies can rest and sun themselves and you'll create a habitat that will keep them around all summer and into autumn.

Although butterflies take nectar from many plants, the larvae of each type of butterfly feed off one specific plant. For example, monarch butterfly caterpillars eat only milkweed plants so that is where the monarch lays her eggs. Other specific hosts for butterfly larvae include alfalfa and clovers for blues and sulphurs; elm, poplar, and willow for mourning cloak and viceroy; hackberry for tawny emperor; carrot, fennel, parsley, and Queen-Anne's-lace for black and anise swallowtail; false and stinging nettles for tortoise shell, painted lady, question mark, and red admiral; thistles, borage, burdock, sunflowers, hollyhock, everlasting, and wormwood for painted lady and silver-spotted skipper; and wild cherry for eastern tiger swallowtail, coral hairstreak, and red-spotted purple. Find out what butterfly species inhabit your region and learn which plants provide food for their larvae.

WEEKEND
PROJECT **#33**

PLANTS FAVORED BY BUTTERFLIES

Annuals:

AGERATUM (FLOSSFLOWER)

CENTAUREA CYANUS (CORNFLOWER)

COSMOS

DAHLIA

HELIANTHUS (SUNFLOWER)

HELIOTROPIUM ARBORESCENS (HELIOTROPE)

LANTANA

LOBULARIA MARITIMA (SWEET ALYSSUM)

TAGETES (MARIGOLD)

VIOLA X *WITTROCKIANA* (PANSY)

ZINNIA

Perennials:

ACHILLEA (YARROW)

ALTHAEA or *ALCEA ROSEA* (HOLLYHOCK)

ASCLEPIAS (BUTTERFLY WEED)

ASTER

CHRYSANTHEMUM X *SUPERBUM* (SHASTA DAISY)

CIMICIFUGA RACEMOSA (SNAKEROOT)

COREOPSIS (TICKSEED)

ECHINACEA PURPUREA (PURPLE CONEFLOWER)

EUPATORIUM (JOE-PYEWEED)

GAILLARDIA (BLANKET FLOWER)

HEMEROCALLIS (DAYLILY)

LIATRIS (BLAZING-STAR)

LILIUM (LILY)

LONICERA (HONEYSUCKLE)

LUPINUS (LUPIN)

MENTHA (MINT)

MONARDA (BEE BALM)

OXEYE DAISY

PHLOX

PRIMULA (PRIMROSE)

PYRETHRUM (PAINTED DAISY)

RUDBECKIA (CONEFLOWER)

SEDUM SPECTABILE (SHOWY STONECROP)

SOLIDAGO (GOLDENROD)

Shrubs:

BUDDLEIA (BUTTERFLY BUSH)

CARYOPTERIS X *CLANDONENSIS* (BLUE MIST)

CLETHRA ALNIFOLIA (SUMMER-SWEET)

HYDRANGEA

KALMIA (MOUNTAIN LAUREL)

KERRIA JAPONICA (JAPANESE ROSE)

KOLKWITZIA (BEAUTY BUSH)

LINDERA BENZOIN (SPICEBUSH)

ROSEA (ROSE)

RHODODENDRON (AZALEA)

SPIRAEA

SYRINGA (LILAC)

VIBURNUM

OPPOSITE PAGE: A garden brimming with colorful perennials is an irresistible magnet for butterflies.

content by sprinkling the bed with a commercial organic or a chemical 5-10-5 fertilizer. Rake into the soil. Dig in some peat moss if you're trying to improve drainage and add lime if your soil tested below a pH of 6. (Most perennials prefer a slightly acid soil with a pH of 6 to 7.) Water thoroughly and, even if you are not planting immediately, add a layer of mulch to aid in moisture retention and limit weed growth.

Planting the Border

To make planting easier, visualize the spacing requirements before you start digging so you won't plant too close together. Outline the shape of each mature plant variety on the surface of the bed with a sprinkling of builder's sand (rain won't wash it away), limestone, or granular 5-10-5 fertilizer. Before actually planting, set the plants on top of the soil to get a better idea of how they'll look as they grow.

When working with bare-root mail-order plants with no top growth, plant within three days of delivery. In the meantime, remove the plants from their packages, trim off any damaged roots, and place the plants in water.

Plant one variety at a time, working from the back to the front of the

ABOVE: This herbaceous perennial border offers a good demonstration of height succession. Edging plants such as lady's-mantle (Alchemilla mollis) and meadow foam (Limnanthes douglasii) soften the edges of the border, and midsize poppies create a bridge to the lupines, which add height in the rear.

OPPOSITE PAGE: Lamb's-ears, used as an edging plant in the Carol Mercer Garden in East Hampton, New York, provides soft color and soft texture. As shown here, the Stachys byzantina variety also can be used to add height when it is in bloom during the summer.

border. Space the plants 6 to 8 inches apart, and separate each variety by 15 to 18 inches. Dig holes wide enough to take the spread of the mature plant's roots and deep enough to allow the crown (the base of the stem) of the plant to remain above soil level. Backfill with soil and tamp down around the plant, leaving a slight depression to catch water. Soak each grouping immediately after planting. If you did not enrich the bed with organic matter, side-dress each grouping when planting time arrives.

If you are planting perennials in pots, space them appropriately, according to their final size and the look you're trying to achieve in your perennial garden. Loosen the root balls and slice through any pot-bound roots. Dig holes the depth of the root ball and set the plant on loose, crumbly earth. Backfill with soil, tamp down, and water thoroughly.

When all of the plantings are in place, water the entire bed, then mulch with a 2-inch layer of shredded bark. This adds a finished look to the garden and keeps moisture in and weeds out.

Growing Perennials from Seed

Growing perennials from seed is easy and less expensive than buying plants. The weekend gardener will be able to germinate seeds indoors by using insulated growing trays equipped with capillary matting, water reservoirs, and greenhouse covers. However, before the young plants can go permanently outdoors, they need to be hardened off for a week or so. To do this, place the plants outdoors during the day and return them to a sheltered place at night. This may be impossible for the weekend gardener, so place them outside for as many hours as possible on Friday and Saturday, then plant them in the garden during the mid- to late afternoon on Sunday. Water the plants thoroughly and cover with lightweight floating row fabric secured along the edges with soil. (Or support the fabric with a frame—see Weekend Project #22.) This cover insulates plants from wind and frost, prevents sunscald, and holds in moisture.

Another way the weekend gardener can harden off transplants is with an automatically ventilated cold frame. The automated window can be set to open for several hours during the hottest part

of the day—from 11 A.M. to 2 P.M. At night, the enclosed plants will experience a drop in temperature, which will harden them off.

If you don't want to go through the hardening-off process, sow seeds right into a prepared bed anytime from April to October. Because tiny seeds can't get a hold in rough soil, break up any clods and rake the soil so it's free of lumps and stones. If your soil isn't enriched with organic matter, work some into the bed.

Dampen the soil, then sprinkle the seeds in short rows or blocks and cover with a ½ inch or so of soil. Tamp down and water gently. To keep the soil warm and moist during the week, cover with

clear plastic. The plastic also will keep critters from digging up the seeds. When the seeds germinate in about two weeks, remove the plastic and replace with a lightweight row cover fabric. Saturate the ground (through the fabric) each weekend during the early spring. The row cover fabric will keep the ground moist and protect the seedlings when temperatures plummet.

During the hotter weather of late spring and summer, the weekend gardener will need to set up an automatic system for watering during the week. Thin the seedlings when they have six to eight leaves, and transplant to their final location.

RIGHT: Take advantage of a wall on your property because it will act as a wind barrier and provide additional heat. Plant the base with perennials and let vines and roses cling to its craggy surface. Here, rose 'Rambling Rector' climbs the wall while delphiniums contribute beauty and height.

Some seeds of woodland plants need to go through a chilling period. Sow these in October; they will lie dormant throughout the winter, then, depending on the severity of the winter, germinate in early to late spring and be established by summer. Sow seeds according to packet directions. After the first hard frost, mulch the soil with several inches of pine straw or shredded leaves. Wait until danger of heavy frosts are over before removing the mulch in early spring. You may not get many blooms the first season, but by the second year, you'll have sturdy, mature perennials for mere pennies.

Caring for Perennials

Perennials are a hardy lot. They don't demand a lot of attention but will thrive for years with just a little care.

- To keep plants blooming, deadhead them periodically by removing flowers as they fade. Because many plants have waves of blooms and open all their flowers simultaneously, wait until there are clumps of dead heads, then shear them off all at once. You'll get another round of blooms lower down the stems. Toward the end of the season, leave some dried heads on the stalks to add interest to the winter

---

A BOG GARDEN

Any area that remains wet or damp throughout the year can be a wonderful natural bog garden. If you don't have such an area, it is easy to create one in a day. If you can't find enough bog varieties at your local nurseries, check in the mail-order catalogs from aquatic nurseries.

An ideal site for a bog garden is in full to partial sun where a natural depression collects rainwater. Or make one where downspouts and underground pipes deposit rainwater.

STEP-BY-STEP INSTRUCTIONS FOR CONTRUCTING A BOG GARDEN

To create an environment that is constantly wet, you'll need to:

1. Dig a 12-inch-deep trench, oval, arc, or whatever shape fits in with your site.
2. Line the pit with 8-mil-thick plastic and backfill with the removed soil plus compost or leaf mold.
3. If desired, dig a deeper hole at one end for one or more of the shrubs or trees from the following list.
4. Plant with moisture-loving perennials, shrubs, and trees, such as those recommended in the following list.

PLANTS FOR THE BOG GARDEN

ASTILBE (SPIRAEA) • HOSTA • *LIGULARIA* (PARSLEY) • *CHELONE LYONII* (TURTLEHEAD) • *OSMUNDA REGALIS* (ROYAL FERN) • *O. CLAYTONIANA* (INTERRUPTED FERN) • *O. CINNAMOMEA* (CINNAMON FERN) • *MIMULUS* (MONKEY FLOWER) • *IRIS ENSATA* (JAPANESE or SWORD-LEAVED IRIS) • *SIBERICA* (SIBERIAN IRIS) • *CALTHA PALUSTRIS* (MARSH MARIGOLD) • *PRIMULA JAPONICA* (JAPANESE PRIMROSE) • *SYMPLOCARPUS FOETIDUS* (SKUNK CABBAGE) • *PONTEDERIA* (PICKEREL WEED) • *ARUM* (BOG ARUM) • *ASCLEPIAS INCARNATA* (SWAMP MILKWEED) • *ACORUS* (SWEET FLAG) • *LOBELIA CARDINALIS* (CARDINAL FLOWER) • *L. SIPHILITICA* (GREAT BLUE LOBELIA) • *MYOSOTIS SYLVATICA* (FORGET-ME-NOT) • and *EUPATORIUM PURPUREUM* (JOE-PYEWEED). Be sure to plant *LYSIMACHIA CLETHROIDES* (GOOSENECK) and *TYPHA* (CATTAIL) in pots to contain their aggressive root systems.

SHRUBS AND TREES FOR THE BOG GARDEN

HIBISCUS MOSCHEUTOS (SWAMPROSE MALLOW) • SWAMP or RED MAPLE • WILLOW • ALDER • and LARCH.

ABOVE, LEFT: A sundial shares center stage in this perennial island bed with several plantings of tree heath (Erica arborea).

ABOVE, RIGHT: A sunny perennial border planted in front of a wall contains variegated Iris 'Wild Echo,' Gladiolus communis sub. byzantinus, and Bergenia 'Ballawley.'

OPPOSITE PAGE: Drifts of red bee balm, white daisies, and yellow columbines make a carefree combination in this garden.

landscape. Plants with attractive dried heads include *ACHILLEA* (YARROW) • *ERYNGIUM MARITIMUM* (SEA HOLLY) • *PAPAVER ORIENTALE* (ORIENTAL POPPY) • *ASTILBE* (SPIRAEA) • *LIATRIS* (BLAZING-STAR) • *IRIS SIBERICA* (SIBERIAN IRIS) and *I. ENSATA* (JAPANESE IRIS) • and *ECHINACEA PURPUREA* (PURPLE CONE-FLOWER—goldfinches and house finches will eat the coneflower seeds all summer through winter).

• During the second year, you will have a better idea of whether your plants are the best choice for your design,

color scheme, and bloom sequence. When one variety doesn't do well, move it—the perennial bed is an ever-changing, evolving garden.

• Every three to five years, divide your perennials to keep them from taking over the bed and to renew them. Plants divided in autumn recover quickly and produce new growth in the early spring, especially those that bloom in the spring and early summer. Autumn-blooming plants such as asters and chrysanthemums should be divided in the spring so they have enough time to recover and flower on cue. In milder climates, divide them in autumn after they've finished flowering.

- To divide, dig up the plant and use a sharp spade or large knife to slice through the roots. Discard any dead areas and remove two-thirds of the top growth. Plant the divisions in loose, prepared soil, with the crown set no lower than the original plant. Tamp down firmly and water thoroughly with a mixture of diluted fish emulsion or 5-10-5 liquid fertilizer. Add several inches of mulch around each plant.

- During autumn, cut perennial foliage to within 1 inch of the soil. After the first hard frost, mulch the plants with 2 inches of pine straw, shredded bark, or shredded leaves. Mulching after the first hard frost helps prevent the soil from thawing during warm winter days. When the soil thaws, then refreezes, it heaves, exposing roots to cold, drying winter winds.

- In the spring, gently draw back the mulch from the tops and around the sides of the plants. Add a layer of compost next to the plants and cover this with additional mulch.

COTTAGE GARDEN

- Newly planted perennials will need watering during dry spells. Established perennials should be able to make it through a hot summer if the bed is well mulched. The mulch keeps moisture in the soil and reduces weeds, which compete for water.

Cottage Gardens

Take a walk through the villages of England's Cotswolds and you'll see magnificent cottage gardens. Nearly every house has a tiny front and back garden in a rainbow of colors. Perennials, biennials, and annuals spill in careful disarray around the lawn. Roses frame doorways, gates, and arbors. Clematis winds its way up tree trunks and weaves through branches.

Although a cottage garden starts with a simple design, it evolves into a spectacular sea of flowers that crowds around the door or spills over onto the pathways. This is an easy garden for you to maintain on weekends, because you can let plants go to seed and grow and mingle together. Once in a while you'll need to restrain a particular plant, but in this care-free garden, none of the plants looks out of place or unsightly. Additionally, in a site so massed with continually blooming plants, weeds find it hard to get a hold.

KEY	QTY	NAME
1	2	*Buddleia davidii* (butterfly bush)
2	2	*Rosa* 'Blaze' (climbing rose)
3	6	*Lavandula angustifolia* (English lavender)
4	6	*Echinacea purpurea* (purple coneflower)
5	4	*Chrysanthemum parthenium* (feverfew)
6	4	*Delphinium* X 'Knights of the Round Table'
7	6	*Dianthus barbatus* (sweet William)
8	8	*Eschscholzia californica* (California poppy)
9	9	*Cosmos* 'Sonata White' (cosmos)
10	6	*Lupinus* 'Russell hybrids' (lupine)
11	6	*Coreopsis* 'Sunray' (tickseed)
12	4	*Gypsophila* (baby's-breath)
13	2	*Rosa* 'Ballerina pink' (shrub rose)
14	6	*Salvia splendens* (scarlet sage)
15	6	*Santolina* (lavender cotton)
16	1	Birdbath
17		Stone pavers
18	1	Bench with arbor

To allow the cottage garden to reach out from its original design into artistic disorder requires planting in drifts and masses. Where you might plant three or five of each variety in a perennial garden, double the quantity in a cottage garden. Use low-growing and creeping plants to soften around the edges, then fill the rest of the garden with midsize and tall flowers so the whole garden retains a harmonious blend of colors and textures. The more crowded the flowers, the better they will look, and the more blooms you'll have for indoor bouquets.

Flowers in the cottage garden will offer continuous color when given six to eight hours of sun. Height plays a key role, so include tall cultivars for blooms that stand above the others and for beautiful bouquets. It is also important

to plant a variety of colors, textures, and shapes. Include the elongated spires and spikes of *AQUILEGIA* (COLUMBINE) • *ALTHAEA* or *ALCEA* (HOLLYHOCK) • *CLEOME* (SPIDER FLOWER) • DELPHINIUM • *DIGITALIS* (FOXGLOVE) • *LIATRIS* (BLAZING-STAR) • LUPINE • *ANTIRRHINUM* (SNAPDRAGON) • *HEUCHERA* (CORALBELLS) • GLADIOLUS • *SALVIA* • *LAVANDULA* (LAVENDER) • *LILIUM* (LILIES) • *VERONICA* (SPEEDWELL) • and *FILIPENDULA* (MEADOWSWEET).

Round blooms pull the eye in and link taller and shorter varieties and one color with another. Consider *RUDBECKIA* or *ECHINACEA* (CONEFLOWER) • CHRYSAN-THEMUM • *DIANTHUS BARBATUS* (SWEET WILLIAM) • *CALENDULA* (MARIGOLD) • *DIANTHUS* (CARNATION) • *PAPAVER* (POPPY) • *CAMPANULA* (BALLOON FLOWER) • *ACHILLEA* (YARROW) • *ASCLEPIAS* (BUTTERFLY WEED) • DAHLIA • *PAEONIA* (PEONY) • *PELARGONIUM* X *HORTORUM* (COMMON GERA-NIUM) • and *ZINNIA*.

Include a variety of sunflower culti-vars; their heights range from 2 to 6 feet, and sturdy stems support blooms 3 to 12 inches in diameter. New hybrids offer colors from palest lemon to deep yellow with centers of honey to choco-late brown.

ABOVE, LEFT: A profusion of annuals, perennials, and shrubs offers continuous color in this cottage garden.

ABOVE, RIGHT: Orange dahlias and pink garden phlox (Phlox paniculata) create swaths of warm color in the herbaceous border throughout the summer months.

ATTRACTING BIRDS WITH A SMALL RAISED POOL OR A WATER TUB

If you don't have the space for a pond, you can easily install a mini water garden in a half-barrel or ceramic container. Planted with a few aquatics, home to a couple of fish, and perhaps equipped with a source of moving water, a mini water garden will attract birds, dragonflies, and other small creatures just like a large pond. Birdbaths need to be filled every day during the summer, but a small water garden will remain full even while you are away. And if the mini water garden is at least 12 inches deep and its surface is partially shaded with aquatic foliage, it won't grow the slimy red algae so commonly found in shallow birdbaths.

Besides barrel or ceramic containers, special tub and kettle kits for small water gardens come complete with container, filter, pump, and a small spouting ornament. Or choose one of the very small fiberglass molded forms. Although most people set them into a 12- to 18-inch-deep hole in the garden, they can be placed on a deck or patio inside a raised-bed frame made from wood, brick, or stone. Position your mini water garden where it will get at least five to six hours of sun.

One simple way to keep a small pool clean and the water recirculating is to purchase a submersible combination pump and filter. Small enough to sit in a tub or mini fiberglass pool, this equipment recirculates the water through narrow tubing and over a simple waterfall made from fiberglass rock, a length of hollow bamboo, or an ornamental spout.

If you are using a half-barrel, first line it with plastic sheeting. Then, for all mini water gardens, place the pump on the bottom of the tub, fiberglass pool, or barrel, and add water to 3 to 4 inches from the top. The level will raise automatically as items are added.

A small water garden will accommodate one dwarf "pygmy" water lily or other floating lily-like aquatic, two marginal plants, and several bunches of oxygenating plants. Root the plants in heavy soil in 6- to 8-inch pots. Layer the top with gravel and thoroughly soak with water before submerging in the pool. Place the water lily pot on the bottom. Anchor the oxygenating plants with rocks on the bottom or between a stack of bricks. Use the bricks to support the marginal plants, which need about 6 inches of water above their crowns. Choose from DWARF PAPYRUS • DWARF BAMBOO • ARROWHEAD • ARUM • CHAMELEON PLANT • PICKEREL WEED • SWEET FLAG • and other small marginal plants. When all the plants are in place, add water to the top of the tub or pool.

Be sure to incorporate smaller varieties, too. Nothing compares to the delicate beauty of *LATHYRUS ODORATUS* (SWEET PEA), the first *GALANTHUS* (SNOWDROPS) of spring, the vibrant oranges of *TROPAEOLUM* (NASTURTIUM), the rich hues of *VIOLA X WITTROCKIANA* (PANSY), and the brilliant reds and purples of ANEMONES.

Provide texture with feathery flowers and foliage such as *TANECETUM* (TANSY) • *GYPSOPHILA* (BABY'S-BREATH) • *ARTEMISIA* (WORMWOOD) • *CENTAUREA CINERARIA* (DUSTY-MILLER) • *THALICTRUM* (MEADOW RUE) • *CHRYSANTHEMUM PARTHENIUM* (FEVERFEW) • *CIMICIFUGA* (BUGBANE) • COSMOS • *LIMONIUM LATIFOLIUM* (STATICE) • *DICENTRA EXIMIA* 'LUXURIANT' (BLEEDING-HEART) • *CROCOSMIA* (MONTEBRETIA) • *STACHYS GRANDIFLORA* (BIG BETONY) • and *SANTOLINA*.

Many of the plantings in a cottage garden are prolific bloomers that respond to constant cutting by sending out more flowers. Toward the end of summer, let some of the blooms go to seed, ripen, and spill over onto the humus-enriched earth. The following year they will fill in even the smallest spaces. Be prepared for a few surprises; annual hybrids usually come up a different shade or color.

Your mini pond will flourish as a natural habitat if you add two or three 2-inch goldfish and about six black snails. The snails will eat the algae, plant, and fish wastes. The fish will eat decaying plant materials, mosquito eggs, and tadpoles. Your small water garden will attract dragonflies to lay eggs, and their larvae will devour mosquito larvae, too. Attract birds and make it easier for them to drink and bathe by positioning a small branch or rock for them to land on.

In the winter, place the marginal plants on the bottom of the pool so their roots don't freeze.

OPPOSITE PAGE: A small raised pool constructed from stone blocks is shallow enough to allow birds to bathe but deep enough to attract frogs. Its location in partial shade encourages the growth of moss on the stones.

ABOVE: A path leading through a garden bursting with foliage and flowers incorporates an element of surprise: a small pool of water that will attract birds and other small creatures.

CARING FOR YOUR COTTAGE GARDEN

Cottage gardens are planted so densely that you will have to feed the soil with organic matter or 5-10-5 granular fertilizer. If your soil is enriched with compost, mulch heavily in the spring and autumn around shrubs and drifts of flowers—anywhere you can see earth. If your soil is not compost-enriched, sprinkle the 5-10-5 over the soil in late spring before you mulch around the plantings.

Up the Garden Path

A garden is not made entirely of flowers and trees. It also includes paths that lead from one place to another—the street to the front door, the back door to the vegetable garden, the patio to the pond or woodland. With creative planning, a path can be a focal point in the garden, leading the eye to some distant view or a key feature in the landscape.

Whether the path is straight or curved, wide or narrow, direct or meandering, it should be covered with a material that suits its function, complements the surrounding landscape, and, particularly important for the weekend gardener, requires little or no upkeep.

If you have an established cement path with straight edges, remember that what you plant alongside the path will take it from boring to beautiful. Soften amu hard, straight lines with edging plants such as *PHLOX SUBULATA* (MOSS PINK) • *THYMUS SERPYLLUM* (MOTHER-OF-THYME) • *ALCHEMILLA* (LADY'S-MANTLE) • and *IBERIS SEMPERVIRENS* (CANDYTUFT).

WEEKEND PROJECT #36

PLANTING HERBS BETWEEN FLAGSTONES AND PATIO SQUARES

Walkways and patios made with bricks, pavers, slabs, or flagstones are ready-made herb gardens. Make this a Saturday afternoon project and enjoy your handiwork just a few hours later. All you need are a few pots of herbs.

Between the cracks is a perfect place to grow hardy thyme varieties. There are hundreds to choose from in a variety of colors and aromas. Some of the prettiest include lemon, silver, variegated, and mother-of-thyme. Thymes are evergreen and bloom profusely for many months, putting on a show of pale to deep purple-red, little flowering spires. They are a big favorite of honeybees, too, so be careful.

Down the sides of the walkway or patio, plant clumps of variegated sage, dill, and chives. Tuck in some tarragon, cilantro, and parsley for fragrance and leaf texture. Globe basil makes a pretty mounding plant, while some of the more exotic basils, such as cinnamon, holy, licorice, and opal, add purple accents and are intensely aromatic.

If you wish to make room for the herbs in a patio area, remove a few stones. Loosen the earth with a shovel, break up the lumps, and dig in a couple of handfuls of compost. Herbs also make a good border around the edges of the patio.

ABOVE: A narrow grass path winds its way through mixed herbaceous borders in an informal garden.

Such low-growing perennials will spill from the bed into sprawling mounds to create a curving effect.

If your landscape and house are formal, use path materials that reflect that. Rectangles of bluestone or gray flagstone are appropriate here. Echo the formality of a path by planting the beds alongside with a colorful collection of stately perennials that don't need staking, such as *EUPHORBIA GRIFFITHII* 'FIRE-GLOW' (SPURGE) • *IRIS PALLIDA* 'VARIEGATA' (VARIEGATED ORRIS IRIS) • *HEMEROCALLIS*

(DAYLILY) • HOSTA • and CHRYSANTHEMUM. Interplant with early- and late-blooming tulips. This walkway will be in bloom from spring to late autumn, and the dying and browning leaves of tulips will be hidden by the long-lasting foliage of daylilies, iris, and mums. Edge the entire length of the beds with *LIRIOPE* (LILY-TURF); though the dried mounds will need cutting back in the early spring, a weed trimmer will easily do the job.

A line of trees underplanted with low-maintenance evergreen ground covers gives a formal feeling to a long walkway or driveway. For spectacular spring color and easy maintenance, plant low-growing WHITE CHERRIES with a horizontal branching habit. *PRUNUS SERRULATA* 'SHIROTAE' grows to just 15 feet. Or try the flowering dogwood *CORNUS KOUSA* 'SUMMER STARS,' which blooms all summer. Both are good choices. If space is at a premium, plant narrow, upright pear trees such as *PYRUS CALLERYANA* 'WHITEHOUSE,' whose mature width is only 8 feet. Underplant with variegated pink, purple, and cream *AJUGA* (BUGLE-WEED), which sends up 6-inch spikes of pink or blue flowers May to June and is evergreen through the winter. Interplant with small bulbs or easy-to-grow *POTENTILLA NEPALENSIS* (CINQUEFOIL). A

good choice is low-growing 'MISS WILLMOT,' which bears brilliant pink flowers all summer.

Use a wide grass pathway in a formal shrubbery garden, and a narrow, winding grass strip in an informal cottage garden. Paths of neatly mowed grass also work well and are easy to maintain. No weeding is necessary; just zip down the path every time you cut the lawn.

The warm tones of bricks are effective as an informal garden path. To set off the earthy tones of the bricks, plant yellows, oranges, and reds found in *CALENDULA OFFICINALIS* (POT MARIGOLD) • *TAGETES PATULA* (FRENCH MARIGOLD) • *TROPAEOLUM* (NASTURTIUM) • and *PELARGONIUM* X *HORTORUM* (COMMON GERANIUM). To make this a permanent border, include the sunset colors of TULIPS and NARCISSUS. Interplant with blue *MUSCARI* (GRAPE HYACINTH) and *PUSCHKINIA*, and multicolored *VIOLA* X *WITTROCKIANA* (PANSY). These all reseed to keep coming up year after year. Add a perennial evergreen such as *VINCA* (PERI-WINKLE); this will spread to fill most of extra space but will allow spring bulbs to push through.

Wood chips, tree trunk slabs, or large irregular stone slabs interplanted with moss are appropriate choices for a walk-

LAYING A STONE WALKWAY

Laying a stone walkway is a simple job. It consists of planning, buying materials, and installing the walkway. If you don't want to spend the whole weekend on the walkway, plan and purchase materials during the week or the preceding weekend.

Before you put your ideas down on paper, go to the local stone quarry and check out the sizes of the slabs available. Whether you choose concrete pavers, flagstones, or irregular slabs cut from sandstone, bluestone, or slate, such materials are usually about 2 inches thick. Your choice will be influenced by the colors of the different stones (they vary from buff to rust and from blue to gray), and whether your walkway will curve around beds, be built on a slope, or go in a straight line on level ground.

Most flags or slabs measure approximately 18 X 18 inches. If you want a one-person path (at least 2 feet wide), lay them side by side.

STEP-BY-STEP INSTRUCTIONS FOR LAYING A STONE WALKWAY

1. Outline the walkway with string and stakes, or use a garden hose if the walkway is to be curved. Remove the sod with a spade, then shovel out the top 4 to 6 inches of soil.

2. If you would like to edge the path, set pressure-treated landscaping ties or other edging along the excavated bed.

3. Fill the excavated walkway with coarse builders' sand or crushed stone. Rake smooth and tread down into the soil. Add layers until the bed is level with the surrounding ground. This base will provide drainage and create a foundation for the flagstones.

4. Set the pavers or flagstones on top of the base, being sure to leave at least 1 inch between each stone. Position the stones so it is comfortable to step from one to another. If you need to cut a stone to fit a tight space, score across the surface with a chisel and then tap along the line with a hammer to remove the unwanted section.

5. Lay one small section at a time, checking the design as you go. If the stones are in the desired position, move them back and forth a little so they settle into the crushed stone.

6. After you have laid all the stones, fill the spaces around them with more of the base material. Pour it over the entire walkway and brush it so that it falls between the stones or slabs. When you are satisfied with the work, water the entire area with a fine sprinkler.

7. You can start walking on the stones immediately; however, the walkway will continue to settle for about a week. After that time, add more crushed stone or sand around the flagstones and spray with water.

OPPOSITE PAGE: Bricks add warmth and beauty to a pathway. Their small, rectangular form can be used to create interesting patterns, as seen in this angled chevron design.

way through a woodland garden. Border natural pathways that are in sun or partial shade with spreading and self-seeding tall varieties such as MONARDA DIDYMA (BEE BALM) • ASCLEPIAS (BUTTERFLY WEED) • GEUM (AVENS) • AQUILEGIA (COLUMBINE) • RUDBECKIA or ECHINACEA (CONEFLOWER) • ASTER • PHYSOSTEGIA (FALSE DRAGONHEAD) • and CHRYSANTHEMUM PARTHENIUM (FEVERFEW). When a path leads through trees that create light or shade, choose a red and white color scheme for the border, underplanted with AZALEAS • IMPATIENS (BALSAM) • GALLIUM ODORATUM (SWEET WOODRUFF) • POLYGONATUM (SOLOMON'S-SEAL) • and ARISAEMA TRIPHYLLUM (JACK-

IN-THE-PULPIT, which also produces red berries in the autumn). Plant red and white varieties of DICENTRA EXIMIA (FRINGED BLEEDING-HEART). A thick layer of mulch and the spreading mat of sweet woodruff will keep out weeds, so the only work for the weekend gardener will be the annual planting of IMPATIENS.

For regions with high temperatures, a path that resembles a riverbed has a cooling effect. It also is in keeping with the natural landscape of any area where plants are resilient to drought and heat. Small stones are a good choice for this pathway. Layer them on top of thick landscaping fabric to keep the path free

of weeds. Anchor it with a line of well-spaced yuccas, and plant heat-resistant varieties between. Choose low-growing, fast-spreading drought-proof ground covers such as VERBENA TENERA 'SISSING-HURST,' with deep pink flowers that bloom all summer into late autumn; ARABIS STURII (ROCK CRESS), with small white spring flowers on top of glossy, 6-inch foliage; and DELOSPERMA COOPERI (HARDY ICEPLANT), with large, vibrant pink daisy heads that bloom all summer on top of succulent gray-green foliage.

Drought-resistant ANACYCLUS DEPRESSUS (MT. ATLAS DAISY) is another good choice. Growing to 2 feet, with a spread

WEEKEND PROJECT #38

DE-ICING WALKWAYS

In late autumn, keep a bucketful of a commercial salt product, kitty litter, slow-release fertilizer pellets, fireplace ashes, or sand near the front door, then sprinkle it on walkways, steps, and the driveway whenever snow or freezing rain make surfaces slick. Because these materials can be trekked indoors, ask people to take their shoes off at the door.

In areas where snow and ice create a hazard for motorists, highway departments spread a mixture of sand and

rock salt (or sodium chloride) so the ice thaws quickly. This may be good for driving conditions, but the briny runoff or spray produced by car wheels is harmful to roadside plantings. To counteract this problem in your own backyard, spend a day in autumn protecting your plants. Install burlap fences and add a thick layer of wood chips around trees to act as barriers against salt penetration. Fill in any deep wells around plantings that would direct runoff to the

roots. On a warm day in the spring, flush around the root areas with a hose to wash away residual salt.

When making future plantings along the roadside, consider those varieties that are more tolerant to salt, such as the Japanese black pine, mugo pine, Austrian pine, Colorado blue spruce, honey locust, black locust, red oak, rugosa rose, and birch.

to 18 inches, and featuring white flowers with large yellow centers and pink stripes, it provides height and cool tones. *ASCLEPIAS* (BUTTERFLY WEED) grows to about the same height and has bright orange, flat heads that bloom for several weeks during midsummer. It self-seeds freely but a long tap root makes it difficult to transplant after the first summer. *ACHILLEA MILLEFOLIUM* 'RED BEAUTY' (YARROW) is especially heat tolerant and grows to 18 inches. Add intense blue to this border with *CAMPANULA ROTUNDIFOLIA* 'OLYMPICA' (BELLFLOWER).

Complement these blues with the deep green foliage and bright yellow flowers of *COREOPSIS VERTICILLATA* (THREADLEAF COREOPSIS or TICKSEED) that bloom throughout the summer. Two exceptional performers in drought conditions are *C.* X 'MOONBEAM,' which is compact and grows 1½ to 2 feet tall, and *C. GRANDIFLORA* 'SUNRAY,' which is also compact and grows only a foot tall.

Ornamental grasses should not be overlooked for dressing up a walkway. With such a wide selection available, grasses make a care-free pathway border filled with interesting shapes and textures. Most are highly resistant to drought, which makes them good planting choices for dry climates.

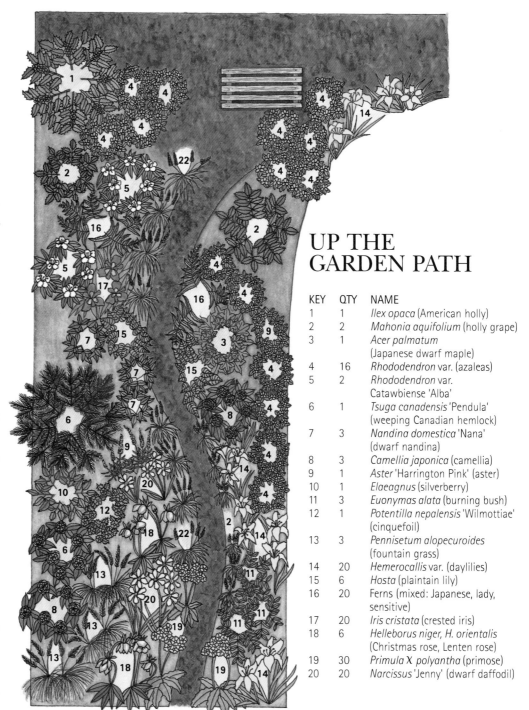

UP THE GARDEN PATH

KEY	QTY	NAME
1	1	*Ilex opaca* (American holly)
2	2	*Mahonia aquifolium* (holly grape)
3	1	*Acer palmatum* (Japanese dwarf maple)
4	16	*Rhododendron* var. (azaleas)
5	2	*Rhododendron* var. Catawbiense 'Alba'
6	1	*Tsuga canadensis* 'Pendula' (weeping Canadian hemlock)
7	3	*Nandina domestica* 'Nana' (dwarf nandina)
8	3	*Camellia japonica* (camellia)
9	1	*Aster* 'Harrington Pink' (aster)
10	1	*Elaeagnus* (silverberry)
11	3	*Euonymas alata* (burning bush)
12	1	*Potentilla nepalensis* 'Wilmottiae' (cinquefoil)
13	3	*Pennisetum alopecuroides* (fountain grass)
14	20	*Hemerocallis* var. (daylilies)
15	6	*Hosta* (plaintain lily)
16	20	Ferns (mixed: Japanese, lady, sensitive)
17	20	*Iris cristata* (crested iris)
18	6	*Helleborus niger, H. orientalis* (Christmas rose, Lenten rose)
19	30	*Primula* X *polyantha* (primose)
20	20	*Narcissus* 'Jenny' (dwarf daffodil)

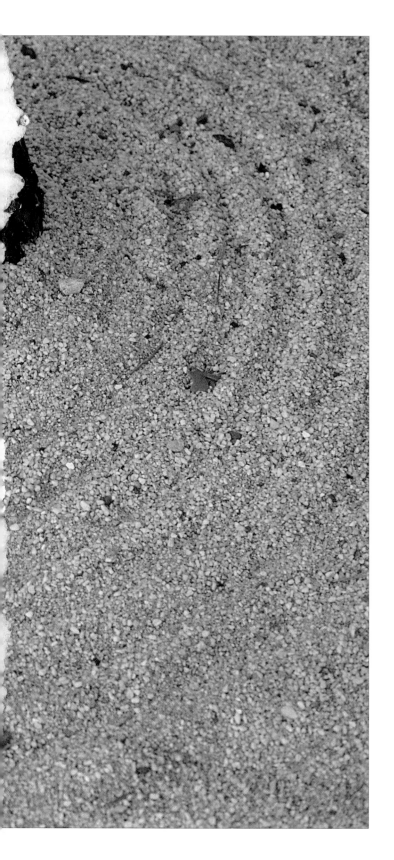

CHAPTER SEVEN

GARDENING BASICS

Make sure your soil is good, and you'll be rewarded with strong, healthy plants that are less vulnerable to disease and insect attacks and better able to withstand the rigors of excessive rain or drought—all of which means less work for you, the gardener. What's the secret to good soil? Available nutrients, organic content, texture, and tilth.

Earthworks

You can tell a lot about soil just by picking up a handful, examining its color, and feeling its texture. If your soil is a rich brown color and crumbly, it is loamy. An excellent growing medium, loamy soil is aerated, drains well, and is easy to work.

If your soil is dense and hard and has a reddish tint, it is probably mostly clay. Though packed with nutrients, clay soil does not allow deep root penetration. It bakes hard during hot, dry weather, and water takes hours to get to the plant roots. The result can be a waterlogged soil that deprives plant roots of oxygen.

LEFT: Landscape fabric covered with a thick layer of gravel can be used to reduce lawn and replace mulch or ground covers.

RIGHT: Before adding ashes, fertilizers, and other chemical amendments to the garden, test the soil to determine nutrient and pH level. Organic compost (FAR RIGHT) can be added at any time to increase the fertility naturally.

Light, sandy soil is not much better. It has few nutrients and, because water drains right through its loose texture, it dries quickly. (Adding lime to sandy soil will help slow the passage of water.)

AMENDING THE SOIL

The solution is to amend clay and sandy soils by adding organic materials such as compost, shredded leaves, finely ground pine bark, aged horse manure, and seaweed, which creates a loose, loamy, moisture-retaining, nutrient-laden soil. Add a 3- to 4-inch layer of organic matter over the beds and till, spade, or fork it in to a depth of at least 8 inches. It is impossible to overload your soil with composted organic matter, so add several inches in the spring and autumn each year.

TESTING THE SOIL

Another important step in soil improvement is to test the soil for the nutrients available to plants. A soil test also determines soil pH—the level of acidity or alkalinity. Have your soil checked by a professional laboratory or by your county extension office. State colleges also have soil-testing facilities. For a small fee, they will interpret the results and recommend ways to amend and improve your soil. You also can buy home soil-test kits but, though helpful in determining the pH, they won't provide accurate information on soil nutrient deficiencies.

Have your soil tested periodically so you know which nutrients it lacks and whether you need to add moderate amounts of diluted liquid fertilizers to

correct the imbalance. Strong concentrations of granular, fast-acting synthetic fertilizers burn plant foliage and tender seedlings, and kill earthworms. They also discourage the presence of beneficial microbes and cause the departure of earthworms, which eventually leads to impoverished soil.

SOIL pH

The pH scale is a measure of acidity or alkalinity, which ranges from 0 to 14. A neutral soil has a reading of 7.0. Soil that tests lower than 7 is acidic; above 7, alkaline. Most vegetables, flowers, trees, shrubs, and earthworms prefer a slightly acid soil—in the range of 6.0 to 6.8. Exceptions include potatoes and blueberries, both of which like a pH of 5.2 to 5.5 (or an alkaline reading of above 7.5), and azaleas, which thrive in a pH of 4.5 to 5.0.

Adding lime is the simplest way to increase alkalinity. To increase your soil pH from 5.5 to 6.5, add 5 pounds of lime to every 100 square feet of heavy clay soil; add 3 pounds to lighter, sandy soils. Although they take a little longer to correct the pH, ground dolmetic or calcitic limes are the best types to use because, unlike quicklime or hydrated lime, they don't rob soil organisms of water or burn plant roots. For maximum benefit, sprinkle the lime over the top of the soil after you've cleaned up the bed in full and turned it over. The lime will work its way into the soil during winter. Your garden will not need another application for three to four years.

Quicklime and hydrated lime work in about half the time with half the quantity. Whichever you decide to use, work it into the soil several weeks before planting. Don't apply lime at the same time you apply chemical fertilizers, dried cow manure, or horse manure—the combination is too strong for plants' root systems. If you have a wood-burning fire and lots of ashes, add them in concentrated amounts to the garden in place of the lime.

Bonemeal, eggshells, and ground oyster shells also increase soil alkalinity. You can add a trowelful into the holes at planting time, or you can sprinkle it around the plants.

TESTING YOUR SOIL

WEEKEND PROJECT #39

It's a good idea to test your soil periodically. The addition of compost, horse manure, straw mulch, leaf mold, and even rainwater can change soil pH from season to season.

Test your soil anytime of the year, but the best time is in the spring before you seed and plant new varieties. Scoop off the top 1 to 2 inches of soil with a shovel. Dig and loosen the soil below to a depth of 5 to 6 inches. Remove small rocks and plant refuse, and crumble the soil until fine (don't use bare hands because this will affect the pH reading). Add water until the soil is muddy. Use your pH meter according to directions. Check several areas of the vegetable and flower beds in this manner.

Get a good idea of the texture of your soil just by squeezing it. After a heavy rainfall (or early in the spring), pick up a lump of soil and squeeze it into a ball. If it sticks together and is very smooth and slippery, it's mostly clay. If it falls apart, and is sharp and gritty, it contains a lot of sand. Silt is fine and powdery. The best garden soil is loam, a combination of all three types. This will cling together and then crumble easily when released.

One way to identify the different soil types in your garden is with a water test. Combine a few soil samples from your vegetable or flower bed and place 1 cup of this mixture in a quart jar. Fill almost to the top with water and cover with a screw-on lid. Shake until thoroughly combined. Allow to settle for 24 hours until layers form. From the bottom up, the layers indicate sand, silt, and clay.

Though many plants will grow in acidic soil, very alkaline soil is high in saline, which is toxic to plants, and low in nutrients. To adjust alkaline soil so it moves one point toward an acid pH, add acidic organic matter. For example, add peat moss at the rate of 5 pounds per 100 square feet or add 2½ pounds of sulfur per 100 square feet. If your soil is so alkaline you are having trouble growing vegetables, use both peat moss and sulfur. Using ammonium sulfate instead of sulfur will add nitrogen to the soil, too.

Spreading 2 to 3 inches of composted material over the beds twice a year will help to keep the pH under control. If you want to maintain an acidic condition, mulch with ground pine bark and needles. To slowly increase acidity, mulch with shredded oak leaves and maple bark or leaves. Sprinkle coffee grounds around plants or over the soil as another natural source of acid.

If hydrangeas are growing in your garden, use them to monitor the soil pH. If the blooms are blue, your soil is in the pH range of 4.5 to 5.0 If the blooms change to or are already pink, your soil leans more toward a neutral 7.0 to alkaline 7.5 pH. (White-flowered hydrangeas are no help because they do not change color.)

ABOVE: *Raised beds in the vegetable garden are rigged with ribbons to keep wildlife pests away.*

OPPOSITE PAGE: *The yellow leaves seen on this tomato plant indicate a nitrogen deficiency.*

pH Preferences of Vegetables

5.0 TO 5.5	ALL POTATOES
6.0 TO 6.5	BEANS, BROCCOLI, BRUSSELS SPROUTS, CARROTS, CAULIFLOWER, COLLARDS, CORN, CUCUMBERS, EGGPLANT, KALE, MUSTARD, PARSLEY, PARSNIPS, PEAS, PEPPERS, RADISHES, SUMMER SQUASH, TOMATOES, TURNIPS, WATERMELON
6.5 TO 7.0	ASPARAGUS, BEETS, CELERY, LEEKS, LETTUCE, MELONS, ONIONS, PEAS, SPINACH, SWISS CHARD, WINTER SQUASH

Soil with adequate nitrogen stimulates leaf growth. Sources of natural nitrogen include cottonseed meal, fish meal, animal manure, soybean meal, grass clippings, and composted legume plants such as peas and beans. Sawdust also is high in nitrogen but takes a long time to break down, so add it to the compost pile instead of directly to the garden bed.

To boost your flower blooms, feed them phosphorus. Use a 10-20-20 fertilizer or sprinkle with organic materials such as colloidal phosphate powder, cottonseed meal, or bonemeal. Wood ashes provide both phosphorus and potassium. Other natural sources of potassium are banana peels and seaweed; add them to the compost pile or directly to the garden beds. Or apply a quarter cup of

INCREASING SOIL FERTILITY

Commercial fertilizers supply and replenish the soil with many nutrients essential for plant growth. The major components are nitrogen, phosphorus (phosphate), and potassium (potash)— or N-P-K. Most gardens need fertilizing once a year in the spring or at planting time. New gardens need about 4 to 5 pounds of 5-10-5 or 5-10-10 fertilizer for each 100 square feet of garden space. Established, nutrient-rich gardens may need only regular additions of composted materials.

Until you know the pH of your soil, avoid chemical fertilizers. Keep adding organic materials to increase soil fertility without upsetting the natural balance.

Plants lacking in nitrogen appear weak and stunted with yellow leaves.

Understanding Fertilizers

The nutrients N-P-K in a fertilizer are measured in percentages of materials in the fertilizer. For example, 5-10-5 indicates that the mixture contains 5 percent nitrogen (N), 10 percent phosphorus (P), 5 percent potassium (K), and the rest inert materials. A fertilizer high in nitrogen is good for leafy greens. One high in phosphorus will help vegetables grow abundant "flowers" and fruits. Potassium produces a strong root system, increasing plant vigor and resistance to disease.

Because plants can absorb nutrients only in liquid form, use liquid fertilizers (or powders you add to water) for

instant benefits. Also, recent research shows that, over the long term, root feeding benefits plants more than foliar feeding (spraying the leaves). If your plants lack a certain element and need a fast fix, however, foliar spraying acts quickly. Because microorganisms in organic fertilizers such as dehydrated or composted cow or horse manures slow down during cool weather, they don't release nitrogen until the soil warms up in late spring. When cool-weather crops need a quick boost, you might want to use synthetic nitrogen fertilizer; it will reach leafy green plants faster in early spring and autumn.

ABOVE, TOP AND BOTTOM: Enrich the soil in your garden with organic materials from the compost pile.

ABOVE, RIGHT: Dehydrated manure can be added directly to the garden. Add fresh manure from nearby stables to the compost pile.

greensand (an iron potassium silicate derived from seabeds) for each square foot of soil.

Organic liquid fertilizers such as manure tea, fish emulsion, and seaweed extracts provide a good source of nitrogen for vegetables, too. Unlike chemical fertilizers, they move quickly through the soil and are easily absorbed by plant roots. Because fish emulsion is particularly high in nitrogen, dilute 1 tablespoon to 1 gallon of water. Don't use when the plants are getting ready to flower and set fruit—too much nitrogen produces more foliage and small fruits, or the blossoms turn yellow at the stem and drop off.

Seaweed extract is lower in nitrogen and contains many trace minerals. For a more balanced liquid fertilizer, use a combination fish emulsion and seaweed extract.

Composting Compendium

You can buy bags of composted materials from a garden center but, because serious soil amendment requires 40 pounds for every 4 X 4-foot area, it is cheaper to buy decomposed organic matter by the truckload from a nearby farm or stables—or better yet, get it free

from your community recycling program. Another part of the solution is to recycle your garden and kitchen vegetable wastes into a compost heap. This is the most practical and convenient way to handle yard wastes such as tree prunings, vegetable and flower stems, wood chips, and weeds. Leave lawn clippings, however, on the grass. They form a light mulch and decompose to feed the roots.

THE COMPOST PILE

Locate your compost pile where it will be convenient. How you construct it is up to you. It can be as simple as a pile on the ground, a bin in the middle of the vegetable bed, a homemade wooden or mesh enclosure, a plastic garbage container with holes in the bottom, or a state-of-the-art compost bin. If you're simply putting it on the ground, aim for a pile that is a minimum of 3 X 3 X 3 feet to ensure it generates adequate heat for decomposition.

A compost pile decomposes rapidly when it contains a good ratio of carbon to nitrogen (a C:N ratio of 25:1 is considered ideal) and its internal temperature is 140 to 160°F (temperatures higher than 160° kill beneficial soil microorganisms).

The traditional method of starting a compost pile is to alternate 6-inch layers of carbon- and nitrogen-rich materials such as chopped up garden stalks (C), grass clippings (N), shredded leaves (C), fresh or aged manure (N), straw (C), vegetable and fruit peelings (N), wood shavings (C), and green weeds or cover crops (N). Add soil to the layers and sprinkle with water occasionally to keep the pile moist. Turn it every three to four weeks with a pitchfork. When made during the summer, a good compost pile should be ready to use in approximately three months. In fact, if you add only shredded material and turn it over twice a week during hot weather, it will be ready in one month.

If you want compost that is more acidic, use shredded oak or maple leaves in one of the layers. You also can increase acidity by adding 1 tablespoon of vinegar to 5 gallons of water and sprinkling it over the compost pile whenever it needs a little moisture.

MAKING A BACK-DOOR COMPOST BIN

When the weather gets chilly, walking to the compost heap in the back of the garden will become an unpleasant chore. Instead, position a compost bin near the back door, behind a log pile, shrub, or lattice screen.

Take two large, plastic garbage bins and cut circles from the bottoms so only narrow edges remain underneath. Stand the bins on the ground near the house, and fill with raw vegetable and fruit wastes throughout the winter. Periodically add a light layer of soil and leaves (if these are accessible). Use the lids to keep out snow and rain (the layer of soil and the lids will keep odors under control, too).

In the spring, keep adding layers of kitchen waste, leaves, and soil. Sprinkle occasionally with water. Keep the lids on so the composted materials don't get soggy from heavy rains.

When the bins are full, lift them and let the compost spill out of the bottom. Shovel any raw vegetable/fruit matter back into the bins and start over. Sprinkle the crumbly composted waste around plantings.

When you have lots of leaves but no manure, add a cup of nitrogen (10-10-10) fertilizer to every square yard of organic litter to help the composting process. Cover with a light sprinkling of soil and make as many layers as you have shredded leaves available.

Decomposition is slow during winter (or when the center of the pile drops below 90°F), but it still helps to turn the pile over once a month. In spring, decomposition takes off, and by midsummer you will have gardener's gold.

COMPOST DOs

Do include these materials in your compost pile:

Paper, sawdust, wood chips, straw, leaves, vegetable and fruit trimmings, legume plants and other garden wastes, peat moss, manure, eggshells, coffee grounds, nut hulls (except black walnuts, which are toxic to most plants), pine needles, salt hay, seaweed, pond weeds, and shredded stalks.

COMPOST DON'Ts

Don't include the following materials in your compost pile:

- Charcoal—it doesn't decay.

- Coal ashes—the sulfur and iron content is toxic to plants.

- Animal food byproducts such as grease, bones, fat, and skin. Not only do these byproducts decay slowly, but they cause the compost pile to smell and attract unwanted animal pests.

- Wastes from pets.

- Large stalks, woody stalks, corncobs, husks, and other tough materials. Unless these items are shredded—or you can let your compost work for a long time—they take too long to break down.

- Diseased plants and weeds with seed heads. Give these materials to your garbage collectors.

COMPOST PROBLEM-SOLVING

- The compost smells bad—not enough aeration; turn it over more often. Don't add animal food leftovers.

- The compost is moist and warm only in the middle—the pile is too small; add more material and mix together.

- The compost pile is damp but is not heating up—it lacks nitrogen and needs materials such as fresh manure or other sources of nitrogen.

- The pile is dry in the center—insufficient water. Turn, then sprinkle with water to moisten. Leave the pile a little depressed on top to collect rain. During periods of heavy rain, cover the top with a tarp or black plastic, but leave the sides open for aeration.

EASY COMPOSTING

The weekend gardener can take advantage of these less-traditional shortcuts for composting:

- Throw all your composting materials onto a patch of garden you plan to make into a new bed. Keep it covered with black plastic so that it breaks down quickly and doesn't look too unsightly. When the cold weather arrives, cover with several inches of straw. In the spring, till it under for an organic-rich bed.

- Locate a space in the garden close to the kitchen door (behind a log pile or a large shrub), and throw all your garden and kitchen vegetable wastes into a bin. You don't even have to turn the pile. Just let it rot naturally and in about two years you will have crumbly compost.

- Regularly add all your chopped or shredded waste underneath the straw or hay mulch covering the vegetable garden.

- Place wire cages in various convenient locations in the garden and fill with shredded organic materials as you work in the garden. In the summer, add a few inches of soil to the top layer of the compost pile and plant nasturtiums, petunias, morning glories, or other trailing annuals around the edges. They'll grow over and down the sides to disguise the cage.

Drop-by-Drop Watering Systems

When you can tend to your garden only on the weekends, set up an automated watering and drip-irrigation system that saves you time and labor. It also will allow you to water your garden during the week when you can't. Before you install a drip-irrigation system, however, amend your soil with organic matter to improve water retention and make it easier for plant roots to absorb available nutrients and moisture.

Drip-emitter or soaker hoses offer a more efficient method of watering than overhead sprinklers because they carry the water directly to the plants' roots. Overhead sprinkling loses water to the air, and if a canopy of thick foliage covers the soil, it stays dry. When emitter or soaker hoses are covered by a layer of mulch, no water is lost to surface evaporation. Also, drip irrigation keeps the plants' leaves dry, greatly reducing the risk of fungal diseases, which spread quickly in hot, humid weather.

If you must use overhead sprinklers, run them early in the morning. Avoid running them in the evening; during the cooler night hours the foliage remains wet, creating the perfect environment for fungal disease.

Soaker hoses are perforated rubber or woven hoses that ooze and trickle water down their entire length. Slow and thorough, they are the best form of irrigation to use in beds planted densely with flowers, herbs, corn, beans, carrots, or any vegetation where the root zones and leaves grow close together.

Drip-emitter hoses are made from rubber or plastic and are equipped with connectors, solid tubes, and emitters. The emitters can be inserted right next to a plant stem. Drip emitters are ideal for use among widely spaced plantings such as tomatoes, peppers, eggplants, roses, shrubs, and specimen trees.

ABOVE, LEFT AND MIDDLE: Drip-irrigation systems efficiently carry water directly to plant roots. They can be equipped with timesaving devices such as an attachment that releases fertilizer automatically into the drip lines. Drip-emitter systems can be used to irrigate rows of strawberries.

ABOVE, RIGHT: Drip emitters also can be snaked through widely spaced plants.

Drip emitters, perforated soakers, or a combination can be customized so several hoses work off one T-connector equipped with valves. The valves can be opened or closed to let one row of plants receive a fast flow of water while another row in the same bed receives just a trickle. Or one row—even one plant—can be completely deprived of water, if necessary.

For raised-bed or container gardens, run a polyflex hose through the beds or from container to container. Arrange the hose so that the emitters, which are usually 18 to 20 inches apart, fall onto each container.

If you don't have a drip-emitter or soaker system, get water directly to plant roots by sinking perforated plastic jugs and bottles next to the larger vegetables at planting time. Fill the bottles or jugs with water, and they will slowly soak the root zones.

Watering

No matter which system you use, water your garden deeply. Shallow watering encourages shallow roots, and when roots grow close to the surface they suffer from the sun's heat. During summer, soil temperature right below the surface can reach close to 120°F. Adding organic matter to the soil will increase water retention. Mulching the beds will help conserve moisture and keep the soil cooler.

Although ornamental and flower beds usually survive without a watering program, most vegetables and annuals need at least an inch of water a week. Depending on your soil type, watering system, and rate of evaporation, applying an inch of water to 100 square feet could take two to four hours.

If your soil drains poorly, be careful not to overwater. Heavy, clay soil gets waterlogged, which can cause plants to wilt—mimicking a sign usually associated with too little water. Feel the soil before you water. If you do have heavy, poor-draining soil, improve drainage by installing raised beds.

Giving your perennial plants, shrubs, and trees a thorough soaking when you put them into the ground gets them off to a good start. During the first summer and autumn, water them periodically to keep them healthy during winter. After the first year or two, many plantings can make it through hot summers with little or no watering, as long as they are surrounded by a good layer of mulch. If drought extends into autumn, however, many shrubs and trees will need watering to get them through winter. This is particularly true of evergreens because they continue to lose moisture through their leaves during winter.

Mulch and More Mulch

If there is one surefire way to cut down on watering and keep the earth from drying out, it is by using mulches. The weekend gardener will want to use them over most of the garden beds—particularly vegetables, annuals, perennials, and small shrubs—because mulches greatly reduce and sometimes eliminate the need for watering. Besides aiding in moisture retention, they also help the soil maintain a uniform temperature by keeping it cool in hot weather and slowing heat loss in cold weather.

Mulches protect plantings, improve the soil, slow down erosion, and help with weed control. Although organic mulches do not eliminate weeding, they make pulling weeds much easier. When weeds germinate in a bulky organic medium, the roots are loose and offer no resistance when pulled.

Organic mulches add nutrients to the soil but rob the soil of nitrogen during the decaying process. To remedy this, periodically apply about 2 pounds of 5-10-5 or 5-10-10 fertilizer per 100 square feet. For the organic garden, sprinkle a half-pound of nitrate of soda or ammonium sulphate per 100 square feet.

Some materials such as wood chips, shredded bark, pine needles, and cocoa hulls are decorative as well as effective mulches. Other organic mulches include rolls of heavy mulch paper, seedless hay, straw, shredded leaves, and sawdust. When using leaves, remember that a layer of whole leaves will mat down and cause what's underneath to die back. Use only shredded leaves when mulching perennials or herbs so new growth can push through the loose covering in the spring.

When adding a layer of heavy mulch such as wood chips or shredded bark, use only a 2- to 3-inch layer. Airy, dry mulches such as straw, hay, or shredded leaves can be up to 8 inches or more.

OPPOSITE PAGE: Don't use small overhead sprinklers to water an expanse of densely foliated garden. Water will be lost to the air and the foliage will keep the soil dry.

ABOVE, CLOCKWISE FROM LEFT: Use large wood chips to mulch around shrubs and trees, and use lightweight materials to mulch around annuals and perennials, such as large, medium, and small wood chips; finely shredded bark; two types of shredded cypress bark; and cocoa hulls.

You also can recycle cardboard and thick layers of black-and-white newspaper (don't use the color sections) and top them with grass clippings.

Even a 1-inch layer of mulch encourages stronger and healthier perennials. It protects the shallow roots from temperature fluctuations and reduces soil heaving in the winter. Mulch in the spring to reduce moisture evaporation and again in December or after the ground freezes. For perennial beds and small shrubs, use shredded bark, shredded leaves, or rotted leaves (leaf mold).

Acid-loving fruit and evergreen shrubs and trees thrive when mulched with shredded pine bark or pine needles. The needles increase or maintain the acidity of the soil and, because they are very light, insulate plants and protect them from heaving.

Vegetables fare better when mulched with at least 8 inches of seedless straw or salt hay. (Be sure to buy salt hay; regular hay is loaded with seeds.) Lay pieces of sprouting potatoes on top of richly organic soil and cover with at least 8 inches of straw. The potatoes grow on

top of the soil and push foliage through the straw. The new potatoes are clean and easy to harvest. Just pull back the mulch and take what you need.

Mulch large shrubs and trees with the larger wood chips. These take longer to break down and need replenishing less frequently.

Keep any mulch a few inches away from the base of trees and shrubs. Mulch that comes right up to the bark creates a safety zone for moles and chipmunks, which will gnaw the tree until the trunk is girdled, causing it to die.

WEEKEND
PROJECT **#41**

WHERE TO FIND FREE MULCH AND WOOD CHIPS

When a few bags of mulch won't cover all of your beds, you could probably use a truckload. The cheapest source for such a large amount is your town's highway department. Garden refuse is collected by disposal companies and trekked to recycling centers, where it is shredded and stored until the winter months. If these materials are requested, many highway departments will deliver

shredded bark, shredded leaves, and wood chips to home owners—at no cost. You also can fill up your own truck, garbage cans, or plastic bags at these recycling centers.

Another source of free wood chips is the electric company, whose maintenance crews prune trees growing into roadside power lines. When you see these crews, ask if they would drop off

the chipped wood at your home instead of taking it to the dump.

If you live in an area where there are horse stables, you've got a free source of manure. Check the classified ads of local newspapers to find out which stables want to get rid of it, though you'll probably have to shovel it yourself. If it's fresh manure, compost it; aged manure can be thrown directly onto the garden.

FAR LEFT: Seedless hay makes a good mulch for rows of flowers or vegetables.

LEFT: To keep weeds at bay, layer marble chips over landscape fabric or plastic.

Also, when mulch touches the bark, it creates a damp zone that is perfect for the development of fungal diseases. It also invites moisture-loving sow bugs (wood louse).

WEED BARRIERS

Weekend gardeners have little time for weeding, so it is important to prevent weeds from continuing their endless cycle. In some locations of the yard, all that is necessary is to use a mower or weed-wacker to keep the growth under control.

In garden beds, you need to eliminate weed growth because it competes with plantings for moisture and nutrients. Rather than harming the soil or adjacent plants with chemicals, control weeds with barriers that reduce or eliminate their existence.

Mulching with organic material is an excellent way to reduce weeds and enrich the soil. Or you may find it more practical to use inorganic weed barriers that last for many years.

INORGANIC MULCHES

Though organic mulches help to control weeds, they don't totally eliminate them. For a weed-free pathway, driveway, or patio area, put down an inorganic barrier such as crushed stone, pebbles, bricks, large stones, slate, treated wood, tightly woven landscape fabric, black plastic, recycled linoleum, or carpeting. They don't break down, and they don't nurture the soil, but they rarely need replacing.

When you are covering an area with crushed stone or pebbles, first put down a layer of heavy-duty landscape fabric or thick black plastic. In order to achieve a totally weed-free area, lay down wooden boards or interconnecting wooden squares.

Before you use plastic as a weed barrier—in a vegetable or bedding garden, for instance—enrich the soil underneath with shredded leaves and composted material and manure. Water the ground thoroughly and lay down the plastic. Make slits wherever necessary and plant through them. Keep in mind that, especially in the vegetable bed, you must remove the plastic at the end of the growing year so you can dig over the bed and enrich it with composted materials.

Both clear and black plastic warm the earth in the spring so crops mature earlier. Clear plastic warms the soil to a greater depth and holds the heat in the soil through the night. It also transmits sunlight, so it can be placed over the soil earlier in the spring to hasten seed germination. Sow seeds in moist soil, water thoroughly, and cover with clear plastic held down with soil or stones. Remove it as soon as the seeds sprout.

Clear plastic, however, also allows the growth of weeds; black plastic does not allow the passage of light, so weeds die. Black plastic also absorbs heat and increases the soil temperature at surface level only, but radiates heat back to the plant foliage at night. This radiated heat sometimes is sufficient to prevent foliage damage from a light frost. Also, cold or frozen soil covered with black plastic takes longer to warm up than uncovered soil or soil covered with clear plastic.

During the past few years, a new type of landscape plastic mulch has been developed by researchers at the University of New Hampshire. Marketed as Infrared Transmitting Mulch (IRT Mulch), it is a combination of clear and black plastic. It blocks the visible radiation that allows plant (weed) growth but allows infrared radiation to pass through to warm the soil. It goes on top of the bed before you plant or seed in late spring.

The disadvantages of plastics are that they don't allow air and water to pass through and the ground beneath is not enriched by organic materials. Also, in the summer the heat transferred by plastic can damage plant roots, so be sure to cover your plants with organic mulch.

ABOVE: Floating row covers protect vegetables from frost, sun, and pests.

LEFT: Black plastic warms the soil in early spring and keeps a bed of spinach transplants weed free.

LANDSCAPE FABRICS

When you are using landscape fabrics for weed control, choose one that is thick and densely woven. For row covers, however, thin, floating-type landscape fabrics are your best choice because they allow light to pass through. These fabrics can be used to protect seeds and seedlings from the elements, insects, and animals.

The dense, felt-like fabrics block the light and do not allow weeds to poke through, but, unlike plastic, they allow air and water (and liquid fertilizers) to get through. However, this type of landscape fabric is unattractive, so you'll want to top it with a decorative mulch such as pebbles, stones, or wood chips. If you top it with wood chips, be prepared to replenish this supply every year or so.

Thick, tightly woven landscape fabrics are virtually indestructible. Some are constructed in three layers; the top layer keeps out weeds, and the middle and bottom layers wick moisture from the surface and keep it in the ground. You can place a soaker or drip-irrigation system over the top of these fabrics, then cover them with a layer of shredded bark or wood chips.

COVER CROPS

Rye, clover, oats, and beans are just a few of the cover crops grown in the vegetable garden during the off-season or to fill an empty space. They grow rapidly to form a dense cover and smother weeds. Before they go to seed, these green manures are tilled or dug into the soil to add organic matter and nitrogen and improve soil tilth. If your soil needs a heavy dose of nitrogen, choose from a variety of legume cover crops, including soy beans, clover, alfalfa, and vetch. If your soil texture needs improving, plant a grain crop such as barley, wheat, rye, or oats.

Cover crops planted in spring and summer will be ready to turn under in autumn. Turn under autumn-planted crops in early spring. If you are working in raised beds, plant a cover crop that can be dug rather than tilled under. The easiest method for the weekend gardener is to interplant late-maturing crops such as tomatoes, squash, and peppers, with succession crops of legumes (soy beans, snap beans, and fava beans) in the summer. Harvest these legume crops as a vegetable in the autumn, and leave the foliage and roots to break down during

ABOVE: Small wood nuggets and shredded bark break down faster than large wood chips. Used in the flower and vegetable beds, they help to enrich the soil.

the winter months. (If you allow the beans to die on the plants, the garden will receive a higher dose of nitrogen.) By early spring, the decayed cover crop will be easy to dig into the soil. Several other cover crops that can be grown in autumn or spring include vetch, clover, barley, oats, rye, wheat, and kale.

If you are preparing a new bed in the spring and want to enrich it first with cover crops, plant peas, buckwheat, and oats for summer tilling and millet for tilling under in autumn.

To make these plantings easier to dig under when they are mature but green, cut them to ground level or flatten them and cover with several layers of newspaper. Wet the newspapers and layer on several inches of organic mulch.

BELOW: Adult lacewings feed on nectar, pollen, aphids, and mealybugs. The predatory larvae of lacewings devour a variety of harmful insects.

Insects, Pests, and Diseases

For the gardener, there are two types of insects: beneficial and destructive. This section will help you tell friend from foe, and suggest ways to elicit the allies to come to your aid and send a clear message to the enemy to stay away.

BENEFICIAL INSECTS

PREDATORY INSECTS

Predatory insects feed on harmful pests. You want to encourage these insects to make a home in your garden.

Ambush bugs. Adults: ½-inch-long, light green flat body with brown markings on wings. Large front legs grab flying prey.

Assassin bugs (kissing bugs). Adults: ½ inch long, pale brown to dark brown. Flat, narrow bodies are equipped with large front legs and sharp, beak-like jaw. Nymphs are orange-colored smaller versions. Both voracious eaters of many insects, including Japanese and other plant-eating beetles, aphids, bees, caterpillars, and leafhoppers.

Big-eyed bugs. Adults: ¼ inch long, olive colored, with large, fly-like eyes. Voracious eaters of leafhoppers, spittlebugs, mites, aphids, and Mexican bean beetles.

Checkered beetles. Adults: ½ inch long, hairy, and black with yellow markings. Larvae: ½ inch long, hairy, and yellow. Prey on wood borer larvae and adults.

Damsel bugs. Adult: ¼-inch-long, dark green bodies, with small heads and eyes. Long front legs used to grab aphids, leafhoppers, treehoppers, psylla, mites, and caterpillars.

Green lacewings. Adults: ¾ inch long, with delicate pale green, lacy wings. Larvae: ½ inch long, gray-brown, and hairy. Larvae's strong jaws grasp mites, caterpillar eggs, thrips, scales, leafhoppers, corn earworms, aphids, and mealybugs. Adults feed on nectar and pollen.

Ground beetles (fiery searcher; European ground beetles). Adults: 1-inch-long, shiny flat body; emit caustic secretions. Fiery searcher is dark brown; European ground beetle is iridescent blue-green. Larvae: 1 inch long, whitish-gray to light brown with strong jaws. Both beetles use strong jaws to grab snails, slugs, cutworms, armyworms, cankerworms, and caterpillars on nocturnal forays. Can't fly but climb trees in search of tent and gypsy moth caterpillars.

WEEKEND PROJECT #42

ATTRACTING BENEFICIAL INSECTS

Whether you purchased a few batches of beneficial predatory insects or they arrived in your garden by chance, encourage them to take up permanent residence by providing them with a variety of their favorite flowers and herbs in your flower borders and vegetable garden: QUEEN-ANNE'S-LACE • EVENING PRIMROSE • SUNFLOWERS • DAISIES • YARROW • BLACK-EYED SUSAN • NASTURTIUM • SAGE • CILANTRO • DILL • FENNEL • CARAWAY • PARSLEY • STRAWFLOWER • and BUTTERCUP. When weeding, leave a few plants of DANDELIONS • LAMB'S QUARTERS • CLOVER • and ALFALFA.

With such a varied menu of nectar and host plants, you'll entice ladybugs, preying mantises, lacewings, parasitic wasps, and predator flies to stay and breed in your garden. These garden-friendly insects will repay you by feasting on a wide variety of bugs.

ATTRACTING INSECT–EATING SPIDERS

Spiders are one of the gardener's best friends. There are about 35,000 species worldwide, and they feast on crawling and flying insects all day long. Orb spiders, the ones that spin large, intricate webs, have a voracious appetite for Japanese beetles and anything else that gets trapped in their webs. The brown wood spider builds its nest in light layers of straw-type mulch, and gobbles grasshoppers and other ground-level insect pests. Wolf spiders don't spin webs but sit in holes and run after their prey. The daddy longlegs (Phalangida family) is a relative of the spider and preys on mites, worms, larvae, spiders, snails, and slugs.

It takes no extra time, just a little thought, to create a spider haven in your garden. Layer inches of airy, straw-like mulches. Don't spray the area with pesticides, and don't destroy spiders' webs. Plant a row of perennials or shrubs near the vegetable garden to provide a regular source of insects for spiders to feast on.

Lady beetles (ladybugs). Adults: ½ inch long, bright orange-red with black spots. Larvae: ½ inch long, flat and skinny, black with orange spots. They hatch from small, cylindrical, orange eggs and often are seen en masse clinging to stems of milkweed and butterfly weed plants. Adults and larvae devour aphids, mealybugs, and scale insects.

Lampyrid beetles (fireflies, lightning bugs, glow worms). Adults: ½ inch long, flat and brown; eat nectar only; glow at night. Larvae: ½ inch long, flat, notched green body equipped with ferocious jaws. Use jaws to bite into heads of snails and slugs to paralyze them.

Mealybug destroyer beetles. Adult: ½-inch-long, shiny black oval bodies with red head. Larvae: ⅓ inch long, yellow, and covered with waxy, white hairs. Both stages gobble up all types of mealybugs.

Praying mantises. Adults: Bright green to brown green, thin, and up to 4 inches long. Clumsy flyers, they walk slowly from plant to plant and sit with long front legs clasped in a praying pose waiting to grasp crickets, moths, grasshoppers, aphids, bugs, bees, wasps, flies, beetles, and other praying mantises. White or light brown egg masses are laid

Attracting lady beetles (OPPOSITE PAGE), praying mantises (ABOVE), and other beneficial insects will help to control aphid infestations.

and "glued" to thin stems or branches in autumn and hatch into insect-eating nymphs in the spring.

Robber flies. Adults: ¾ inch long, with large, hairy thorax (middle portion). Larvae: ¾ inch long, thin, and white with black heads. Adults' beak-like, hairy mouths grasp onto moths, butterflies, grasshoppers, bees, flies, and flying beetles. Larvae are subterranean and feed on (lawn) grubs and beetle pupae.

Rove beetles. Adults: 1-inch-long, flat black or brown bodies, similar to earwigs. Prey on aphids, other small insects, and eggs. Larvae eat red spider larvae and various cabbage maggots and caterpillars.

Soldier beetles. Adults: Pennsylvania leatherwing soldier beetles are ½ inch long, with yellow or orange body marked with black on head and wing tips. Downy leatherwing soldier beetles are ½ inch long with black body and soft hairs. Larvae: 1 inch long, flat, white, and hairy. Adults eat caterpillars, grasshopper eggs, and cucumber beetles.

Spined soldier bugs. Adult: ½-inch-long, brown shield-shaped flat bodies. Beak-

WEEKEND PROJECT   #44

WELCOMING TOADS TO YOUR GARDEN

Once the sun goes down, toads venture out of their damp holes and feast on gobs of garden pests, including cutworms, ants, chinch bugs, potato beetles, and slugs. Welcome them to your garden by providing them with daytime hiding places that keep their skin cool and moist. They'll burrow into enriched moist earth, dig under boards, hop into upturned plant pots, nap under leaves, and take refuge under low-growing shrubbery and ground covers.

Attract them in the spring by placing plant saucers of water throughout the garden. Make toad abodes out of clay flowerpots: Chip a 3-inch arch off the top, then push the open end down into the soil, leaving an access through the little archway. Add inches of straw around your vegetables and toads will dig underneath the mulch where it's cool and moist. Lay down two or three wooden boards in the vegetable garden so toads will take refuge underneath and gobble up the slugs that crawl beneath at sunup.

Toads hibernate by burying themselves several inches deep in crumbly earth. When turning over the ground in the early spring, do so very carefully so that you don't harm any napping toads.

ABOVE, TOP: Soldier beetles prey on cucumber beetles.

ABOVE, BOTTOM: Cocoons of the parasitic Braconid wasp on Sphinx moth larvae.

OPPOSITE PAGE: Larvae of this parasitic tachinid fly feed on many insect pests.

like mouth used to attack and impale more than 100 garden pests, ranging from large caterpillars to Mexican bean beetles. Nymph soldier bugs are just as voracious but eat smaller insects closer to their own size. Soldier bugs paralyze their victims before sucking out the juices. Available through mail-order catalogs, they are said to provide pest control for 85 days or longer after release in the garden.

Syrphid flies (hover flies; flowerflies). Adults: ½ inch long and thin, with yellow and black bands. Larvae: ½ inch long, pale green, and grub-like. Adults eat nectar only. Larvae suck the juices from aphids, leafhoppers, mealybugs, and scales.

Vedalia beetles (also called lady beetles). Adults: Similar to lady beetle. Larvae: ⅓ inch long, pink with black markings. Eggs are red ovals. Both adults and larvae feed on soft-bodied insects, including cotton-cushion scale.

PARASITIC INSECTS

Some beneficial insects are parasitic rather than predatory. The adults deposit their eggs on or in the larvae and pupae of many moths (also some butterflies), aphids, scales, flies, and beetles. The hatched juveniles feed on or within the body of the host, killing it. Parasitic adult wasps and flies fuel up on flower nectar and pollen only.

Braconid wasps. Adults: Tiny and red with black wings. Use a long, black ovipositer to deposit eggs and larvae on gypsy moths, tent caterpillars, hornworms, cutworms, cabbageworms, and larvae of codling moths, oriental fruit moths, aphids, and many beetles.

Chalcid wasps. Adults: Tiny, thin metallic brown and fly-like. Deposit eggs on the larvae of beetles, moths, and butterflies.

Ichneumonid wasp. Adults: Tiny, thin, and black or brown with long black ovipositor used to deposit eggs on the larvae of moths, cabbage butterflies, larch sawflies, and corn borers.

Tachinid flies. Adults: ½ inch long, brown, and hairy. Deposit eggs on the body of host insects or on plants frequented by hosts. Larvae: Tiny maggots that feed internally on beetles, grasshoppers, caterpillars, corn borer larvae, cutworms, Japanese beetles, gypsy moth larvae, squash bugs, and sawflies.

Trichogramma wasps. Adults: Used commercially to control mealybugs, aphids, and scale. These tiny wasps deposit their eggs on the eggs and larvae of cabbageworms, cabbage loopers, hornworms, corn earworms, cutworms, armyworms, gypsy moths, codling moths (and other pest moths), and cabbage butterflies.

HARMFUL AND DESTRUCTIVE INSECTS

Your garden may be host to all kinds of pests that will destroy your gardening efforts and make more work for you. Watch for indications of these troublemakers and take care of them promptly. Solving a small problem is a lot easier than handling a big one. For more earth-friendly techniques to rid or control the following pests, see "Cultural and Biological Controls" on page 194.

Aphids. Adults and nymphs: Pinhead size, pear-shaped, winged or wingless insects. Colors range from light yellow-

green to dark brown-black. HOST PLANTS: Anything with plant sap. DAMAGE: Suck sap from leaves, causing yellowing and shriveling. Carry disease from plant to plant. Aphids excrete excess sap sugars, which trigger the growth of black sooty mold. CONTROLS: Spray with insecticidal soap or rotenone. Prune larger infected branches. Attract aphids to yellow dishes or yellow cardboard coated with a sticky substance such as Tanglefoot or thick oil. Use a fast spray of water to wash them off plants and shrubs. Spray branches with ultrafine oil to smother eggs. Many predatory insects feed on aphids.

Cabbage loopers and cabbageworms. Adults: Both moths. Cabbage "butterfly" is cream with black-tipped wings; nocturnal looper moth has brown, silvery wings. Similar larvae: 1-inch-long bright green caterpillars with fine yellow stripes on each side. Loopers form a vertical loop when they walk by drawing back legs up to front legs. HOST PLANTS: Cabbage, cauliflower, broccoli, mustard, kohlrabi, and kale. Loopers also feed on leaves of potatoes, tomatoes, radishes, spinach, parsley, and peas. DAMAGE: Can devour entire crop if not checked. CONTROLS: Cover crops with floating row covers to deter butterflies from lay-ing eggs or spray plants with pyrethrin or rotenone. Hand-pick eggs and caterpil-lars. Spray large infestations of caterpillars with Bacillus thuringiensis (BT, available as Dipel or Thuricide). Delay planting until autumn, when but-terflies have departed. Encourage beneficial insects.

Colorado potato beetles. Adults: ¼-inch-long yellow-and-black-striped beetle. Larvae are same size as adults, but red with row of black spots along each side. Eggs are large and orange. HOST PLANTS: Solanaceae (nightshade) fam-ily of potatoes, eggplant, peppers, and tomatoes. DAMAGE: Adults and larvae feed on leaves until plants are defoli-ated. CONTROLS: Use floating row covers. Mulch plants with 1-foot layer of straw. Hand-pick the eggs, adults, and larvae. Spray plants with rotenone or pyrethrin and the larvae with Bacillus thuringiensis (BT, available as Dipel or Thuricide). Parasitic nematodes placed in the soil also will destroy the larvae when they move from the plants into the ground before they develop into adults. Predatory insects include lady beetles and ground beetles.

Cutworms. Adults: Nocturnal, 1- to 2-inch-long gray-brown fat grubs that curl up when touched. HOST PLANTS: All vegetables. DAMAGE: Cut off young stems at ground level. Some cutworms also eat leaves. CONTROLS: Buy para-sitic nematodes and add to soil before planting or seeding. Dust diatomaceous earth around the base of seedlings and transplants. Cut bottoms off cans, foam cups, or milk cartons and place around seedlings. Secure by pushing ½ inch or more into the ground. When turning over the earth, check for cutworms; hand-pick and destroy (drop into pond).

Hornworms. Adults: Large moths with narrow brown and white wings and orange-spotted body. Larvae: Huge 3- to 4-inch-long, bright green caterpillars with diagonal white stripes down each side. Long black horn at rear. Eggs laid singly under leaves. HOST PLANTS: Tomatoes, potatoes, peppers, and egg-plants. DAMAGE: Major chewing; entire leaf and plant can disappear quickly. CONTROLS: Hand-picking—carefully, these insects can pinch—is easiest and fastest. Or spray with BT or rotenone.

LEFT: Colorado potato beetles and their larvae will defoliate plants.

Hornworms bearing a mass of white egg bumps have been parasitized by trichogramma or braconid wasps. When wasp eggs hatch, the larvae survive by living off the hornworms' gastric juices, thus killing hornworms, then maturing to inject other hornworms.

Japanese beetles. Adults: ½-inch round iridescent green-bronze beetles. Larvae:

Subterranean 1-inch-long fat white grubs with brown head. HOST PLANTS: Roses, raspberries, grapes, peaches, apples, cherries, plums, evening primroses, tomatoes, beans, corn, and many other plants and weeds. DAMAGE: Adults feed and skeletonize the leaves. Larvae chew on roots, stunting plants and reducing yields. CONTROLS: Spray

parasitic nematodes on the soil or the lawn to control larvae. Moles devour grubs (and will depart when the parasitic nematodes reduce the grub population). Spray adults with insecticidal soap or rotenone. Hand-pick (sweep them off or shake them) into a jar or bucket of soapy water. Predator insects also feed on grubs.

WEEKEND PROJECT #45

GET RID OF MOLES BY ELIMINATING JAPANESE BEETLES

If your lawn is a network of mole tunnels, you have a Japanese beetle problem. Moles burrow into an area and take up residence where beetle larvae are plentiful. By eliminating one, you eliminate the other.

The adult Japanese beetle is identified by its bronze-green iridescence. It devours the leaves of roses, tomatoes, and a host of other vegetables and flowers. It also destroys the lawn. Its cycle is simple but nasty.

Japanese beetles lay their eggs in clipped grass, and the newly hatched grubs burrow into the soil where they

eat the roots of the turf grass (and destroy your lawn). Roll back a section of dead turf, and you'll see curled-up, nickel-size white grubs with dark brown heads. The moles move in and thrive on the abundance of grubs.

Although you can hang pheromone traps for adult beetles, the best way to get rid of them is to go after the larvae that overwinter in your lawn. In spring, after the last frost and before the adult beetles emerge in late June, treat the surface of the lawn with Parasitic Nematodes Hb. For a lawn of 600 square feet, buy a packet containing 10 million

nematodes, mix with water, and spray the surface. This Hb strain of nematodes starts to work immediately. One application lasts three months, so do a second spraying in August, when the female beetles lay eggs. This will kill off the current year's grubs.

Because winter frosts kill the nematodes, yearly applications are necessary. Look for nematodes in mail-order catalogs and at your local garden centers.

NESTING BOX FOR BIRDS

Birds are a natural pest control. During nesting season, when they have four to six mouths to feed, they catch insects and grubs 12 hours a day. Don't miss out on this beneficial feeding frenzy. Put up several bird boxes to encourage birds to come to your garden.

Winter, when your garden is taking care of itself, is a good time to make a few nesting boxes. Once you have materials, you can construct three or four boxes in one afternoon (if you're using an electric jigsaw to cut the wood, you can do it in half the time). Put the boxes outside in March, before the birds start looking for nesting spaces.

Although songbird species, such as bluebirds, tree swallows, titmice, nuthatches, chickadees, and wrens, vary in size, many will use a box with a 1½-inch entrance hole.

Attract different species by putting the boxes in desirable habitats. For bluebirds and tree swallows, place the boxes in the middle of the lawn (or a grazed field) facing a fence or overhead telephone wires. Titmice and nuthatches prefer boxes on woodland edges. Chickadees and wrens also like to be close to trees but will nest in boxes placed near the house, the deck, or a woodpile.

To protect birds from predators, place the boxes on poles 5 feet off the ground. Do not add perches to the boxes. Nesting adults can land directly on the entrances, while perches provide landing places for jays, who will steal the eggs. To prevent raccoons, squirrels, and other predators from reaching into the boxes to pull out eggs or nestlings, nail 1-inch-thick wooden guards to the outside of the entrance holes (this is a 2 X 2-inch square of wood with a hole, the same dimensions as the entrance, bored in the center). Also, cone-shaped metal baffles inverted halfway up the pole will stop pesky predators from climbing up.

You will need a piece of 1-inch-thick cedar, cypress, or redwood, 5 feet X 6 inches. You also can use pine (though it is not as durable) or exterior plywood (though it is not as attractive so you will want to paint the outside of the box light gray or beige). Don't paint the inside of the box; fledglings use the rough texture to climb up to the entrance hole so they can get out.

You'll also need a handsaw or an electric jigsaw, and nails: twenty-two 1⅔-inch-long galvanized siding nails; two 1½-inch smooth-shanked pivot nails; and one 1½-inch-long round-headed screw.

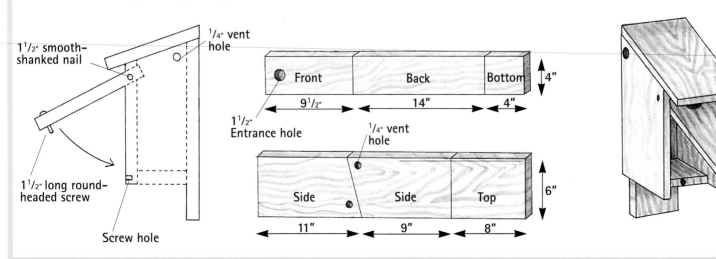

1½" smooth-shanked nail

¼" vent hole

1½" long round-headed screw

Screw hole

1½" Entrance hole

Front — 9½"

Back — 14"

Bottom — 4" / 4"

¼" vent hole

Side — 11"

Side — 9"

Top — 8"

6"

STEP-BY-STEP INSTRUCTIONS FOR CONSTRUCTING A SIMPLE NESTING BOX

1. Using a drill with a ¼-inch bit, bore five ¼-inch drainage holes in the bottom section: one in the center and one 2½ inches in from each corner. Drill a ¼-inch vent hole in the middle of each side section about 1½ inch from the top. Using a 1½ inch bit, drill an entrance hole 2½ inches from the top and centered in the front section.

2. Nail the back between the two sides using four siding nails on each side.

3. Nail the bottom section inside the two side sections; flush against the back section using two siding nails on each side.

4. Position the front section between the sides so the bottoms are even. Hammer the two pivot nails through the sides into the front, 1 inch down from the top.

5. Drill one hole through the center of the bottom of the front section and another hole ½ inch into the center of the end of the floor section. Use a round-headed screw to secure the two together. A round-headed screw is easier to remove when cleaning out the box.

6. Nail the roof on with two siding nails along each side, three across the back.

7. Affix the box to a 6-foot-long 4X4 sunk 1 foot into the ground.

LEFT: Stake or cage tomato plants to avoid damage from slugs.

Mealybugs. Tiny, soft-bodied scale insects covered in white powdery substance. Live in colonies. HOST PLANTS: Houseplants, fruit trees, and vegetables. DAMAGE: Congregate under leaves and suck sap from leaves, which yellow and shrivel. Black sooty mold sometimes grows on the excreted sugar sap. CONTROLS: Remove with forceful spray of water or spray with insecticidal soap. On small infestations, dab each mealybug with rubbing alcohol applied to a cotton-tipped swab. Buy mealybug destroyers and encourage beneficial insects.

Mexican bean beetles. Adults: ¼-inch-long, round yellowish-brown body with sixteen black spots. Larvae: ¼ inch long, bright yellow, and hairy. HOST PLANTS: Beans. DAMAGE: Adults and larvae skeletonize the leaves and devour entire rows very quickly. CONTROLS: Hand-pick into jars of soapy water or spray with rotenone or pyrethrin. Plant resistant bean varieties and use floating row covers. Grow nectar- and pollen-producing plants to attract predatory assassin bugs and parasitic wasps.

Slugs and snails. Slimy, gray-brown mollusks that grow to 3 inches long. Eyes protrude from head on tentacles. Slugs look like snails without a shell. Jelly-like egg masses laid under boards and rocks in moist areas. Nocturnal, they hide in holes in soil and under boards during day. HOST PLANTS: Vegetable greens and tender foliage of many plants. CONTROLS: Boards laid flat in planting beds provide daytime shelter; hand-pick and throw into pond or bucket of soapy water. Or spread diatomaceous earth, wood ashes, or crushed eggshells around plants to repel major infestations. Attract to shallow saucers filled with beer

or sugar-water. Preyed on by ground beetles and lampyrid beetles (firefly larvae). Attract adult fireflies with low-growing vegetation and nectar-producing plants. Ground beetles like to hide under rocks.
Squash bugs. Adults: ½ inch long and dark brown. Nymphs live in colonies, have green bodies with reddish-orange heads and legs. Both emit a strong odor when crushed. Clusters of orange-brown eggs are laid on underside of squash leaves. HOST PLANTS: Pumpkins, melons, cucumbers, and winter squash. DAMAGE: Suck sap from leaves causing young plants to wilt and die. CONTROLS: Early in season, use floating row covers. Hand-pick egg clusters and bugs and remove straw from around vines. Spray colonies of nymphs with insecticidal soap or sabadilla. Rotate crops annually and plant resistant varieties.
Squash vine borers. Adults: 1-inch-long moth with clear wings and black and red body. Eggs laid on underside of leaves. Larvae: 1-inch-long white grub with brown head. HOST PLANTS: Summer and winter squash, gourds, cucumbers, and melons. DAMAGE: Larvae bore into stems and runners: leaves wilt and plant dies. CONTROLS: Place foil on ground under plant to disorient moth. Hand-pick eggs. Cover plant with floating row

cover during late June/early July to deter moth. Make slits in stems where mounds of "sawdust" accumulate and remove borers (can be many in one spot). Cover stems with soil to encourage new root growth. Dust squash vines weekly with rotenone. Inject predatory nematodes into vines or apply to soil when temperatures are above 60°F. Rotate plants annually and plant resistant strains of squash.
Stink bugs. Brown or bright green, depending on region. Adult: flattish ½-inch-long, shield-shaped bodies. They "stink" when touched. Nymphs are round and brownish beige. HOST PLANTS: Cabbages, corn, peaches, tomatoes, potatoes, and beans. DAM-

AGE: Puncture fruits to feed on flesh and juice. Tomatoes develop white lumps under skin; fruit develops black pits and drops prematurely. Green stink bugs also feed on leaves and stems. CONTROLS: Hand-pick eggs and bugs or spray with insecticidal soap. For large infestations and extensive damage, dust or spray with sabadilla or pyrethrin. Eaten by praying mantises.
Whiteflies. Tiny, $1/16$-inch-long white flies that rise en masse when host plant is touched. HOST PLANTS: Many vegetables and fruits and most houseplants. DAMAGE: Suck juices from leaves and deposit sticky secretions. Leaves yellow, shrivel, and drop off. CONTROLS: Plant dies unless treated with insecticidal soap or ryania. Whiteflies are attracted to yellow. Place yellow plate or cardboard coated with Tanglefoot or something sticky to trap them. Encourage lacewings and lady beetles. When bringing houseplants indoors or buying plants at the nursery, check carefully for whiteflies.

ABOVE: Squash bugs lay their eggs on the underside of leaves.

OPPOSITE PAGE: A gazebo adds a formal backdrop to a carefree cottage garden. These self-seeding, fast-growing annuals and perennials are attractive to butterflies, beneficial insects, birds, and other creatures that thrive in a natural garden.

**CULTURAL AND
BIOLOGICAL CONTROLS**

Your beds are filled with blooms for butterflies and hummingbirds. You've planted berries and put up boxes for bluebirds. Your water garden is a home to turtles and frogs, a playground for toads and kingbirds. To safeguard their existence and keep wildlife coming back, use plant-derived insecticides like rotenone, pyrethrin, sabadilla, and insecticidal soaps made from natural fats and oils. Natural botanical pesticides are made from flowers, roots, leaves, and stems and put together in potent packages. They also are less harmful to wildlife because they break down quickly and are not stored in plant tissues or animal fat. Like all pesticides, however, they should be used in moderation, or you'll eliminate the beneficial insects you're trying to entice.

Another option is to practice integrated pest management (IPM). This method of gardening embraces the idea of combining organic gardening techniques and cultural and biological controls with small doses of synthetic fertilizers and pesticides. With IPM, you fall back on moderate applications of chemical pesticides only when necessary.

WEEKEND PROJECT **#47**

SQUIRREL-PROOFING YOUR BIRD FEEDERS

Spend a little time in the beginning of the bird-feeding season to outwit the squirrels, and you and the birds will have a more peaceful winter. Although you can buy mesh-enclosed feeders, it only takes a few minutes to enclose them yourself or to make an enclosed tray. The best way to do this is to surround them with galvanized or plastic-coated wire with 1 X 2-inch mesh.

An effective method to keep squirrels out is to put your feeders on poles, then position them 15 feet away from trees, fences, or buildings so squirrels can't jump to them. Protect feeders that are suspended from trees by hanging them from long lengths of twine. Hang your feeder at least 4 feet off the ground and 15 feet away from the tree trunk.

You can also stand two 10-foot poles in the middle of the lawn. Space them at least 10 feet apart and stretch a piece of twine or very fine wire between (both are too unstable to support a squirrel). Hang small feeders from the center, 4 feet off the ground. If you have no choice but to use a thicker wire or twine, thread it with anything that revolves,

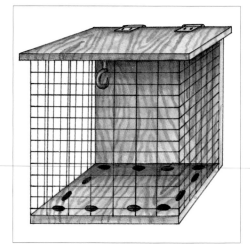

such as beads, bobbins, or small pieces of hollow tubing, for several feet on either side of the feeders.

FAR LEFT: Pure rotenone can be used safely on crops, but like any insecticide, it should be used with caution and in moderation.

LEFT: Insecticidal soap is not a preventative; it must be sprayed directly on squash bug nymphs or other insect pests in order to destroy them.

CULTURAL CONTROLS

The kindest methods of control are the cultural ones. They not only save you from poisoning your environment but also save you work. Try these as your first line of defense:

- Mulch to keep weeds down and soil-borne diseases away from plant foliage.

- Mow, pull, or whack weeds before they go to seed and start a new cycle or attract insects to your beds by providing food and hiding places.

- Avoid watering plants overhead at night. When foliage can't dry off quickly, fungal diseases are more prone to strike. Install a drip-irrigation system or soaker hoses, at least in your vegetable beds. Give disease-prone tomatoes enough space so air can circulate between plants.

- Rotate crops annually to avoid attack from the same soil-borne diseases and grubs from the previous year. Plant disease- and insect-resistant plants.

- Don't put all your eggs in one basket: Plant squash in four corners of the garden so if one or two die from squash vine borers, you still have two healthy plants. Plant snap and pole beans in separate beds to keep Mexican beetles from destroying entire rows.

- Use barriers to deter insect attacks: gallon milk jugs, hot caps, floating fabric rows, and sharp grit around plants. Protect seedlings and transplants with collars. Take 8 X 2-inch strips of cardboard and staple them into bands. Press "collars" an inch or more into the soil around the plants.

- Lay aluminum foil beneath squash plants to deter moths from laying eggs that hatch into white, 1-inch-long grubs, which infest roots and stalks. Or, cover squash plants in June with landscape fabric so moths can't get at the leaves to lay eggs. Remove in July to allow for pollination.

CROW-PROOFING YOUR FEEDERS

Chickadees, Carolina wrens, downy woodpeckers, titmice, and nuthatches love to feed on peanut butter mixes. So do crows, but if you stuff the mix into recycled cans, crows can't get to it. Neither can squirrels, if you make sure you hang the cans so they are inaccessible (see Weekend Project #47). Here are two methods that really work for birds.

Method #1: Take a 1-pound coffee can or a ½-pound mixed nuts can and cut a 1½-inch opening in the center or lower half of the plastic lid (remove the bottom if you have an extra plastic lid). Tie string or twine around the center

and hang it horizontally. Do not attach a perch for it will encourage jays and starlings to land and feed. If you want to encourage cardinals, bluebirds, and evening grosbeaks to come, be sure to add a perch.

Method #2: Take a ½-pound can and push a hole through the bottom. Thread a piece of string from the inside out so the can can be hung vertically. Take a small piece of plastic-coated, small-mesh wire and form a cup shape that will fit into, and hang slightly out of, the can. Remove the cup and fill with a peanut butter mix, then reinsert in the can.

- Seed squash in mid-June so they don't fruit until the end of July, after moths have laid their eggs in someone else's garden.

- Plant strongly aromatic plants among or near flower and vegetable beds. Some plants have a built-in natural resistance to certain insects and work as "companion" plants. Try marigolds, tansy, santolina, thyme, garlic chives, mint, and rosemary.

- Don't suspend Japanese beetle traps near vegetable or flower beds. They just attract more beetles to your garden. Studies show that less than half end up in the traps.

- Don't use bug zappers! Mosquitoes go after human sweat, not ultraviolet light. Zappers kill more beneficial insects and harmless (and beautiful) moths than insect pests.

- Hand-pick beetles, caterpillars, slugs, and other visible pests. Put a plastic bag over a section of the plant and shake the insects into the bag. Or, use the bag as a glove, grab the offenders, and pull the bag off your hand inside out. Tie a knot on the top, and the insects remain inside. Discard the bag in the garbage or empty its contents into a pond.

LEFT: Mulching and covering tender transplants will protect them from slugs, snails, cutworms, and frost.

- Where slugs are a problem in the garden, put down wooden boards. They will hide under the boards during the day, making them easy to catch. Dispose of the slugs by dropping them into a jar of soapy water or put them in a pail and feed them to pond dwellers.

- Use mulches of pine needles, bean hulls, and other rough materials to deter slugs and snails. Spread diatomaceous earth around plants—the sharp, crushed shells (made from sea creatures) pierce the slimy skin. You also can use builders' sand, crushed eggshells, crushed oyster shells, and wood ashes.

- Spread yellow containers with Tanglefoot or another sticky residue to attract aphids and whiteflies.

- Encourage birds to take up residence by providing them with nesting sites, food, water, and shelter (see Weekend Project #46).

- Hang a bat box in a protected, sunny area. Bats consume flying insects from dusk to dawn (see Weekend Project #49.)

- Clean up garden debris at the end of the summer so insects and larvae don't overwinter in your beds.

INVITING A BAT TO DINE

WEEKEND PROJECT **#49**

Navigating by radar, bats feed on the wing from dusk to dawn. Because one small brown bat can devour as many as 600 flying insects per hour, a colony can effectively control vast numbers of mosquitoes, June bugs, and other night-flying pests.

You can attract bats to your property if you provide them with roosting places, a source of water (such as a small pool), and a bat box that is placed in a favorable location.

Put up the bat box in the spring or summer. Position it 12 to 20 feet above the ground where it gets morning sun and is protected from wind. You can mount it on a pole, on the side of a house, or on a tree trunk. Make sure there are no wires or branches in the flight path of the box. If bats haven't taken up residence after a year but you still see them flying around the area, move the box to a warmer, more open location.

How can you tell if bats are occupying the box? Place a sheet of paper on the ground below the box and check for guano droppings a day or two later.

- Avoid damaging plants, shrubs, and trees when you prune and mow. Take care not to tear stems when you remove vegetables and snip flowers. Such damage invites diseases and insects.

BIOLOGICAL CONTROLS

- Make your garden inviting to beneficial insects. Most are available from mail-order companies.

- Introduce microbial pathogens that cause diseases in gypsy moth, tent, and other noxious caterpillars and in Japanese beetle grubs. Spray destructive caterpillars, cornworms, armyworms, and cutworms with Bacillus thuringiensis (BT, available as Dipel or Thuricide). Infect the ground with parasitic nematodes to destroy Japanese beetle grub populations.

- Use sulfur fungicide to control mildew, rust, and leaf spot on vegetables and ornamentals.

- Make your own insecticidal soap by adding 3 tablespoons soap flakes to 1 gallon of water. Spray directly on the insects. Don't use on plants in full sun; the plants can suffer leaf loss. Wait for a cloudy day or spray after the sun goes down. Insecticidal soaps will effectively control aphids, leafhoppers, mealybugs, mites, pear psyllas, thrips, and whiteflies.

HOMEMADE INSECT REPELLENTS

For green gardeners, organic alternatives to chemical pesticides are plentiful. Some can be ordered from mail-order companies, and others can be found on your kitchen shelves or growing in your garden.

- Combine 1 cup of cut-up hot peppers, several cloves of garlic, and 2 quarts of water. Allow to stand overnight, strain, and spray on insects and leaves.

- Cover 1 cup of chopped garlic with mineral or vegetable oil and let stand one or two days. Strain and combine the oil with ¼ cup of insecticidal soap or 1 tablespoon dishwashing liquid soap and 2 quarts of water. Spray the mixture under the leaves directly onto mealybugs, whiteflies, and aphids.

- Place some honey or sugar-water in shallow dishes or jar tops to attract insects away from ripening fruits. (Note that this also will attract wasps, bees, and ants.)

- Combine 1 tablespoon of liquid soap and 1 quart of water to protect against Japanese beetles. Pour into a wide-necked bottle and scoop beetles off roses, tomatoes, and beans into the liquid. Replace the lid, and leave beetles until they are dead.

- Wear gloves and use a hand cultivator to carefully rake apart a nest of ants.

Cover the disturbed ground with paper towels or old rags soaked in vinegar for several hours until the ants move out.

- Place fresh orange rinds around plantings or wood piles infested by wasps, ants, or other undesirable insects. The bitter oil in the rind is an effective insect repellent. When the rinds dry up, they are not noticeable. Replace them frequently.

OPPOSITE PAGE, LEFT: Wait for a cloudy day to spray plants with insecticidal soap.

OPPOSITE PAGE, RIGHT: A thick layer of straw keeps moisture in the soil and weeds under control in this garden. Bars of soap suspended from stakes deter deer from browsing.

LEFT: Some plants such as asters, phlox, roses, and verbena suffer from powdery mildew. To control this disease, provide more air circulation between plants, dust with sulfur, or buy the newer resistant varieties.

COMMON DISEASES

You can expect to find four major forms of disease in your garden:

- Bacteria—microorganisms that attack garden plants by entering cut wounds, openings, and bruises. Symptoms include leaf spots, wilting, and rotting of fruit, stems, and roots.

- Fungii—various kinds of parasitic spores that thrive in a moist environment under or above the ground. Symptoms include decomposing tissues—oozing, rotting, and blackening on fruit, stems, leaves, and roots.

- Parasitic nematodes—microscopic worm-like parasites that dwell and spread in the soil.

- Viruses—submicroscopic, subcellular particles that multiply and spread.

These diseases are spread by soil, seed, rain, water, wind, insects, and animals. They also can be spread when a gardener touches a diseased plant, then works in another part of the garden.

RIGHT: Student gardeners at Longwood Gardens in Kennett Square, Pennsylvania, use bird netting to protect fruit and vegetable crops from raccoons and other wildlife.

CONTROLLING THE SPREAD OF DISEASES

You may be unable to eliminate diseases, but you can minimize their spread with these precautions:

- Buy disease-resistant plants and seeds whenever possible.

- Don't harvest and work in the garden when plants are wet from rain, dew, or humidity.

- After pruning diseased stems and branches, clean tools between cuts in a mild solution of ¾ cup of bleach to 1 gallon of water.

- Pull and destroy diseased plants, stems, or branches.

- Rotate plants every year. With some diseases, it may be necessary to wait three to four years before planting in the same location. Don't follow one member of a family with another member of the same family. Don't follow tomatoes, for instance, with peppers or eggplants; they all belong to the same family (Solanaceae).

- Use cultural controls to deal with insects and weeds.

- In humid environments, allow plenty of space between plants for proper air circulation.

- Buy a good reference book on disease identification and learn to recognize diseases at an early stage.

- Use the services available from your county extension office. It is staffed with professionals and volunteer master gardeners, who will diagnose plant diseases at no cost.

A Natural Brew for Diseases

A solution of baking soda and insecticidal soap can help prevent black spot fungal disease on roses and phlox. Mix 1 generous tablespoon of baking soda into 1 gallon of water. Add a few drops of insecticidal soap to help the mixture spray evenly. Spray weekly throughout the summer. Spray on a cloudy day or when the sun has gone down to prevent possible leaf burn.

GARDEN WILDLIFE

When you provide shelter, food, and water for wildlife, you also risk inviting the creatures to raid your garden.

The solution is to plant a little extra (far away from tasty tomatoes) and to take precautions to protect your fair share of the garden.

- Install an electric fence, preferably at a 40-degree angle, to deter deer (see Weekend Project #51.)

DEER-REPELLENT SPRAYS

WEEKEND PROJECT #50

If erecting a fence is not practical, other proven solutions to deer problems include hanging blocks of soap in the garden and spraying plants with liquid repellents.

Hang blocks of soap 3 feet apart around the area you want to protect. Cut the soap into 2- to 4-inch chunks, tie string around each chunk, and hang from plant branches. Rain will reduce the pieces but will also renew the odor.

Spray repellents on shrubs, trees, and other plantings as soon as you see deer in your neighborhood. Repellents that

taste bitter to deer contain a toxic fungicide called Thiram. Organic sprays deter deer by exuding an offensive odor. They may contain tar oil, ammonium soaps, or putrescent egg. Besides mixing up your own putrescent mixture from eggs and water, there are several organic brands readily available including Magic Circle, Hinder, Deer Away, Natural Scent, and MGK Big Game Repellent.

Because deer love to eat young buds, spray your plantings two weeks before buds break (this may be as early as January in some areas). Then spray

every two weeks until after the buds have opened.

Branches broken and bark torn 2 to 3 feet up the trunks of young spruces, hemlocks, and pines have been damaged by male deer. During the mating season in November and December, they rub their antlers on young trees to remove the velvet growth. If the trunk of a tree is girdled during this aggressive ritual, the tree will die. To avoid this, start spraying with repellents in October, and erect chicken-wire barriers around specimen trees.

CONSTRUCTING A DEER FENCE

You've planted your garden and are looking forward to enjoying the fruits of your labors. However, hungry deer threaten to steal all the benefits of your hard work. To stop a deer problem quickly, take care of it the first weekend you notice it.

The simplest way to keep deer (and other smaller mammals) from browsing in your vegetable garden, orchard, or flowering ornamentals is to erect an electric fence. It is easy to surround a small garden area in no more than a few hours.

Here are several ways to build a fence that will deter deer and smaller animals:

1. Construct a 40-inch-high double fence 36 inches apart. String electric wires on the outside every 6 inches for the first 18 inches up (this narrow width keeps out smaller animals, such as rabbits, skunks, or woodchucks), then two more spaced at 28 inches and 38 inches.

2. Erect a single, 7- to 10-foot-high fence. String with electric wire every 8 to 10 inches.

3. For the best protection, according to the New York State Department of Agriculture, erect a fence with 7-foot posts placed 8 feet apart and slanted away from the garden at a 40-degree angle. Support with 4-foot posts sunk 12 inches into the ground on the outside, elevating the fence line to 4 feet. String with electric wires every 12 inches. The slant of the fence and the electricity are major deterrents.

No matter which method you use, check the tension on the wires every few months, releasing them slightly during the winter and readjusting them again in the spring. Keep electric fences free of plants and fallen branches; anything that interferes with the wires can cause a short in the fence.

Livestock electric wire kits are available at most feed and seed stores and some garden centers. You can also purchase battery-powered electric fence systems through mail-order catalogs.

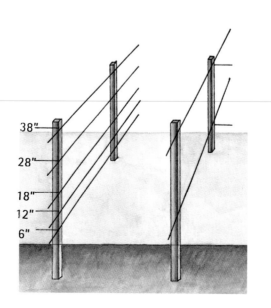

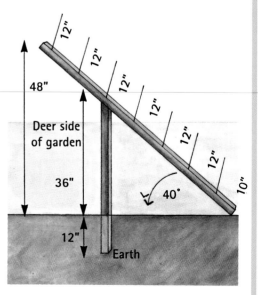

LEFT: *Yarrow, geraniums, nasturtiums, and a carpet of thyme surround a small stone birdbath, which also provides a refreshing drink for the resident feline.*

- Bury small-mesh wire 6 to 12 inches deep to keep rabbits and woodchucks from burrowing under a fence.

- Create an overhang on top of a fence to keep raccoons from climbing over it.

To protect plantings without the aid of a fence:

- Surround young trees with wire mesh cages so rabbits and deer can't eat the tender foliage.

- Surround the trunk of mature trees with 6- to 8-foot-tall wire mesh to keep deer from rubbing their antlers against the rough bark. This can girdle the trunks and cause the trees to die.

- Go vertical. Plant climbing peas and beans. Train melons, pumpkins, winter squash, sweet potatoes, and tomatoes up trellises and bamboo tepees so most of the leaves and the harvest are out of reach. Summer squash and cucumbers are not prime targets for wildlife.

- Use long, low cages or floating row covers over peppers, eggplants, and other small plantings.

- Cover fruit trees and bushes with netting to deter birds, raccoons, and other critters. Remember that animals take fruits before they're fully ripe, so put up preventive measures early.

- Apply liquid wildlife repellents frequently, changing the brands periodically so animals don't get accustomed to them. (Note that chemical repellents containing thiram are highly toxic to humans and to the environment. Several safe, organic repellents are available that contain kitchen ingredients or fatty-acid soaps.)

- Hang bars of soap from all the stakes and cages in your garden or on several branches of trees and shrubs to deter deer.

- Some gardeners use a sonar installation that also triggers a light system. The double effect startles the deer.

- Use moving scarecrows. Stationary scarecrows are ineffective, so construct ones that move and flutter in the breeze (see Weekend Project #20.)

- Use floating row covers to keep birds off ripening fruits. Deer chew right through this lightweight fabric, so add chicken mesh for better protection.

Essential Gardening Tools

These basic tools will answer most gardeners' needs. Have them on hand so you don't spend precious time running to the garden center to get them.

Cultivator: With three to five prongs, this tool will help you loosen earth and dig out weeds without straining your back. Use a cultivator to draw lines for sowing seeds.

Garden rake: Use this metal rake to smooth soil, and free it of stones and debris, spread compost and fertilizer, and level and grade the soil.

RIGHT: Early summer color in the sunny border is provided by gay-feathers, ornamental onions, evening primroses (Oenothera), lilies 'Golden Clarion', and annual shirley poppies (Papaver rhoeas).

YEAR-ROUND TOOL MAINTENANCE

A few minutes spent on maintenance after using your tools and at the end of the gardening season will ensure that they stay in good condition for many more hours of use.

Each time you use a tool, wipe it clean. An easy way to clean it is to keep a 5-gallon bucket filled with a mixture of sand and 1 pint of (recycled) motor oil in the shed or garage. Then, to clean and oil your tool at the same time, plunge it into the bucket, and work up and down vigorously.

To keep bladed tools effective throughout the gardening season, sharpen them after each use. Remove rust on shears, loppers, saws, and sickles with a fine-metal cloth. Sharpen the blades with a sharpening stone or a file. Follow up by rubbing lightly with oil.

To keep small tools handy but protected from the elements, install a mailbox near your vegetable or herb garden to store garden gloves, a trowel, hand hoe and rake, or other small garden necessities.

Before you put away your tools at the end of the gardening season, take a little time to clean away encrusted soil, dried foliage, or any rust spots. Spray with water and wash clean. Dry thoroughly with old rags or paper towels. Drop small-headed tools, such as weeders, hand rakes, bulb planters, and trowels, into a bucket of sudsy water. Swish them around and wipe dry.

Thrust the washed and dried tools into the bucket of sand and oil, or pour a little motor oil onto a rag and rub it over the metal parts.

Drain water from hoses and hang up during winter months to avoid cracking.

Remove matted grass from the mower, empty the gasoline chamber, then clean and sharpen blades.

Finally, hang a tool rack in a shed or the garage to hold your tools. Store chemical or organic pesticides, herbicides, and fertilizers on a high shelf away from curious children and animals.

Hand hoe and hand cultivator: These short-handled versions give more control and are especially useful in densely planted beds.

Hand trowel: This short-handled, miniature shovel is used to plant annuals, herbs, and transplants.

Hoe: Use to cut out weeds and break up soil without bending. Some are fitted with a straight edge; others have two prongs for digging furrows.

Leaf rake: Available in metal, plastic, or bamboo. Use to rake leaves off a lawn or garden bed.

Spade: With its straight-edged bottom, use to slice sod, to cut borders around beds, and for heavy-duty digging.

Spading fork: Use to turn over soil, break up clods, and fork over compost or matted leaves.

Shovel: The rounded, slightly pointed tip cuts into the earth for preparing holes for trees and perennials.

Water timer: Electric water timers offer a range of automatic programming. They are attached to faucets and garden hoses connected to sprinkler systems, soaker hoses, or drip-irrigation systems.

Wheelbarrows and garden carts: These come in all sizes and colors, in lightweight metal and wood. Indispensible for carting rubbish, leaves, and plants.

LEFT: Use hand pruning shears to make clean cuts when clipping roses.

OPPOSITE PAGE: These dense plantings of shrubs and perennials—delphiniums, roses, and bellflowers—leave no room for weeds to poke through in this low-maintenance garden.

PRUNING TOOLS

The weekend gardener will want to keep pruning chores to a minimum. Some plantings, however, benefit from moderate annual trimming: Many shrubs and vines produce bigger and better blooms on new growth; some perennials can be coaxed into a second bloom if they are sheared after the first flowering; trees and shrubs will grow into healthier specimens when diseased wood is removed.

Curved pruning saw: Identical to an extension-pole pruner except it is held by hand. Use it for sawing hardwood branches more than 2 inches in diameter.

Extension-pole pruners: These telescoping shears are operated by pulling a string. Some models have a hooked saw attached to the shears. Lightweight aluminium and plastic poles tire your arms less than wooden poles.

Hand-pruning shears: The handles of these shears fit snugly into your hand. Use them for nipping off small branches up to ½ inch in diameter.

Hedge shears: Equipped with long, flat blades and short, sturdy handles, these shears are used for trimming hedges and shearing perennials at the end of the season.

Lopping shears: These have two long handles, one held in each hand. Use them to slice through branches up to 2 inches in diameter.

GARDEN RESOURCES

ALPINE PLANTS

Colorado Alpines, Inc.
P.O. Box 2708
Avon, CO 81620

Heaths and Heathers
P.O. Box 850
Elma, WA 98541

The Primrose Path
RD 2, Box 110
Scottdale, PA 15683

Rice Creek Gardens
1315 66th Avenue NE
Minneapolis, MN 55432

Siskiyou Rare Plant Nursery
2825 Cummings Road
Medford, OR 97501

BIOLOGICAL
CONTROLS AND
ORGANIC PROUCTS

Age-Old Organics
P.O. Box 1556
Boulder, CO 80306

Gardens Alive
5100 Schenley Place
Lawrenceburg, IN 47025

Nature's Control
P.O. Box 35
Medford, OR 97501

The Necessary Trading Co.
P.O. Box 305
New Castle, VA 24127

BULBS, CORMS,
AND TUBERS

American Daylily &
  Perennials
P.O. Box 210
Grain Valley, MO 64029

Breck's Reservation Center
6523 North Galena Road
Peoria, IL 61632

Cooper's Garden
212 West County Road
Roseville, MN 55113

Daffodil Mart
Route 3, Box 794
Gloucester, VA 23061

Dutch Gardens, Inc.
P.O. Box 200
Adelphia, NJ 07710

Honeywood Lilies
P.O. Box 63
Parkside, SK SOJ 2AO
Canada

Jackson and Perkins
60 Rose Lane
Medford, OR 97501

John Scheepers, Inc.
63 Wall Street
New York, NY 10005

McClure & Zimmerman
108 West Winnebago
Friesland, WI 53935

Netherland Bulb Co.
13 McFadden Road
Easton, PA 18042

Park Seed Co.
Cokesbury Road
Greenwood, SC 29647

Peter de Jager Bulb Co.
188 Asbury Street
Hamilton, MA 01982

South Van Bourgondien Bros.
245 Farmingdale Road
Route 9, Box A
Babylon, NY 11702

Van Engelen Inc.
Stillbrook Farm
313 Maple Street
Litchfield, CT 06759

The Waushara Gardens
Route 2, Box 570
Plainfield, WI 54966

Wayside Gardens
1 Garden Lane
Hodges, SC 29695-0001

FERNS AND
SHADE PLANTS

Fancy Fronds
1911 4th Avenue West
Seattle, WA 98119

Shady Oaks Nursery
700 19th Avenue NE
Waseca, MN 56093

GROUND COVERS
AND VINES

Gilson Gardens
3059 U.S. Route 20
Perry, OH 44081

Ivies of the World
P.O. Box 408
Weirsdale, FL 32191

HERBS

Capriland's Herb Farm
534 Silver Street
Coventry, CT 06238

Dutchmill Herbfarm
Route 2, Box 190
Forest Grove, OR 97116

Hedgehog Hill Farm
RFD 2, Box 2010
Buckfield, ME 04220

Hemlock Hill Herb Farm
Hemlock Hill Road
Litchfield, CT 06759

Le Jardin du Gourmet
P.O. Box 75
St. Johnsbury, VT 05863

Nichols Garden Nursery
1190 North Pacific Highway
Albany, OR 97321

Taylor's Herb Garden, Inc.
1535 Lone Oak Road
Vista, CA 92083

Well-Sweep Herb Farm
317 Mt. Bethel Road
Port Murray, NJ 07865

MUSHROOM KITS

Field and Forest Products Inc.
3296 Kozuzek Road
Peshtigo, WI 54157

Fungi Perfecti
P.O. Box 7634
Olympia, WA 98507

Gardener's Supply Co.
128 Intervale Road
Burlington, VT 05401

Hardscrabble Enterprises, Inc.
HC 71, Box 2
Circleville, WV 26804

Morel Moutain
6300 Trillium Trail
Mason, MI 48854

Mushroompeople
P.O. Box 220
Summertown, TN 38483

Park Seed Co.
Cokesbury Road
Greenwood, SC 29647

River Valley Ranch
P.O. Box 898
New Munster, WI 53152

Western Biologicals
P.O. Box 283
Aldergrove, BC V4W 2T8
Canada

ORNAMENTAL GRASSES

Kurt Bluemel, Inc.
2740 Greene Lane
Baldwin, MD 21013-9523

Limerock Ornamental Grasses
RD 1, Box 111-C
Port Matilda, PA 16870

PERENNIAL SPECIALISTS

Andre Viette Farm & Nursery
Route 1, Box 16
Fishersville, VA 22939

Bobeleta Gardens, Inc.
15980 Canby Avenue
Farlbault, MI 55021

Caprice Farm Nursery
15425 SW Pleasant Hill Road
Sherwood, OR 97140

Carrol Gardens
444 East Main Street
Westminster, MD 21157

Charles Klehm & Son
  Nursery
4210 North Duncan Road
Champaign, IL 61820

Mileager's Gardens
4838 Douglas Avenue
Racine, WI 53402-2498

Wayside Gardens
1 Garden Lane
Hodges, SC 29695-0001

White Flower Farm
Route 63, P.O. Box 50
Litchfield, CT 06759-0050

ROSES

Jackson and Perkins
60 Rose Lane
Medford, OR 97501

Roses of Yesterday and Today
802 Brown's Valley Road
Watsonville, CA 95076

Stocking Rose Nursery
785 North Capitol Avenue
San Jose, CA 95133

Wayside Gardens
1 Garden Lane
Hodges, SC 29695-0001

SEEDS

Abundant Life
P.O. Box 772
Port Townsend, WA 98368

Comstock, Ferre & Co.
263 Main Street
Wethersfield, CT 06109

The Cook's Garden
P.O. Box 535
Londonderry, VT 05148

D. Landreth Seed Co.
180-188 West Ostend Street
Baltimore, MD 21230

Johnny's Selected Seeds
Foss Hill Road
Albion, ME 04910

Joseph Harris Co. Inc.
Moreton Farm
Rochester, NY 14624

Pinetree Garden Seeds
Box 300
New Gloucester, ME 04260

Seeds Blum
Idaho City Stage
Boise, ID 83706

Seeds of Change
P.O. Box 15700
Santa Fe, NM 87506-5700

Shepherd's Garden Seeds
30 Irene Street
Torrington, CT 06790

Southern Exposure Seed
  Exchange
P.O. Box 170
Earlysville, VA 22936

Stokes Seeds, Inc.
Box 548
Buffalo, NY 14240

Thompson and Morgan
P.O. Box 1308
Jackson, NJ 08527-0308

Vermont Bean Seed Co.
Garden Lane
Fari Haven, VT 05743

W. Atlee Burpee Co.
300 Park Avenue
Warminster, PA 18974

SHRUBS AND TREES

Ferris Nurseries
811 Fourth Street NE
Hampton, IA 50441

Forest Farm
990 Tetherow Road
Williams, OR 97544-9599

Foxborough Nursery
3611 Miller Road
Street, MD 21154

Girard Nurseries
Box 428
Geneva, OH 44041

Greer Gardens
1280 Goodpasture Island Road
Eugene, OR 97401

Wayside Gardens
1 Garden Lane
Hodges, SC 29695-0001

TOOL AND GARDEN EQUIPMENT SPECIALISTS

A.M. Leonard, Inc.
6665 Spiker Road
Piqua, OH 45356

Gardener's Eden
P.O. Box 7307
San Francisco, CA 94120-7307

Gardener's Supply Co.
128 Intervale Road
Burlington, VT 05401

Langenbach Fine Tool Co.
P.O. Box 453
Blairstown, NJ 07825

Smith & Hawkin
25 Corte Madera
Mill Valley, CA 94941

WATER GARDEN SPECIALISTS

Charleston Aquatic
   Nurseries
Johns Island
Charleston, SC 29455

Lilypons Water Gardens
P.O. Box 10
Lilypons, MD 21717-0010

Maryland Aquatic Nurseries
3427 North Furnace Road
Jarrettsville, MD 21084

Slocum Water Gardens
1101 Cypress Gardens
   Boulevard
Winter Haven, FL 33884

Van Ness Water Gardens
2460 North Euclid Avenue
Upland, CA 91786-1199

Waterford Gardens
74 East Allendale Road
Saddle River, NJ 07458

William Tricker, Inc.
7125 Tanglewood Drive
Independence, OH 44131

WILDFLOWERS AND NATIVE PLANTS

Appalachian Wildflower
   Nursery
Route 1, Box 275-A
Reedsville, PA 17084
(plants only)

Brookside Wildflowers
Route 3, Box 740
Boone, NC 28607

Clyde Robin Seed Co. Inc.
Box 2855
Castrol Valley, CA 94546

Goodwin Creek Gardens
P.O. Box 83
Williams, OR 97544

Illini Gardens
Box 125
Oakford, IL 62673
(plants only)

National Wildflower
   Research Center
2600 FM 973 North
Austin, Texas 78725-4201
(advice on cultivation &
propagation)

Native Gardens
Route 1, Box 494
Greenback, TN 37742

New England Rootstock
   Association
Box 76
Cambridge, NY 12816
(plants only)

Plants of the Southwest
Agua Fria
Route 6, Box 11-A
Sante Fe, NM 87501

The Redwood City Seed Co.
P.O. Box 361
Redwood City, CA 94064

The Vermont
   Wildflower Farm
P.O. Box 5, Route 7
Charlotte, VT 05445-0005
(seeds only)

We-Du Nurseries
Route 5, Box 724
Marion, NC 28752

WILDLIFE GARDEN KITS

National Wildlife Federation
Backyard Wildlife Habitat
   Program
8925 Leesburg Pike
Vienna, VA 22184

BIBLIOGRAPHY

Ball, Jeff. *Rodale's Garden Problem Solver: Vegetables, Fruits, and Herbs*. Emmaus, Penn.: Rodale Press, 1988.

Bartholomew, Mel. *Square Foot Gardening*. Emmaus, Penn.: Rodale Press, 1981.

Bisgrove, Richard. *The Flower Garden*. New York: Viking-Penguin, Inc., 1989.

Clausen, Ruth Rogers, and Nicolas H. Ekstrom. *Perennials for American Gardens*. New York: Random House, 1989.

Cox, Jeff and Marilyn. *The Perennial Garden*. Emmaus, Penn.: Rodale Press, 1985.

Fell, Derek. *The Easiest Flowers to Grow*. San Ramon, Calif.: Ortho Books, 1990.

The Garden Home Companion. New York: Macmillan Publishing Company, 1991.

National Gardening Association. *The Complete Guide to Growing America's Favorite Fruits & Vegetables*. Reading, Mass.: Addison-Wesley Publishing Company, 1986.

Phillips, Ellen, and C. Colston Burrell. *Rodale's Illustrated Encyclopedia of Perennials*. Emmaus, Penn.: Rodale Press, 1993.

Reader's Digest Illustrated Guide to Gardening. Pleasantville, N.Y.: Reader's Digest, 1978.

INDEX